M000204204

**Conversations with
Donald Hall**

Literary Conversations Series
Monika Gehlawat
General Editor

Conversations with Donald Hall

Edited by John Martin-Joy,
Allan Cooper, and Richard Rohfritch

University Press of Mississippi / Jackson

The University Press of Mississippi is the scholarly publishing agency of the Mississippi Institutions of Higher Learning: Alcorn State University, Delta State University, Jackson State University, Mississippi State University, Mississippi University for Women, Mississippi Valley State University, University of Mississippi, and University of Southern Mississippi.

www.upress.state.ms.us

The University Press of Mississippi is a member of the Association of University Presses.

First printing 2021
∞

Library of Congress Cataloging-in-Publication Data

Names: Hall, Donald, 1928–2018, interviewee. | Martin-Joy, John, editor. |
    Cooper, Allan, 1954– editor. | Rohfritch, Richard, editor.
Title: Conversations with Donald Hall / edited by John Martin-Joy, Allan Cooper,
    and Richard Rohfritch.
Other titles: Literary conversations series.
Description: Jackson : University Press of Mississippi, 2021. | Series:
    Literary conversations series | Includes bibliographical references and index.
Identifiers: LCCN 2020053613 (print) | LCCN 2020053614 (ebook) |
    ISBN 9781496822468 (hardback) | ISBN 9781496822475 (trade paperback) |
    ISBN 9781496822482 (epub) | ISBN 9781496822499 (epub) | ISBN 9781496822505
    (pdf) | ISBN 9781496822512 (pdf)
Subjects: LCSH: Hall, Donald, 1928–2018—Interviews. | Poets, American—
    20th century—Interviews.
Classification: LCC PS3515.A3152 Z46 2021 (print) | LCC PS3515.A3152 (ebook) |
    DDC 811/.54 [B]—dc23
LC record available at https://lccn.loc.gov/2020053613
LC ebook record available at https://lccn.loc.gov/2020053614

British Library Cataloging-in-Publication Data available

Contents

Introduction   vii
   John Martin-Joy, M.D., Allan Cooper, and Richard J. Rohfritch

Chronology   xvii
   Richard J. Rohfritch

Publications by Donald Hall   xxiii
   Richard J. Rohfritch

The Poetic Situation: An Interview with Donald Hall   3
   David Ray / 1958

Poems Without Legs: An Interview with Donald Hall   10
   J. R. S. Davies, Ian Hamilton, and Bill Byrom / 1963

An Interview with Donald Hall   15
   Scott Chisholm / 1971

An Interview with Donald Hall   37
   David Hamilton / 1983

"Names of Horses": An Interview with Donald Hall   53
   Alberta T. Turner / 1985

Donald Hall: An Interview   60
   Liam Rector / 1989

Donald Hall, The Art of Poetry No. 43   78
   Peter A. Stitt / 1991

"Ox Cart Man"   104
Jay Woodruff / 1992

A Conversation with Donald Hall and Jane Kenyon   118
Marian Blue / 1993

Donald Hall: Without and Within   130
Steven Ratiner / 1997

It's about Orgasm; It's Not about a Musk Ox: Interview with Former
US Poet Laureate Donald Hall   148
Anne Loecher / 2012

Writing Naked: Donald Hall on Poetry and Metaphor in Journalism   157
Mike Pride / 2013

Poetry, Aging, and Loss: An Interview with Donald Hall   162
John Martin-Joy, MD / 2015

Additional Resources   173

Index   177

Introduction

Over the last seventy years, thousands of interviews have been conducted with poets, playwrights, novelists, musicians, and artists of all genres. Many commentators, including academics, have debated whether the interview is a true form of art. Not all artists engage easily in conversation, and not all interviewers are concise and thoughtful. But every now and then a poet or a sculptor comes along—a Donald Hall or a Henry Moore—who raises the bar, lifting the common interview into the realm of conversational art.

The unique voice of Donald Hall—prolific poet, writer of essays, memoirs, and children's books, editor of influential anthologies and textbooks—can be heard in almost 170 vibrant interviews conducted over the course of a long and distinguished career. Hall, who served as the first poetry editor of the *Paris Review*, conducted the inaugural interview of the magazine's "Art of Poetry" feature with T. S. Eliot in 1959, followed by interviews with Marianne Moore in 1961 and Ezra Pound in 1962. *Paris Review* interviews have become the benchmark for the modern interview form, with their particular emphasis on the engagement between interviewer and interviewee. Those conducted by Donald Hall have become an invaluable source for educators and writers alike. Hall clearly learned a great deal while interviewing those poets and applied that experience when he was being interviewed by others.

The interviews collected in *Conversations with Donald Hall* are wide-ranging and compelling. Spanning a period from 1958 to 2015, they cover in detail three distinct periods of Hall's creative life: the early years of accomplishment when he lived in Ann Arbor and taught at the University of Michigan (1957–75); the New Hampshire years in which Hall and his wife, the poet Jane Kenyon, lived together as freelance writers and poets; and the lonely but immensely creative years in New Hampshire following Kenyon's death in 1995. Throughout, Hall shows himself to be a master of the riveting interview. Hall spoke powerfully of his ambitions, his joys, his daily life, and finally of his pain. Above all he spoke of his dedication to his craft. Perhaps most characteristic of all was a simple announcement that he made in passing but that might well stand as his poetic credo: "I play with sentences."

Hall's early interviews "The Poetic Situation" (1958) and "Poems Without Legs" (1963) appeared at a time when American poetry was undergoing a radical change. Born in suburban Connecticut in 1928 and educated at Harvard and Oxford, Hall was part of a rich generation of American poets that included Robert Bly, James Wright, Louis Simpson, John Ashbery, and Adrienne Rich, among others. Most of these poets knew each another, and all began by writing and publishing formal verse. By the late 1950s the development of their work had moved quickly from formal verse to a new kind of free verse, in large part due to Robert Bly's influential poetry magazine *The Fifties* (it would be retitled *The Sixties* and *The Seventies* in subsequent decades). The magazine provided a roadmap for many poets: criticism of the formal poetry being written at the time; in-depth analysis of the work of James Dickey, Denise Levertov, and others; poems by new and innovative American poets; and translations of poetry from several languages including Spanish, German, and Norwegian.

Hall had already achieved early success as a formalist. He won the Newdigate Prize for his poem "Exile" in 1952 when he was twenty-five. His first collection, *Exiles and Marriages* (1955), garnered enough praise that he and his work were featured in *Time* magazine. The early poem "My Son My Executioner" was vivid and memorable, and it has endured. But the language in that first book was sometimes decorous and there were critics who disparaged it for being too witty or superficial. He began to be called an "academic poet." It was not necessarily a compliment.

And Hall wasn't satisfied. In "The Poetic Situation" he said prophetically, "I think we have passed out of a formal period into a wild one." By the time "Poems Without Legs" appeared in *Isis* in 1963, he was emphasizing the importance of the imagination and inwardness. In that interview he discussed Bly's game-changing book *Silence in the Snowy Fields* and James Wright's startling new collection *The Branch Will Not Break*. Hall had been writing new free-verse poems, eventually gathered in his 1964 collection *A Roof of Tiger Lilies*. In "The Grass," he wrote "everything builds or alters itself." Hall's poetry and poetics were in a state of creative change.

Change was also a growing theme in Hall's personal life. Unhappy in his marriage and drinking too much, he entered psychotherapy in Ann Arbor with the psychoanalyst M. M. Frohlich. As Hall told John Martin-Joy, his problem was not depression but "ignorance of my own feelings. As I have often said, for 'love,' read 'hate' throughout." Hall had been reading Freud for some time, and he found Freud's work "exciting" and said it went places. Hall disliked Jung but said, "Freud is as nasty as the world and as human life is." Freud's thinking about free association came to inform Hall's approach to writing, with valuable results. But the marriage could not be saved, and by the late 1960s Hall and his wife Kirby Thompson had divorced.

Hall's period of creative experimentation ran roughly from the sixties to the mid-seventies. During this time he published three more books of poems: *The Alligator Bride: Poems New and Selected* (1969); *The Yellow Room: Love Poems* (1971); and *The Town of Hill* (1975). In these books, Hall explored a number of different themes and styles, including surrealism and the prose poem form. While Hall occasionally disparaged poems from those collections, *The Town of Hill* contains at least two well-known poems from that era: "Transcontinent" and "White Apples," a line from which he chose for the title of his 2006 volume of selected poems, *White Apples and the Taste of Stone.* After *The Town of Hill* was published by Godine, Hall said, "Very soon, immediately, I felt this wonderful access to language. Words began coming to me. At the same time I began 'O Cheese' and 'Kicking the Leaves.' They came in a long line, which I'd never written before." Like all seminal poets, Hall had been searching for a kind of poem that he hadn't fully developed yet. In a 1971 interview with Scott Chisholm, Hall talked about the kind of poem he was aiming for:

> I am mainly interested in trying to write a poem in which, as Galway [Kinnell] said to me in conversation last fall, you bring everything that you have done, everything that you know, together at once. That's not quoting Galway exactly, that's what I got from what he said. That kind of poem involves knowing yourself. You have to be able to get at the truth of your feeling and not to distort it. This is where I want to go now, and where I hope I am going.

When Chisholm noted that Hall had once insisted that control and formality were the best approaches in poetry and asked if he had modified his views, Hall replied: "I haven't modified them; I've just reversed them." A moment later, he candidly admitted that "the old way ran out."

In 1969 Jane Kenyon enrolled in one of Hall's large lecture courses at the University of Michigan, and she later submitted work for Hall's poetry workshop. Hall didn't know Kenyon, but he chose her as one of twelve students for his workshop based on the quality of her poems. Over time they dated, became inseparable, and finally married in 1972. Their move to his grandparents' New Hampshire homestead, Eagle Pond Farm, proved to be crucial for them both.

Kenyon recognized New Hampshire's importance to Hall. As a child he had spent summers at his grandparents' farm, and he came to appreciate what he saw as the community's tolerance of eccentricity and difference. His 1963 memoir *String Too Short to Be Saved* chronicled those early years, and not only won him a devoted readership but brought him, as he told Chisholm, "tremendous satisfaction." Kenyon urged Hall to leave his professorship so that they could live at Eagle Pond Farm together and write. The sense of belonging to a rural community, the presence of the past, the close relationship with changing seasons and the natural world fed the imaginations of both poets. Starting in 1975, they lived in what Hall called the "double solitude" of two poets living under one roof.

Hall had written the title poem of *Kicking the Leaves* while still living in Ann Arbor, but the blossoming of his poetry (Hall called it his "big break-through") happened after the move. Like his nonfiction, his poems celebrated his return to a beloved rural landscape. Reviewers praised the poems in *Kicking the Leaves* for the elegance and simplicity of their long musical lines. In the interview with Alberta T. Turner about his poem "Names of Horses," Hall reflected:

> I didn't choose the long line; it chose me. On several occasions during the last thirty years, the sound of my poems has altered; it has become exciting to make a new noise. After years of working with short-lined percussive, enjambed free verse, in the fall of 1974 I found this long line coming . . . When I began this poem—in 1975, I think—it arrived in a line that made the new music. Over the many drafts, over years of working, gradually these stanzas found their present shape.

The long line, inherited from Walt Whitman, gave Hall's work a more musical, symphonic sound than was possible to achieve in the staccato of short lines. He continued to develop the form through two critically acclaimed volumes, *The Happy Man* and *The One Day*. As he recalled in the *Paris Review* interview,

> This material started to arrive during my years of flailing about. It came in great volcanic eruptions of language. I couldn't drive to the supermarket without taking a notepad with me. I kept accumulating fragments without reading them or rewriting; it was as if I was finding the stone that I would eventually carve a sculpture from.

Always a relentless reviser, Hall spoke of sixty to eighty drafts over long periods of time. With *The One Day*, he began by organizing the material as "a long asymmetric free verse poem in thirty or forty sections . . . No good. Later I discovered the ten-line blocks that I could build with." In their 1993 interview about "Ox Cart Man," Hall and Jay Woodruff delved deeply into Hall's process of revision. As Hall told us later, singling out this interview for praise, "we really got intimate with the act of writing a poem." On this topic, as on many others, we find Hall reflecting on himself in retrospect. As Woodruff carefully reviewed Hall's drafts of "Ox-Cart Man," Hall reflected aloud: "It interests and amuses me to realize that I have been lying about this poem for years. . . . I've said for years that it took me two years to write this poem, and at least fifty or sixty drafts. Well, we have found something like nineteen drafts, and if anything is missing it's not much." Hall told us that this interview was "the only intimate account of the long revision of a poem."

By 1994 Hall and Kenyon had spent twenty years together at Eagle Pond Farm, working together, living a life together. In the *Paris Review* interview Hall made it clear how important she was to him: "Everything that my life has come to—coming here, the church, my poems of the last fifteen years— derives from my marriage to Jane in 1972. And I've watched her grow into a *poet*. Amazing . . . But it's living with her that has made all the difference for me."

Marian Blue's intimate 1993 interview, which included both poets, revealed their working partnership in detail. Often Hall answered first, while Kenyon quietly added a humorous response that seemed to underline a point and make it sharper:

> **BLUE:** How did that type of tension affect your ability to critique each other's work?
>
> **HALL:** Jane and I were student and teacher and friends for some time before anything romantic happened. When we were first married, we had to cope with that earlier relationship. I couldn't criticize her poems, because then I became the teacher. It was psychically confusing; her husband suddenly turns into Professor Hall. The solution—and this is comic—was that we needed a third person. When Gregory Orr would join us, then I could say anything about Jane's poems and she could say everything about mine. Greg's presence made it a workshop in which we were equals.
>
> **KENYON:** That was a very felicitous discovery.

They had survived the awkwardness of being professor and student, and the patronizing inquiries about the great poet's "little wife." Then, just as

Kenyon's career was taking off, Hall was diagnosed with liver cancer. *Life Work*, a paean to the writer's work ethic and perhaps the best of Hall's midlife nonfiction, was nearly derailed by the discovery of his cancer. Kenyon cared for her husband though his surgeries and searched for the meaning of his illness. In her poem "Afternoon at MacDowell" Kenyon walks to the car with a noticeably thin Donald Hall and asks herself: "I believe in the miracles of art, but what/ Prodigy will keep you safe beside me. . . ." But in 1995, after being diagnosed with leukemia and undergoing a harrowing series of treatments, Kenyon died at Eagle Pond Farm.

The pain of losing Jane Kenyon erupted in Hall's late collections *Without* (1998) and *The Painted Bed* (2002). These volumes, which won Hall much critical acclaim and a new and larger audience, are incomparable in modern American poetry. Hall poured out his grief in personal and searing language: ". . . I go to bed early, reading / *The Man without Qualities* / With insufficient attention / Because I keep watching you die." The directness was new and painful for him. Louis Begley wrote that while Hall had always had an awareness of mortality, in new poems like "Without" he presented the reader with "a laconic and scary factual report from the killing fields." If *Without* was a new departure for Hall, in some ways it also marked a return to formal verse, influenced by his love for Thomas Hardy and, as he acknowledged in interviews, his connection to Jane Kenyon's own emotionally powerful work. These late poems are as crucial to Hall's legacy as the long free-verse poems of *Kicking the Leaves*. At the same time they were also as crucial to his psychological survival as anything he ever wrote. As he recalled in his interview with Martin-Joy, "*Without* kept me alive after Jane's death. It was as if I could do something about her dying."

Steven Ratiner, who drove to Eagle Pond Farm in 1997 to interview Hall, found a changed man. The once clean-shaven Hall had "grown a scruffy beard," and his long hair was wild. Asked about the change, Hall said:

> I haven't let my hair grow by deciding to; I just haven't been going to the barber. And I'm aware that Jane was my barber for twenty years of marriage and more, perhaps that's why. . . . Life has totally changed, my life has totally changed and it's as if with the beard I've acknowledged this change.

Hall explained how raw his grief still was, and how compulsive his need was to share it: "People often say, 'How courageous of you to speak of it'; well, it wasn't courageous at all, I couldn't not. I felt like the Ancient Mariner, who had to tell his story." The turn in Hall's work—what he later termed necropoetics—led him to reflecting on medical care, grief, and the process of dying. In old age Hall wrote his final poetry, spoke to medical audiences, and published reminiscences of Jane Kenyon. Poetry diminished, but in a last remarkable burst of creativity he returned to prose. Hall published three critically acclaimed books of essays, beginning with *Unpacking the Boxes: A Memoir of a Life in Poetry.* As the subtitle of that book showed, Hall was very much interested in revisiting and summing up his life and career. And his long dedication to literature was rewarded: he was named Poet Laureate of the United States in 2006, and he received the National Medal of Arts from President Barack Obama in 2011.

The last interview in this collection, conducted by Martin-Joy in 2015, captures Hall reflecting on aging, creativity, and loss. He speaks of his book *Essays After Eighty*, and how his poetry, always a sensual experience for him, eventually ran out. But the death of Jane Kenyon remains at the center of his world. Hall comes alive as he recounts his intense experiences as a witness and a survivor. He was pleased that this interview would appear last in our collection. "It's not long but it is thorough and it is special," he said, "and it will feel rather terminal!"

These interviews were conducted in various circumstances. Some, like those by David Ray and the Oxford undergraduates Ian Hamilton and J. R. S. Davies, took place in front of a live audience, where Hall excelled. Mike Pride spoke with Hall alone at Eagle Pond Farm. Others were conducted by mail. Stitt's 1991 *Paris Review* conversation, perhaps Hall's most famous, is a hybrid. It took place in person but evolved over several years: the first two sessions at Eagle Pond Farm in 1983 and 1988, and the third on stage at the 92nd Street Y in New York.

However an interview started, Hall liked to edit and polish the transcript afterward. Though his editing was often light, his attention to detail and tone gave his interviews power and precision. What is remarkable is that Hall's presence—at times informal, direct, or humorous—comes through so vividly.

The emotional give and take in these interviews evolved over time. In the first, the young poet is provocative, abrasive. In the second he argues stubbornly with J. R. S. Davies, Bill Byrom, and Ian Hamilton, disputing practically all of their assertions. Perhaps in this way the young Hall defined and developed his own aesthetic of poetry. Over the years, however, the confrontation softens. In its place we find a kind of humorous patience and playfulness that has more dramatic value than the young poet could have mustered. Hall would not be pretentious enough to call it wisdom. But it is the voice of a writer who has brought the full weight of his experience to bear in his responses.

The impact of these conversations on the interviewers was often long-lasting and profound. Some, like Liam Rector, were already close friends with Hall when they interviewed him. For others, a single interview with Hall has stayed vivid in memory for decades. Jay Woodruff, who interviewed Hall about "Ox Cart Man," told us that he recalls being "impressed (and maybe a little intimidated) by Don's responsiveness: those envelopes with the Eagle Pond Farm return address came back fast!" For Woodruff it is Hall's generosity—with thoughts, with drafts, and with time—that stands out twenty-five years later. By phone or by letter, Hall had "a remarkable combination of directness and kindness" that Woodruff never forgot.

John Updike once said that anthology-making, "like sculpturing in marble, is in large measure an art of taking away." An anthologist himself, perpetually fascinated by Henry Moore, Hall would have appreciated the remark. Of the 170 interviews that Richard Rohfritch unearthed in Hall's archives at the University of New Hampshire, we gave serious consideration to about sixty and finally agreed on the thirteen interviews collected in *Conversations with Donald Hall*. Throughout 2017 and the first months of 2018, Hall sent us his detailed recollections of the interviews that interested us and shared his lively opinions on what to include. Hall did not agree with us on every choice. Ian Hamilton's masterful interview from 2000 was a favorite of Hall's despite, or perhaps because of, his interviewer's challenging attitude. Fortunately, the book-length interview is still in print.

Hall was pleased with our idea of creating a kind of biography through the interviews we chose, and he was thrilled with the final result. We believe this collection of interviews makes a lively statement about Hall's life and literary preoccupations of the moment. Taken together, they chart the literary development and personal journey of one of the most remarkable poets and essayists of our time.

About a year before Donald Hall's death, Richard Rohfritch spent many Saturday mornings at Eagle Pond Farm speaking with the poet. Rohfritch's reflections give us a final snapshot of Hall at age eighty-eight. Sitting in his favorite blue wing chair with the working version of *A Carnival of Losses* nearby, Hall spoke rapidly and enthusiastically in the soft, gravelly voice of his later years. His hair was long, his beard wild, his eyebrows often raised. Rohfritch recalls:

Don spoke in stories. He pointed to the couch directly across from his chair and told how Robert Creeley had sat there and composed a good poem in a few minutes—impressing Don, who revised religiously. He proudly pointed out a Henry Moore maquette that Moore had given him when Don published his book on Moore's sculpture. I imagined a maquette to be large, and didn't at first notice the small object on the table until an exasperated Don told me to pick it up.

Typically I would ask about a specific event or person, and Don would take over. He complained about lapses in his short-term memory, but his long-term memory was phenomenal: he corrected the title of a poem he published seventy-one years ago that I had mangled.

From Rohfritch's description, it is clear that Hall's drive, intensity, and charisma remained intact. Like Woodruff a quarter century earlier, Rohfritch was struck by Hall's generosity.

Hall remarked in these pages that only a fool would be afraid of death. In early 2018, while helping us arrange permissions for this book, he e-mailed us with his typical good humor: "I'll try to stick around to see my *Conversations*!" In May, however, at age eighty-nine, he became ill. Hall entered the hospital and abruptly stopped answering letters. He asked his assistant Kendel Currier to let us know. Hall entered hospice care and returned to Eagle Pond Farm, where he died on June 23. His memorial service was held on a hot June day at South Danbury Christian Church in New Hampshire. Afterward he was buried beside Jane Kenyon in the Proctor Cemetery. Though Donald Hall's remarkable voice is silent now, there is some comfort in knowing that these conversations, in his own words, will live on in the pages of this book.

We would like to acknowledge Bill Ross, head of Special Collections at the Dimond Library, University of New Hampshire, for graciously granting us access to the Hall papers; Kendel Currier, Donald Hall's longtime assistant, for much spirited help; Katie Keene, Mary Heath, and the staff of the University Press of Mississippi for guidance and help on the project; our families, for their support; and Donald Hall himself, for his inspiration, his example, and his friendship.

JMJ
AC
RR

Chronology

1928   Donald Andrew Hall Jr. is born in New Haven, Connecticut, on September 20, the only child of Donald Andrew Hall and Lucy Wells. The family lives on the top floor of a rented house on Corum Street.

1934   Father purchases house on Ardmore Street in Spring Glen in Hamden. Hall enters Spring Glen Elementary School, Hamden, Connecticut. His fourth-grade teacher, Gladys Keeley, remarks in his report card: "Donald needs help in written language."

1935   Starts to devour books, reading prose and poetry including Tom Swift, the Hardy Boys, the novels of Albert Payson Terhune, and the novels and poems of Roy Helton.

1940   Reads Poe, Keats, Shelley, Byron, and Blake. Writes first poem, "The End of All." Begins spending summers at the farm of his grandparents, Wesley and Kate Wells, in Wilmot, New Hampshire.

1942   Attends Hamden High School. Meets fellow young poets, including freshmen at nearby Yale, and starts reading modern poetry. Early poems appear in the Hamden High School literary magazine, *The Cupola*.

1944   Attends Bread Loaf Writers' Conference at age sixteen; plays softball with Robert Frost. Enters Phillips Exeter Academy in Exeter, New Hampshire. Discovers Wallace Stevens, William Carlos Williams, and Marianne Moore. Poems appear in the *Philips Exeter Review*.

1945   Publishes first poems without pay in small magazines, including *Trails, Matrix,* and *Experiment.*

1947   Graduates from Philips Exeter Academy, where he is selected as class poet. Enters Harvard. Elected to the editorial board of the *Harvard Advocate*, in which many of his poems and essays appear. Meets Robert Bly, Adrienne Rich, Frank O'Hara, Kenneth Koch, L. E. Sissman, Peter Davison, John Ashbery, Robert Creeley, and Richard Wilbur. His teachers include John Ciardi, Archibald

MacLeish, and Harry Levin. Wins Lloyd McKim Garrison Poetry Prize for "A Single Look" and the John Osborne Sergeant Translation Prize for a metrical translation of Horace.

1950   Edits his first book, *The Harvard Advocate Anthology*. Meets Kirby Thompson, a student at Radcliffe, on a blind date.

1951   Graduates from Harvard with a B.A., *magna cum laude*, and is elected to Phi Beta Kappa. Writes and directs his first play, *The Minstrel's Progress*.

1952   Attends Christ Church College, Oxford University, as a Henry Fellow. "Passage to Worship," the first poem for which Hall is paid, appears in *World Review*, London. Poem "The End of January" is broadcast on the BBC. Wins Newdigate Prize for poem "Exile." *Time* magazine features Hall in an article called "The Yanks at Oxford." The *Times Literary Supplement* reviews Hall's poems. As President of the Oxford University Poetry Society, edits the weekly Oxford student magazine, *Isis*. On September 13, Hall marries Kirby Thompson in Princeton, NJ. They take a honeymoon drive through France, Germany, Austria, Yugoslavia, and Greece.

1953   Becomes first poetry editor of the *Paris Review*. Hall's grandfather, Wesley Wells, dies while Hall is at Oxford. After receiving his B.Litt., Hall attends Stanford University as a creative writing fellow, studying under Yvor Winters. Publishes first poems in the *New Yorker* and *Poetry*.

1954   Returns to Harvard as a Junior Fellow, Society of Fellows. Son Andrew is born.

1955   Viking Press publishes *Exiles and Marriages*, Hall's first book of poetry. The book wins the Lamont Poetry Prize, is nominated for the National Book Award, and receives favorable reviews on the front pages of the major newspaper book supplements and in newspapers. Two days after the book appears, Donald Hall Sr. dies at age fifty-two.

1956   First paid poetry reading at New York City YMCA. Wins Edna St. Vincent Millay Award, Poetry Society of America.

1957   Appointed as assistant professor of English at the University of Michigan. Coeditor with Robert Pack and Louis Simpson, *The New Poets of England and America*.

1958   Book of poetry, *The Dark Houses*. Member of editorial board, Wesleyan University Press Poetry Series (1958–64).

1959   One year leave in England. Meets Henry Moore and interviews him for *Horizon* (published 1960). Hall's interview with T. S. Eliot appears in the *Paris Review*. Begins writing about his memories of life and childhood on his grandfather's farm. Publishes first of eleven children's books, *Andrew the Lion Farmer*. Daughter Philippa is born.

1961   First prose book, *String Too Short to Be Saved*, is published.

1962   Editor, *Contemporary American Poetry* (anthology).

1963   Guggenheim Fellowship for Poetry; returns to England for a further year of leave from Michigan. Writes criticism and reviews for the *New Statesman, Encounter*, and BBC radio scripts. Again interviews Henry Moore and his friends for a *New Yorker* profile (published in 1965).

1964   *A Roof of Tiger Lilies*, a book of poetry, is published.

1965   *The Faber Book of Modern Verse*, Third Revised Edition (editor). Consultant, editor, and scout for new writers for Harper & Row (1965–81).

1966   Promoted to full professor at University of Michigan.

1967   Marches on Washington with son Andrew to protest the Vietnam War. Hall and Kirby separate.

1969   Hall and Kirby divorce. Hall begins drinking more than before; he writes less poetry. He spends several years in psychotherapy with M. M. Frohlich, a psychoanalyst in Ann Arbor. *The Alligator Bride: Poems New and Selected* is published. Jane Kenyon enrolls as a student in Hall's lecture class "An Introduction to Poetry for Non-English Majors." Hall does not know her, but based on her work, he later selects her as one of twelve students for a poetry workshop.

1970   *Marianne Moore: The Cage and the Animal. As the Eye Moves: A Sculpture by Henry Moore*, with photos by David Finn, is published. Kenyon graduates from University of Michigan with a B.A.

1971   *The Yellow Room: Love Poems*.

1972   Marries Jane Kenyon. She earns her M.A. at the University of Michigan. Hall wins his second Guggenheim Fellowship for Poetry and travels to England with Kenyon.

1973   *Writing Well*, a textbook that eventually reaches nine editions.

1974   First sports book, *Playing Around: The Million Dollar Infield Goes to Florida*, is published.

1975   Hall resigns from the University of Michigan. In August, he and Jane Kenyon move to Eagle Pond Farm in Wilmot, New

Hampshire, the ancestral farmhouse his great-grandfather bought in 1865. Hall's grandmother Kate Wells dies at ninety-seven; Hall buys Eagle Pond Farm from her heirs. In October, "Kicking the Leaves" appears in the *New York Times*.

1976   *Kicking the Leaves: A Poem in Seven Parts. Dock Ellis in the Country of Baseball*, with Dock Ellis, is published. *A Writer's Reader*, a textbook, is published and eventually appears in nine editions. Hall and Kenyon begin attending the South Danbury Christian Church and become deacons.

1977   Teaches modern poetry for a semester at Dartmouth College.

1978   *Kicking the Leaves*, a book of poetry; *Remembering Poets*; *Goatfoot Milktongue Twinbird: Interviews, Essays, and Notes on Poetry, 1970–76*.

1979   Hall's third children's book, *Ox Cart Man*, appears. It wins the Caldecott Prize and is eventually published in seven other languages.

1980   Receives honorary doctorate from Plymouth State College (now University), Plymouth, New Hampshire, the first of twelve he will eventually receive. *To Keep Moving: Essays, 1959–1969*.

1981   *To Read Literature, Fiction, Poetry, Drama*, textbook.

1982   *The Weather for Poetry: Essays, Reviews and Notes on Poetry, 1977–81*; *To Read Poetry* (textbook); *Claims for Poetry* (editor).

1983   Wins Sarah Josepha Hale Award for Distinction in Literature.

1984   Appointed Poet Laureate of New Hampshire.

1985   Travels to Italy with Jane Kenyon; visits Milan, Florence, and Rome. *Fathers Playing Catch with Sons* (on sports); *The Oxford Book of Children's Verse in America* (editor).

1986   Hall and Kenyon travel to China and Japan for six weeks for the United States Information Agency (USIA). *The Happy Man*, a book of poetry, appears; it later wins the Lenore Marshall/Nation Poetry Prize.

1987   *Seasons at Eagle Pond* (essays) and *To Read Fiction* (textbook).

1988   Travel to Rome and Florence. *The One Day: A Poem in Three Parts* appears and later wins the National Book Critics Circle Award and the Los Angeles Times Book Prize. *Poetry and Ambition: Essays: 1982–88*.

1989   Elected to the American Academy and Institute of Arts and Letters. Diagnosed with colon cancer and undergoes successful surgery.

1990	Publishes *Old and New Poems* and *Here at Eagle Pond*, a book of essays.
1991	Receives honorary doctorate from Bates College, Lewiston, Maine, his parents' alma mater. Receives Robert Frost Silver Medal from Poetry Society of America. Appointed a council member of the National Council on the Arts and of the Council of the National Endowment for the Arts. First trip to India with Jane Kenyon for the USIA.
1992	*Their Ancient Glittering Eyes: Remembering Poets and More Poets.* Hall's cancer recurs and metastasizes to liver. Half of his liver is surgically removed.
1993	Honorary doctorate from the University of Michigan. Hall and Kenyon make their second trip to India for the USIA. *The Museum of Clear Ideas*, a book of poetry, and *Life Work* (nonfiction).
1994	Hall and Kenyon become associate faculty at the graduate writing seminars at Bennington College, Vermont. Jane Kenyon is diagnosed with acute lymphoblastic leukemia. She enters Dartmouth-Hitchcock Medical Center for chemotherapy. In October, Hall and Kenyon fly to Seattle, where Kenyon receives a bone marrow transplant at the Hutchinson Cancer Research Center. Hall's mother dies at age ninety. Kendel Currier, Hall's distant cousin, becomes his amanuensis, typing his manuscripts and correspondence. *Death to the Death of Poetry: Essays, Reviews, Notes, Interviews* and three children's books are published. Receives Ruth Lilly Poetry Prize.
1995	Jane Kenyon is appointed New Hampshire Poet Laureate. On April 11, lab work shows that her leukemia has recurred. Kenyon and Hall, knowing her death is near, choose poems for a collection of her work. On April 22, at age forty-seven, she dies at home at Eagle Pond Farm. Hall is appointed New Hampshire Poet Laureate for second time.
1996	Hall experiences a three-month manic episode and then a depression; he receives treatment. *The Old Life*, a book of poetry.
1998	*Without*, a book of poems. The book sells 20,000 copies in its first year and wins the L. Winship/PEN New England Award.
1999	Meets Linda Kunhardt, a schoolteacher and aspiring poet, at a poetry reading in New Hampshire. Linda becomes his companion.
2001	Receives honorary doctorate from Dartmouth College. Suffers a stroke in January while visiting Bennington College. Undergoes a successful endarterectomy to unclog his right carotid artery.

2002	*The Painted Bed* (poetry).
2003	*Breakfast Served Any Time All Day* (essays on poetics).
2005	*The Best Day the Worst Day: Life with Jane Kenyon.*
2006	Hall is appointed Fourteenth US Poet Laureate. *White Apples and the Taste of Stone, Selected Poems, 1946–2006.*
2008	*Unpacking the Boxes* (memoir). Hall's ex-wife Kirby dies of cancer at age seventy-six.
2011	In March, President Barack Obama presents Hall with the 2010 National Medal of Arts at the White House. *The Back Chamber,* poetry collection, is published. Hall announces he has stopped writing poetry but will continue to write essays.
2012	Essay "Out the Window" appears in the *New Yorker*.
2014	*Essays After Eighty* is published.
2015	Nineteenth book of poetry, *The Selected Poems of Donald Hall*, is published. New Hampshire Literary Hall of Fame Honoree.
2016	Admitted to the New London Medical Center in January and again in February; he is diagnosed with congestive heart disease.
2017	Nominated for the 2017 Gold Medal for Belles Lettres and Criticism by the American Academy of Arts and Letters for lifetime achievement.
2018	In May, Hall falls ill. After a brief hospital stay, he enters hospice care and returns to Eagle Pond Farm. On June 23, Donald Hall dies in the front parlor of his ancestral home. A memorial service is held at South Danbury Christian Church, and he is buried beside Jane Kenyon. In July, his forty-seventh book, *A Carnival of Losses: Notes Nearing Ninety*, appears.

Publications by Donald Hall

During his lifetime, Hall published nineteen collections of poetry, eight books of essays, and twenty books of nonfiction. As a writer, editor, and anthologist, he is credited with over 130 publications.

Poetry

Poetry Collections

Exiles and Marriages. New York: Viking Press, 1955.

The Dark Houses. New York: Viking Press, 1958.

A Roof of Tiger Lilies. New York: Viking Press, 1964. London: Andre Deutsch, 1964.

The Alligator Bride: Poems New and Selected. New York: Harper & Row, 1969.

The Yellow Room: Love Poems. New York: Harper & Row, 1971.

The Town of Hill. Boston: David R. Godine, 1975.

A Blue Wing Tilts at the Edge of the Sea: Selected Poems, 1964–1974. London: Secker & Warburg, 1975. Consists of poems from *The Alligator Bride* and *The Town of Hill.*

Kicking the Leaves. New York: Harper & Row, 1978. London: Secker & Warburg, 1979.

The Happy Man. New York: Random House, 1986. London: Secker & Warburg, 1986.

The One Day: A Poem in Three Parts. New York: Ticknor & Fields/Houghton Mifflin, 1988.

Old and New Poems. New York: Ticknor & Fields/Houghton Mifflin, 1990. New Delhi, India: Affiliated East-West Press, 1993.

The One Day and Poems 1947–1990. Manchester, UK: Carcanet Press, 1991. Consists of poems from *The One Day* and *Old and New Poems.*

The Museum of Clear Ideas. New York: Ticknor & Fields/Houghton Mifflin, 1993.

The Old Life. Boston: Houghton Mifflin, 1996.

Without. Boston: Houghton Mifflin, 1998.

The Painted Bed. Boston: Houghton Mifflin, 2002.

White Apples and the Taste of Stone: Selected Poems 1946–2006. Boston: Houghton Mifflin, 2006.

The Back Chamber. Boston: Houghton Mifflin Harcourt, 2011.

The Selected Poems of Donald Hall. Boston: Houghton Mifflin Harcourt, 2015. Boston: Mariner Books, 2017.

Limericks

The Gentleman's Alphabet Book. New York: Dutton, 1972.

Poetry Translations

Den Enda Dagen. Lund, Sweden: Ellerstroms Forlag, 1995. Swedish translation of *The One Day: A Poem in Three Parts.*

La Cama Pintada. Cordoba, Spain: Ediciones Aristas, 2002. Spanish translation of eight selected poems from *The Painted Bed.*

La Cama Pintada. Granada, Spain: Valparaiso Ediciones, 2014. Spanish translation of *The Painted Bed.*

Without. Madrid: Ediciones Vitruvio, 2014. Spanish translation of *Without.* Poems also printed in English.

Eagle Pond, Jane Kenyon and Donald Hall. Granada, Spain: Valparaiso Ediciones, 2015. Spanish translation of poems selected from Jane Kenyon, *The Collected Poems of Jane Kenyon*, and Donald Hall, *White Apples and the Taste of Stone, Selected Poems 1946–2006.*

Poetry Chapbooks, Booklets, and Pamphlets

Exile, the Newdigate Prize Poem. Oxford, UK: Fantasy Press, 1952.

Donald Hall. Oxford, UK: Fantasy Press, 1952

To the Loud Wind and Other Poems. Cambridge, MA: Pegasus/Harvard Advocate, 1955.

The Alligator Bride. Menomonie, WI: Ox Head Press, 1968.

Kicking the Leaves: A Poem in Seven Parts. Mt. Horeb, WI: Perishable Press, 1976.

O Cheese. Lexington, KY: The King Library Press, University of Kentucky, 1979.

The Toy Bone. Brockport, NY: BOA Editions, 1979.

The Twelve Seasons. Dublin, Ireland and Deerfield, MA: Gallery Press and Deerfield Press, 1983.

Brief Lives: Seven Epigrams. Concord, NH: William B. Ewert, 1983.

Couplet: Old Timer's Day, Fenway Park, 1 May 1982. Berkeley, CA: Tom Clark, 1984.

Great Day in the Cows' House. Mt. Carmel, CT: Ives Street Press, 1984.

1,2,3,4 Stories. Sweden, ME: Ives Street Press, 1989.

Daylilies on the Hill. Concord, NH: William B. Ewert, 1992.

Two Poems. Donald Hall and Robert Bly. Brownsville, OR: Story Line Press, 1994.

Apples and Peaches. Edgewood, KY: R. L. Barth, 1995.

Ric's Progress. Northampton, MA: Warwick Press, 1996.

Winter Poems from Eagle Pond. San Antonio, TX: Wings Press, 1999.

The Purpose of a Chair. Waldron Island, WA: Brooding Heron Press, 2000.

Two by Two: Poems by Donald Hall and Richard Wilbur. Easthampton, MA: Warwick Press, 2000.

Ric's Progress. Medford, MA: Arrowsmith, 2007.

Prose Publications

String Too Short to Be Saved. New York: Viking Press, 1961

Henry Moore: The Life and Work of a Great Sculptor. New York: Harper & Row, 1966. London: Victor Gollancz, 1966.

Marianne Moore: The Cage and the Animal. New York: Pegasus, 1970.

As the Eye Moves: A Sculpture by Henry Moore. With David Finn. New York: Abrams, 1970.

Playing Around: The Million Dollar Infield Goes to Florida. [With others.] Boston: Little, Brown, 1974.

Dock Ellis in the Country of Baseball. With Dock Ellis. New York: Coward, McCann & Geoghegan, 1976. Second revised ed., New York: Fireside/Simon & Schuster, 1989.

Remembering Poets: Reminiscences and Opinions: Dylan Thomas, Robert Frost, T. S. Eliot, Ezra Pound. New York: Harper & Row, 1978.

Goatfoot Milktongue Twinbird: Interviews, Essays, and Notes on Poetry, 1970–76. Ann Arbor: University of Michigan Press, 1978.

To Keep Moving: Essays, 1959–1969. Geneva, NY: Hobart & William College Press, 1980.

The Weather for Poetry: Essays, Reviews and Notes on Poetry, 1977–81. Ann Arbor: University of Michigan Press, 1982.

Christmas Snow: A Story. Tilton, NH: Sant Bani Press, 1982.

Fathers Playing Catch with Sons: Essays on Sport (Mostly Baseball). San Francisco: North Point Press, 1985.

The Bone Ring: A Verse Play (originally *Ragged Mountain Elegies*). Santa Cruz, CA: Story Line Press/The Reaper, 1987.

The Ideal Bakery: Stories. San Francisco: North Point Press 1987.

Seasons at Eagle Pond. New York: Ticknor & Fields/Houghton Mifflin, 1987.

Poetry and Ambition: Essays, 1982–88. Ann Arbor: University of Michigan Press, 1988.

Here at Eagle Pond. New York: Ticknor & Fields/Houghton Mifflin, 1990.

Anecdotes of Modern Art: From Rousseau to Warhol. With Pat Corrington Wykes. New York: Oxford University Press, 1990.

Their Ancient Glittering Eyes: Remembering Poets and More Poets: Robert Frost, Dylan Thomas, T. S. Eliot, Archibald MacLeish, Yvor Winters, Marianne Moore, Ezra Pound. New York: Ticknor & Fields/Houghton Mifflin, 1992.

Life Work. Boston: Beacon Press, 1993.

Poetry: The Unsayable Said: An Essay. Port Townsend, WA: Copper Canyon Press, 1993.

Death to the Death of Poetry: Essays, Reviews, Notes, Interviews. Ann Arbor: University of Michigan Press, 1994.

Principal Products of Portugal: Prose Pieces. Boston, Beacon Press, 1995.

Breakfast Served Any Time All Day. Ann Arbor: University of Michigan Press, 2003.

Willow Temple: New and Selected Stories. Boston: Houghton Mifflin, 2003.

Samtal Med Pound: Ezra Pound Intervjuad. Lund, Sweden: Ellerstroms, 2003. Swedish translation of Ezra Pound interview.

The Best Day the Worst Day: Life with Jane Kenyon. Boston: Houghton Mifflin, 2005.

Eagle Pond. Boston: Houghton Mifflin, 2007. Reprinted as *On Eagle Pond.* Boston: David R. Godine, 2016.

Unpacking the Boxes. Boston: Houghton Mifflin, 2008.

A Good Foot of Snow: A Story. Jamaica Plain, MA: Marsolais Press, 2009.

Christmas at Eagle Pond. Boston: Houghton Mifflin, 2012. Reprinted in paperback by David R. Godine, 2017.

Essays After Eighty. Boston: Houghton Mifflin Harcourt, 2014.

On Eagle Pond. Boston: Nonpareil Book/David R. Godine, 2016.

Ensayos Despues de Los Ochenta. Granada, Spain: Valparaiso Ediciones, 2017. Spanish translation of *Essays After Eighty.*

A Carnival of Losses: Notes Nearing Ninety. Boston: Houghton Mifflin Harcourt, 2018

Edited Publications and Textbooks

The Harvard Advocate Anthology. New York: Twayne, 1950.

Lotte Zurndorfer: Poems. With Oscar Mellor. Oxford, UK: Fantasy Poets, 1952. Pamphlet.

Martin Seymour-Smith: Poems. With Oscar Mellor. Oxford, UK: Fantasy Poets, 1952. Pamphlet.

Geoffrey Hill: Poems. With Oscar Mellor. Oxford, UK: Fantasy Poets, 1952. Pamphlet.

Adrienne Cecile Rich: Poems. With Oscar Mellor. Oxford, UK: Fantasy Poets, 1952. Pamphlet.

Michael Shanks: Poems. With Oscar Mellor. Oxford, UK: Fantasy Poets, 1952. Pamphlet.

Michael Raper: Poems. With Oscar Mellor. Oxford, UK: Fantasy Poets, 1952. Pamphlet.

A. Alvarez: Poems. With Oscar Mellor. Oxford, UK: Fantasy Poets, 1952. Pamphlet.

New Poems. Oxford, UK: Fantasy Press, 1952. Poems by nine poets, including Hall.
  Pamphlet.
New Poems. Oxford, UK: Fantasy Press, 1952. Poems by ten poets, including Hall. Pamphlet.
Thom Gunn: Poems. With Oscar Mellor. Oxford, UK: Fantasy Poets, 1953. Pamphlet.
Anthony Twaite: Poems. With Oscar Mellor. Oxford, UK: Fantasy Poets, 1953. Pamphlet.
Arthur Boyars: Poems. With Oscar Mellor. Oxford, UK: Fantasy Poets, 1953. Pamphlet.
New Poems. Oxford, UK: Fantasy Press, 1953. Poems by nine poets. Pamphlet.
New Poems. Oxford, UK: Fantasy Press, 1953. Poems by seven poets. Pamphlet.
New Poems. Oxford, UK: Fantasy Press, 1953. Poems by nine poets, including Hall.
  Pamphlet.
Oxford Poetry 1953. With Geoffrey Hill. Oxford, UK: Fantasy Press, 1953. Poems by
  fifteen poets, including Hall and Hill.
The New Poets of England and America. With Robert Pack and Louis Simpson. New
  York: Meridian Books, 1957.
Whittier. New York: Dell, 1960.
A Poetry Sampler. New York: Franklin Watts, 1962.
The Faber Book of Modern Verse. Michael Roberts. London: Faber and Faber, first
  published 1936. third rev. ed. edited by Donald Hall [adding American poets and
  new English ones], 1965.
New Poets of England and America: Second Selection. With Robert Pack. Cleveland:
  Meridian, 1962.
Contemporary American Poetry. Baltimore, MD: Penguin, 1962.
Concise Encyclopedia of English and American Poets and Poetry. With Stephen Spender.
  New York: Hawthorn Books, 1963.
Poetry in English. With Warren Taylor. New York: Macmillan, 1963.
Man and Boy: An Anthology. New York: Franklin Watts, 1968.
The Modern Stylists: Writers on the Art of Writing. New York: Free Press, 1968.
A Choice of Whitman's Verse. London: Faber & Faber, 1968.
American Poetry: An Introductory Anthology. London: Faber, 1969.
The Pleasures of Poetry. New York: Harper & Row, 1971.
Writing Well. Boston: Little, Brown, 1973. Nine editions to 2007.
Teaching Writing Well. With D. L. Emblen. Boston: Little, Brown, 1973. Four editions
  to 1982.
A Writer's Reader. With D. L. Emblen. Boston: Little, Brown, 1976. Nine editions to 2002.
Poets on Poetry Series (fifty-six books of prose by poets) and *Under Discussion Series*
  (sixteen books about poets). Founding general editor. Ann Arbor: University of
  Michigan Press, 1978–96.
To Read Literature, Fiction, Poetry, Drama. New York: Holt, 1981. Three editions to 1992.

The Oxford Book of American Literary Anecdotes. New York: Oxford University Press, 1981.

To Read Poetry. New York: Holt, Rinehart & Winston, 1982.

Claims for Poetry. Ann Arbor: University of Michigan Press, 1982.

The Contemporary Essay. New York: Bedford/St. Martin's Press, 1984. Three editions to 1994.

The Oxford Book of Children's Verse in America. New York: Oxford University Press, 1985.

To Read Fiction. New York: Holt, Rinehart & Winston, 1987.

New Voices: University and College Poetry Prizes, 1984–1988. 7th edition. New York: Academy of American Poets, 1989.

Best American Poetry 1989. Donald Hall, guest editor. New York: Macmillan, 1989.

The Essential Marvel. New York: Ecco Press, 1991.

To Read a Poem, second ed. Ft. Worth, TX: Harcourt Brace Jovanovich College Publishers; Heinle & Heinle (Australia), 1992.

The Essential Robinson. New York: Ecco Press, 1993.

The Oxford Illustrated Book of American Children's Poems. New York: Oxford University Press, 1999.

Children's Books

Andrew the Lion Farmer. New York: F. Watts, 1959.

Riddle Rat. New York: F. Warne, 1977.

Ox Cart Man. New York: Viking Press, 1979.

The Man Who Lived Alone. Boston: David R. Godine, 1984.

I Am the Dog I Am the Cat. New York: Dial, 1994.

The Farm Summer 1942. New York: Dial, 1994.

Lucy's Christmas. San Diego: Browndeer Press/Harcourt Brace Jovanovich, 1994.

Lucy's Summer. San Diego: Browndeer Press/Harcourt Brace Jovanovich, 1995.

Old Home Day. San Diego: Browndeer Press, 1996.

When Willard Met Babe Ruth. San Diego: Browndeer Press, 1996.

The Milkman's Boy. New York: Walker, 1997.

Conversations with
Donald Hall

The Poetic Situation: An Interview with Donald Hall

David Ray / 1958

From *Southwest Review*, vol. 43, no. 1, Winter 1958, pp. 47–52. Reprinted by permission of David Ray.

When Donald Hall read his poetry at the 1020 Art Center in Chicago recently, David Ray arranged an interview with him the next day. The following is a transcript.

David Ray: We might as well start out with a big one. Do you approve of the trend, in so many of the younger American poets, back to formal and even intricate technical concerns in their work? Yesterday, for example, you read a poem in terza rima and a little later, a sestina.

Donald Hall: I think you are behind the times with your *trends*. In a gross, popularizing way (the only way in which trends exist or matter) I think we have passed out of a formal period into a wild one. *Time* and *Life* have been calling for artists to behave like artists for a long time now, and those people out in San Francisco have responded. They will have their rewards, for a time, and you may be sure that the word *academic* will be tossed around even more than it has been. The question of form, or trends in form, is not serious. It is certainly dangerous, and of course absurd, when the question of form is regarded as some sort of opposition between constriction and freedom. There is no freedom in art, from automatic writing to anagrams. Freedom is the expression of the will and art is not free because the will is a servant of the Muse, which is the personification of the artist's intuition of excellence. Anyone who finds an opposition between freedom and bondage in art should be given a PhD. Form vs. free verse is not a problem for the intelligence. All and no verse is free . . . sestinas and cantos are as good and bad as you make them. Besides, in what sense is the "trend toward form" a fact at all?

DR: A symptom if not a fact.

DH: Well, sestinas were rescued from Swinburne by the lyrical Mr. Pound. Who are the revolutionaries after whom has come the conservative reaction? Auden was being formal in 1929; Hart Crane wrote practically no free verse. Eliot is always close to regularity and Pound is often perfectly regular. Wallace Stevens has written the best blank verse since Wordsworth. Is Yeats conservative? Then is Richard Wilbur? The idea of recent literary history most of us have is screwy. The revolution that existed was largely a revolution of diction not of metrics. I'm talking about what really happened, not about what people said was happening. There is more cant about contemporary poetry than there is bad poetry, which must be a record of some sort. Considerations of gross form (as opposed to minute formal qualities of a poem, the style) are usually irrelevant, and evasive. The word *sonnet* does not describe a poem very accurately, yet William Carlos Williams (who is about as repetitive as Swinburne in his rhythms) thinks so. Evasion of the real issue, by concentrating on some false issue, is historically a proven method of failure. What matters for any artist is to keep his eye on the apple, and not get distracted into evasion like the great majority of his would-be colleagues. I suppose the apple is the most efficient use of language—words used fully to describe and judge human experience, leaving nothing out. Of course one may decide, with good reasons either historical or personal, that one writes best, or should write best, in one particular gross form or lack of it. One may attempt a new way of writing for the sake of its difficulty. I find poets now capable of great technical extension, the best of them, and I cannot regret it. Wilbur and Merwin, very different poets, are both capable of excellent translation. The vulgar trend, though, as I said before, is against this kind of writing. The same people who think that growing a beard, or going to bed with another man when they really prefer women, is going to help them write poems, make an equation between formlessness and life, an old mistake and a powerful one. Watch out for people whose programs as artists really concern only behavior. Most likely they are vicious fakes. Their eyes are not on the apple, they are evasive, and they substitute behavior as artists for making art.

DR: Speaking of people who don't have their eyes on the apple, what do you think of the tendency to generalize about artistic productivity? For example, "Artists have to be ascetic" (the sublimation routine), "have to lead the good life," "have to explore experience" (in an obvious sense—invariably invoking the name of Hart Crane, Baudelaire, or Poe). You've already indicated discontent with this sort of thing, but do you have anything more specific to say about it?

DH: It is the hobby of idiots. Artists don't have to *do* anything in particular except be artists. Lawrence Lipton to the contrary, they can even be rich, or insurance executives, or Fascists. Art refuses to fit the categories of the casuist. A poet at least has to be intelligent, but he doesn't have to behave in any particular way. Emphasis on behavior, or the attempt to discern a pattern, is again mere evasion of the serious center of the problem. People don't want to admit that there is no philosopher's stone for art. They keep looking for the recipe that makes artists, thinking "If I go to Hartford and get a job with Hartford Accident and Indemnity I will write *"Sunday Morning"* or "If I get syphilis I will write *"Les Fleurs du Mal."* Art is no stimulus-response commodity. Fascists, Communists, heterosexuals, homosexuals, bourgeois businessmen, have all written excellent poetry. Anybody can write poems, if he is a poet. This redundancy excludes fools who demand conformities, currently nonconformist, of behavior.

DR: Let's go from formulas to the conditions, the environment, of artistic workmanship. Could you compare the effects, for a practicing poet, of the atmospheres provided by teaching at a university, or studying there, an arrangement such as that at Stanford or Iowa, and that provided by having a job completely unrelated to the arts? You must admit that these are different influences, despite their failure to produce mere given responses.

DH: I have to speak largely in ignorance. I think again that no prescriptions hold. If you like a job unrelated to the arts, fine, but never do it because you think it will help your poetry! Never do anything because it will help your poetry. I think the poet whose livelihood is unrelated to the arts is a rarity, and I just mean to be descriptive. Stevens is the contemporary example. Most poets, though, have managed to spend a great deal of time in association with other artists, or even hangers-on of the arts, people who talk their language and share their concerns. The lone artist, of whatever quality, is extraordinarily rare. Hopkins's correspondence with Bridges and Patmore was surely necessary for him. I find nothing to object to, but the name, in a writers' workshop. The most stimulating thing for most artists is contact with the best work of their own generation. If, as at Iowa now, there are five or six serious and talented men, these five or six will maybe profit by being at a writers' workshop and knowing each other. I never attended a workshop, so I am being speculative. When I was at Stanford, there were only four of us working at verse, and that's scarcely a workshop.

DR: Of course you were there as a student, but next year you'll be teaching. Does that involve any change of viewpoint for you? Or do you think it will have much influence on your work?

DH: Ask me again in a year. I doubt, of course, that teaching will do anything to my poetry except decrease its quantity, because it will decrease my free ruminating time, walking and reading and talking, all in an undisciplined way. I have had four years free of the necessity to do anything in particular, and God knows I have liked it! Now I have to work for a living at a job which is not what I want to do most, a disability I share with the rest of the world.

DR: A good many young poets are comfortably established in teaching or the publishing industry, though.

DH: Who is in the publishing industry? Louis Simpson fled in glee to the Columbia campus after five years in publishing. Howard Moss is with the *New Yorker*. Is there any other poet who is a publisher or magazine worker? Ciardi is more a teacher than an *SR* editor. Publishing is an infernal cross between business and art, and poets do well to steer clear of it. I know Eliot managed, but then I've been saying that no prescriptions work. About the universities, the word "comfortably" is sneaky. Most poets are—merely to twist your meaning—*uncomfortable* about being in the universities, because of teaching loads, fuddy-duddy colleagues, and second-rate students. I'm not dodging your question, but I think the stereotype of the remove, the quiet of the university is totally false. It is much more alive to problems, even to horrors, that the commuters of Happy Valley or the workers in the canning factory. We tend to accept a rather medieval stereotype of the university. It is a sensitized point, and it is not under anesthesia. Perhaps you were asking if it is a good thing to be comfortable. It would be hard to insist that it was, but at any rate I am radical enough to believe in the irrelevance of personal discomfort to art. It is relevant enough when you are so uncomfortable—hunger, cancer of the liver, etc.—that you *cannot* write. Comfort is not to be equated with complacency, which is the enemy. I have known complacent college professors, and desperate ones. I have known exceedingly complacent anarchists. *Faute de mieux*, the university is the best place for most writers today. Summers off, ability to some extent to rearrange working hours to suit writing hours, association if it is stimulating. Some poets not teaching live in university towns, like Frost in Cambridge. All these reasons are well known. One other is important. It is the one profession from which you can take a year or more off at a time, whenever you can afford to. Try doing that in publishing or business! If you work in a factory, you lose seniority and get laid off quicker. Physical work gets you too damned tired, anyway. It's no way out. The great American hatred of the academic has nothing to do with the academy; in part it is the old American singsong about No More Teachers, No More Books, but more than that it is the simple anti-intellectualism of the second-rate romantic mind. Poets have tended historically more often to respect intelligence than to despise it, and intelligence is at least slightly more apt to reside in a university than outside it. The university in America at its best preserves the books and the ideas, while it criticizes American society; its unique value is that it can do the second with the aid of the first. I do not mean to praise the fuddy-duddies, the bandwagon jumpers, the goons, and the fools. There are others.

DR: I suppose the divorce of artist and university is more complete among novelists than among poets, anyway. But it has always seemed regrettable that there was such a separation, whether necessary or not. I don't quite share your view that it is the fault of the second-rate romantic with his anti-intellectualism, though that is a feature of it. I believe the universities are discouraging to a large extent, that they do a lot of unnecessary things to alienate the artist, to make it rough for him. The anecdotes professors love to tell about the later famous artists who quit school bitterly aren't very funny. The schools seem peculiarly inflexible; they won't budge an inch to make room or leave room for the individualist, who of course at the same time is making a great effort to meet the demands of the institution. I'm not personally bitter because I've been able to weather it out, at least for my M.A., but I've seen a lot of valuable people washed out because the university wouldn't make the slightest effort at understanding.

DH: This sounds cry-baby. A university is not a person but a set of rules. If you resent a set of rules as if they were a person you are being sentimental. The saddest thing I know is the hypocrite who is not quite enough of an anarchist to get into trouble, but talks like a dangerous man when the authorities are not listening. The kind of a man who writes dirty words on a wall at night to express his disapproval of bourgeois morality. Institutions are bothersome but if you have any sense you know what they are and are not and understand your own relationship to them. Plenty of people wouldn't go to a college if they had the guts not to, and I have no great sympathy for them if they persist in making small demonstrations of their difference. A university is not like a government, which it is up to everybody to change. A university only changes itself.

DR: We've talked now about creativity and the environment for it. Let's shift to its final resting place—its expression in print, or on records. Lawrence Lipton has been referring to "the vocal tradition," that is, the revival of public readings and the increasing practice of recording. Do you think it will result in any misevaluations? I've heard statements to the effect that Thomas's reputation was somewhat aided by his rhetorical competence in the sound studios.

DH: Thomas's overinflated reputation is more due to his reputed behavior than to his ability as an actor. He fulfilled, in the Merry Tales of Master Dylan, the stereotype demanded of the poet. His apotheosis by the popular magazine—*Ladies' Home Journal* recently had a story called "Hank, Judy, and Dylan Thomas," not to speak of *Time*—results from this pattern of acceptable behavior. I wouldn't blame Thomas for this. No one has read his poetry, but a line or two sounds satisfactory. Ignorant palates prefer strong seasoning.

DR: Speaking of reputations, what ones do you think overblown today and who do you think is primarily responsible for this evaluation?

DH: I think Randall Jarrell's the most seriously overblown reputation. The others I don't worry about. I suppose Jarrell's war poems started his popularity. They are made of the weepy, pseudo-tough sentimentality demanded of war poems. Then he turned to writing reviews which are popular because they are full of jokes, and articles which are popular because they affirm received taste—"ooh" and "aah" about Robert Frost, William Carlos Williams, Walt Whitman, Marianne Moore, and the rest of the cast. Finally he collected enough two-line gags to make a novel. He would have made a decent writer of Bob Hope's monologues, but he's no poet. I see no conspiracy in his reputation. These things happen. A few good people seem to like his poetry, and they mean it, but they are wrong.

DR: Who do you think underrated?

DH: Stanley Kunitz, Yvor Winters, J. V. Cunningham, Norman Cameron, Howard Nemerov, Reed Whittemore, among middle-aged writers. Cameron is dead.

DR: I'll certainly agree with you about J. V. Cunningham, one of the best poets of our time. I'd put Karl Shapiro in that list too. The anthologists were good to him only to turn around and treat him with a gross unfairness and neglect. What do you think of the practices of present-day anthologists, incidentally? Do you think they're doing much harm or good?

DH: More often than not, I squirm at the taste displayed in anthologies, and often I doubt motives for the inclusion of certain poets; doubtless I am becoming another in the long, distinguished list of literary paranoids. I don't know. A recent poet-anthologist included in his collection one poem each by Louis Untermeyer and Oscar Williams, an obvious attempt to curry favor, we would say—but the anthologist is W. H. Auden, in his horrible

Criterion Book of Modern American Verse, and Auden scarcely needs to butter up anthologists. Here the attribution of motive must be mistaken, so perhaps it is elsewhere. You might as well grant your enemy sincerity. An anthology like Auden's will do considerable harm, for it misrepresents, and in effect belittles, American poetry in England (Faber did it first, and it is designed for the British). International understanding, in poetic areas, is set back ten years by this irresponsible, cynical job, which Louise Bogan, fantastically, called "definitive" in her *New Yorker* review. Auden is not content with bad taste in choosing his poets, a great many represented by one poem each, but he cannot even spell the names of his poets or get their dates right. The better poets he prints he invariably represents by inferior work, and when he disapproves of a poet he chooses one piece. Karl Shapiro has one poem, Chester Kallman three. John Ciardi's *Mid-Century Anthology* was the most helpful one I know about. I think Williams is the best of the regular anthologists, with a talent for finding the surprising poem. With the exception of the thematic, or directed, anthologies, like Auden's and Ciardi's, I don't think they are very important. As a rule they reflect reputation more than they create it. I just edited one with Louis Simpson and Robert Pack, an anthology of young poets for Meridian Books; so I know how hard it is to do. We try to get a generation. You'll see what you think of it.

DR: I'll certainly agree that the Auden anthology was a good example of unfair editing, though I respect the man tremendously. Unfortunately the people he slighted have no recourse—they are consigned to oblivion as far as that book is concerned. And it merely takes a few injustices of this sort to damage a poet greatly. I don't share your view that the anthologies are merely reflective of reputations. But what about magazines? Some are falsely credited with a salutary influence on poetry; some are just coasting on their reputations, while others, not necessarily given credit, are doing a lot for poetry of permanent value.

DH: No magazine satisfies me. Shades of gray.

DR: Is there anything you want to say about the situation of poetry in general?

DH: Not much. There is more variety of poetic line available to young poets than there has been in years. I am hoping that the ability to write, in a lot of people, will come up against more subject matter. A pious hope, to be sure, but at least there's something to start from. I make no predictions.

Poems Without Legs:
An Interview with Donald Hall

J. R. S. Davies, Ian Hamilton, and Bill Byrom / 1963

From *Isis* (Oxford, UK), November 13, 1963, pp. 18–20. Reprinted by permission of the Ian Hamilton estate. The text of James Wright's poem, included in the original, is omitted here.

In his introduction to the Penguin *Contemporary American Poetry* (published at the end of last year), Donald Hall said that "a new kind of imagination seems to be working" in the recent poetry of Robert Bly and James Wright, among others—"so new that I lack words for it." Mr. Hall was in Oxford earlier this term to address the Poetry Society, so we took the opportunity of recording the following interview with him, in order to discuss further these recent developments in American poetry. Most of the poems referred to are in the Penguin anthology, and so are easily accessible; we print James Wright's poem "Eisenhower's Visit to Franco, 1959" below. Acknowledgments are due to Longmans, Green and Co., who have recently published *The Branch Will Not Break*, by James Wright, from which the poem is taken. I would also like to thank Ian Hamilton and Bill Byrom for their part in the ensuing discussion.

—J. R. S. Davies

Donald Hall: Colin Falck was talking the other day about "poems without legs." I think this describes exactly what I want in poetry now, and what Robert Bly and James Wright, for instance, are doing.

Question: The best of these poems do have legs which one can define as dramatic legs: they concern themselves with an area of activity which is generally shared and generally agreed upon. . . .

DH: Maybe I should say "poems without crutches" because they will not all necessarily lack some thread of narrative or conventional discourse, but they won't depend on it; their real energy will come not from the conventional structure of the poem, but from the images themselves as they are juxtaposed. A "poem without legs" does not rely on these old methods of construction which have come to turn the poem into, for the most part, a kind of "argument" poem.

Q: Yes, but at the same time in their theory they [these poets] do talk about irrational poetry springing from a rational source. . . . It seems to me in some ways that what they are saying is related to a total attitude to the world—it's impossible to say things about the world, it's impossible even to use ordinary descriptions because these descriptions might not be true. . . .

DH: At the beginning of Bly's book of poems that came out in America last year, there is a quotation from Jacob Boehme: "We are all asleep in the outward man." The only "real" world is the world that we all share unconsciously, inwardly. This is the world to which poetry really must make reference. Of course, this is a startling thing in the context of English and American poetry in the last thirty years. American poetry has been so concerned with *things*: English poetry has concerned itself with replacing the informal essay—writing occasional poems, poems that are bits and pieces of the objective world. These poems have nothing to do with Imagism or Objectivism, technically, but spiritually they are identical. If you look back at what T. E. Hulme says at the start of the modern movement, it is all an attempt to move poetry outside, towards getting in facts, opinions, and generalizations. Poetry is becoming impoverished by facts. The poetry we're talking about now concerns itself with fantasy, with imagination. . . . I think Bly is a revolutionary, but the revolution that he wants is an inward one, not an exterior one. When that revolution takes place then we shall see the Shell-stations in a new light, as in his poem "The Possibility of New Poetry." When that revolution comes there is social change because he believes that the inward world contains a way of feeling which changes our exterior actions. In Bly's poems, the recognition of this interior world and the employment of imagination is in itself a criticism of the world of bourgeois capitalists. It happens when you allow the imagination to work so that you have metamorphoses and strange connections. For instance, another poem of Bly's, "After the Industrial Revolution, All Things Happen at Once"—all these things are bits of the exterior world, yes, but putting them together is an act of the imagination. Putting them together without conjunctions, without any legs.

Q: But he's not just putting them together, he's putting them one after another: surely that implies a time sequence?

DH: I don't think so. In literature we are always cursed with the necessity to put one thing after another, but increasingly modern writers have wanted to cancel out time and work for simultaneity. By omitting conjunctions, anything that makes things go together—this would include the order of logic—by omitting these things, one gets a sense of duplication and therefore simultaneity. It is like a stack of transparent objects; you see them all at once. One moves toward simultaneity even though the art of literature is necessarily a time art, an art of sequence. I was interested in something someone said when I spoke to the Poetry Society here—"You want, then, a poetry without conjunctions?" I agreed that conjunctions would not be part of my poetry because I wanted the sense of simultaneity, the kind of effect you get from juxtaposing things without leading the reader to a particular kind of intellectual relationship among them. But later I realized perhaps I would like the kind of conjunctions that don't make any sense by acting to deny the sense of conjunction. I mean, you say that the grass is green because—there was a fire yesterday in Timbuctoo. That ridicules conjunctionism. In the same way narrative "legs" can be used to make a nonsensical narrative which itself can be a narrative of imagination.

Q: This new poetry will open the floodgates to a lot of crap, surely?

DH: Definitely! Any new poetry will—even Wordsworth opened the floodgates to a lot of crap. . . .

Q: Yes, but it's very difficult to work out ways in which you begin to discriminate between kinds of nonsense. . . . Since we are talking in theoretical terms, I find what I'm troubled by is the permissive element in this theory.

DH: It is a danger, and a danger that I am perfectly happy to undertake for the sake of the possible gains. I think you are right in implying that there are probably more possible ways to fail here—because the judgment that one can give to this kind of poem is not really analytical. No, this kind of poem takes assent or dissent. You either say yes to it or you say—crap.

Q: But it seems to me the more you particularize in your dream world the more eccentric it's going to seem. The more you allow it to turn on grand absolutes of light and dark the more you keep to this very general sort of abstract center. But the more you give it some kind of individual particularity, the more it's likely to be written in a sort of egocentric eccentric dream world. . . .

DH: Are you saying that you are approving of a more general kind . . . ?

Q: But, I mean, if it has to turn on abstracts it also turns on clichés. . . .

DH: I suspect that what you say is really false and that there are more sets of symbols and interior references with a generalizable meaning available to poets if they dig deeply enough. One need not go to the eccentric, to the merely individual, to find them. I think that the difficulty with this kind of poetry for most people is that they are applying a kind of reading which is inappropriate to the poem. You must lay yourself open to it and not translate as you go along—try to accept the images into yourself and let them happen. One should not try to resist eccentricity, but find in oneself a response to the images.

Q: Are these poems constructed like any other English or American poems that you can think of?

DH: Let's take a little poem by James Wright—"Lying in a Hammock . . ."—which starts out with the poet lying in a hammock seeing certain things—turds, horses' droppings, "blaze into golden stones." Now that has absolutely nothing to do with the kind of discourse that people like Philip Larkin wish to enter into—it has no apparent relationship to the last line, "I have wasted my life." Finally one can go back and see that everything is changing in the poem and that everything he's looking at is somehow getting better—even turds are blazing into golden stones. . . . The distance between the dropping of horses and a man lying in a hammock is so extraordinary a distance compared with, for instance, in Larkin's "The Whitsun Weddings," the poet alone and all the other chaps married. The huge imaginative leap from the one thing to another is close enough for me to having no legs. . . .

[reads James Wright, "Lying in a Hammock"]

Images are the units of speech from one unconscious mind to another. With an objective image one feels visual (or aural, or whatever) recognition: yes, that's the way it looks. With the "interior" image the subject is not anything in the exterior world; the subject is a feeling—something as general as that—a feeling, a sense. A poem can be united by the title "Miners," it can be united by a subject which is implicit without the title. Obviously, it must have some form, some sort of unity—it must provide a sense of *completion*. It has to be improvised out of images towards a sense of completion without depending, primarily, at any rate, upon the legs of logical discourse or narrative. I think that Wright's poem has tremendous effect ending this way.

Q: Wouldn't you say that, for instance, Wright's poem on Eisenhower's visit to Franco was using a traditional ironic structure?

DH: I wouldn't describe the poem that way at all. It seems to work on contrast, yes. Now Cleanth Brooks generalizes irony so much that practically anything that contrasts is irony. I mean, if you mention light, then dark, ah, that's ironic. But I don't think that's a very useful idea of irony.

Q: But if you contrast politicians like Franco with the sort of poor people . . .

DH: That's not irony, is it?

Q: Well, here light applies to all the glittering that's going on in Madrid with the planes arriving: the dark is in respect of the poor people and yet Franco is promising that all dark things will be hunted down. By which he means something quite different from what the poem implies by dark.

DH: I don't think he does. I think the poet regards him as being the enemy of all those things that he calls dark. Franco is the enemy of "the mouths of old men," the enemy of wine and so on. If you think that that's ironic language because light is usually assumed to be good and dark bad, well, then we have to throw out a lot of Blake and a lot of Lawrence—no, not throw them out, but consider that they were being ironical! I think Wright is taking light quite clearly. The metallic kind of light and glitter that he's talking about is a bad thing.

Q: It's been perverted, surely?

DH: It's a bad thing, while everything about the dark is good. I don't see any irony. Irony seems to me to happen when you use light honorifically and then let it sneak in finally that light is not all that it seems. That light has its dark side.

Q: I mean, I thought he was playing on the traditional properties of light etcetera associated with virtue and showing that in this case . . .

DH: He's not doing it here because it seems to me that there is a huge modern tradition to establish the goodness of dark things. And this comes immediately to mind when one sees how he's doing it. One doesn't have any sense, "oh, he means light to be dark this time, how clever of him!" The way I see the poem, it works on a series of *expressive* images in contrast. There is no double-take of any kind. Irony always seems to me to employ a double-take and a moment of uncertainty before one sees where the real force lies. The beauty of these images seems to me that they are absolutely clear in their affect from the moment they are uttered. And their affect is the whole point of them; they're expressionist images. We have simple sets of contrasts, delicately worked out, and the result is a marvelous kind of impeachment and a real political statement in which, to go back to what we were saying earlier, the dark world, the world of the imagination, is a judgment upon the world of metallic light. We have had so many *terrible* antifascist poems, for God's sake, and the reason most of them are terrible is that the opposition, the thing that we have to be anti-fascist about, is something as weak as doing good or being nice to people. You know, the usual wishy-washy liberalism. In this poem we don't have that: we have an enormous affect on the other side of it—the darkness, the wine in the mouths of old men—an affect contained in images. . . .

An Interview with Donald Hall

Scott Chisholm / 1971

From *Tennessee Poetry Journal*, vol. 4, no. 2, Winter 1971. The lightly edited version below is from Donald Hall, *Goatfoot Milktongue Twinbird: Interviews, Essays, and Notes on Poetry, 1970–76* (University of Michigan Press, 1978). Reprinted with permission of *Tennessee Poetry Journal*.

Question: Mr. Hall, you were born and raised in New England. Would you comment on early influences which led you to write in the first place?

Answer: It's always a series of trivialities and accidents. I grew up in the suburbs of New Haven, Connecticut—a town called Hamden. I spent all my summers on a farm in New Hampshire where my mother's father and mother lived. They were one-horse farmers. It was not economical to run small farms anymore. My grandmother is still there, at ninety-two. It's the house she was born in. That is the place where I kept to myself and daydreamed. From twelve on, I wrote poems there. I loved my grandfather very much. We'd be in the tie-up and he'd be milking and he would recite poems to entertain me. They weren't good poems; they were pieces he used to recite at the Lyceum when he was a young man. He was a great piece-speaker—very dramatic, great gestures.

When I was about twelve, and in seventh grade, I got interested in *being* something romantic and appealing. (You can begin any art for a silly reason, and then the art itself can take hold of you.) I was a lousy athlete, and I wanted some alternative way to get attention, especially from girls. Cheerleaders. I was interested in acting and writing. I wrote my first poem then. I wrote a few more, and I tried to write some fiction. Then, when I was fourteen, I became enormously excited about poetry. The friends that I gradually made at high school mostly had some interest in the arts. The girls I dated *were* going to be actresses; one boy wanted to become a composer. We were the oddballs in high school; but even being strange—that sense of alienation—was something I wanted and liked and fed upon. So I kept on writing poems. I used to come home from school, frequently after rehearsing a play, and work on poems for a couple of hours. One thing that strikes me as strange is that, right away, I began revising poems. I would finish a poem, and then I would start it over again, making changes. As far as my parents were concerned, I was to do what I liked. When I was sixteen, they sent me to Bread Loaf Writers' Conference, where I met Robert Frost.

I got excited about being a poet at fourteen, and I just kept on. My girl friends who were going to be actresses stopped. I don't think I had any more talent at fourteen than anybody else did. I just kept on. I wanted to, so much. Really, I never hesitated; there was never any dramatic point in my life where I made a decision or looked back and saw that I had made a decision.

Q: I suppose that a person could say that a great deal of your work involves the sense of loss. In your prose pieces, especially in *String Too Short to Be Saved*, there is the sense of lost people, places, events—and a good deal about your grandfather. Those characteristics carry over to your poetry in poems like "Old Home Day." Are you aware of the sense of loss as a motivating factor in your work?

A: I'm aware when I read it; I'm not aware of it as a motivation to become a poet, for instance. Of course, a tremendous amount of poetry is elegiac—not just over death, but over the loss of youth, or the loss or friends.

I used to think that this was a temperamental thing with me. I used to think that it was connected with New Hampshire, a disappearing country, a place where, every year there were more farms abandoned, and where, when you walked through the woods in the pastureland you had to watch where you put your feet for fear you might fall into a well or an old cellar hole. I used to think that this was my conditioning. But now I think my conditioning must have been earlier, and that's one reason why I liked New Hampshire, because it fulfilled the sense of loss I already had. I've come to think that the sense of being abandoned is central to my spirit. Sometimes I think we might get this from the memory of being born. Being born is a kind of abandonment and loss—loss of that comfort of the fluid and warmth inside the womb, out into the hostile air that makes you cry. I don't know. I can only talk out of my feelings and make guesses. Certainly, it could go back to wailing in your crib when your mother has gone next door to talk to a neighbor, or when someone who is supposed to look after you forgets you for a while. The sense of loss or abandonment wells up strong in your life when something in the present touches down on that old feeling.

I think that poems happen mostly when something in the present—something that you observe, something that moves you—reaches back into something very deep and probably very old in your head. It's like when two pieces of the mineral get together in an arc light: a spark jumps across it. Poetry happens in this near-collision of the two things; the words start coming, the images start forming.

And so the poem, insofar as a poem is about anything, is about these two distinct events. This accounts for the fact that poems are written in layers —a top side of the poem that the poet and his audience may be immediately aware of, an underside of the poem which the poet is not aware of at the point of composition, which he may never be aware of, and which the audience in reading may not be aware of—but which, in fact, moves the poet to write and moves the reader to respond. This communication is not intellectual. It is the communication of one inside speaking to another inside.

Q: You didn't always talk the same way about poetry, did you? At Oxford, for example, you once said, "The best poems are utterly controlled and formal," and on another occasion you wrote that, "All doctrines of inspiration have been invented by amateurs and poseurs." Do you still hold to these attitudes—or have you modified them? (laughter)

A: I haven't modified them; I've just reversed them.

That statement was partly a reaction to Englishmen talking about inspiration in a wispy way which simply meant that they wouldn't take poetry seriously. But it's only partly that. What I hear mostly in those sentences is a shriek of terror—a fear of inspiration, a fear of the imagination, a fear of the loss of control.

Earlier, you asked me about the influence of New England. Now, I don't know if this is the influence of New England or not (it sounds as if it could be) but I certainly grew up with two opposite things in my head concerning poetry. One was that I loved it; I loved the form of it, the feel of it, the beauty of it. A good poem has a sensual body: they're lovely and beautiful, like women, like sculpture.

On the other side—the second side—there was a part of me that really knew that poetry was wicked. Poetry was associated with things like opium dens, the white slave trade. I mean, it was a wicked thing to do. Like women! [laughter] The proper thing to do, I suppose, was to be the business man— putting in his hours of work for his family. Poetry was an exotic thing. It was like being captain of a pirate ship or something. I use these childish descriptions because I think it was like that.

I wanted it both ways. You try to satisfy both sides of your ambivalence. And so I made poems that were controlled by technique and reason.

I asserted control because the real freedom of poetry, the loosening of the impulse of unconscious things that are primitive and conventionally reprehensible—that loosening frightened me. A lot of New England, a lot of Harvard, and a lot of Oxford went along with this fear about poetry. I wrote poetry that was antipoetic. Eventually, in my life, I got over much of this fear, so that I could love the sensual body of the poem and try to make poems which are, in themselves as objects, beautiful. But I used to be frightened of what the content might reveal to other people. I think that in the concentration on technique, on control, in the denial of inspiration, you hear a man saying, "Please. I don't want to hear anything inside myself that isn't upright, moral, true, loyal"—the whole Boy Scout Oath.

Q: Speaking of technique, you once wrote that "All American writers, in one way or another, are obsessed with their technique." Do you feel that this is an obsession which opposes certain freedoms or innovations in poetry?

A: I think it's a device by which we often keep ourselves from innovation. But it goes both ways, as I say about everything. Whenever I make a spiritual innovation in poetry, for myself, something happens which is technically different. The poem makes a different noise. Years ago, it seemed to me that by experimenting with the technical side of poetry, I allowed voices to speak out of me that hadn't been able to speak before. Now I'm suspicious of the order of events. Perhaps, the first thing was really the voice wanting to speak. Perhaps the voice was really running me and disguising itself as a search for new technique, in order to let me ride it. in order to let it come out. I talk as if I'm running a boardinghouse inside myself.

If concentration on technique allows poets to grow, it's fine. Many people, however, get stuck in technique and don't go any further. This was especially true for many of us who were beginning to write poetry after the Second World War. The concentration on technique can become infantile. You can get stuck in the "playing" aspect of words. I do not regret, at the moment, that I spent so much time thinking about line breaks, and vowels, because I think that in the preconscious—not the unconscious but the preconscious—I gathered a lot of knowledge. It's like an athlete, practicing a lot, who learns to make moves which, in a particular game, he does without thinking. He moves as if by instinct—but it's not instinct: it's something learned which resides in you without you thinking about it.

Obviously, you learn tremendously from reading the poets and loving them. This knowledge enters your preconscious and forms your idea of what the sensual body of a poem may be. But you also learn by your own writing and devising. When I write poems now, I never think about wit or technique—about showing off and playing with words. I revise what doesn't sound right to something that sounds better. I think the sounding-not-so-right and the sounding-right arc simultaneously matters of the sensual body of the poem—which is, to a degree, a matter of what I used to call technique—and matters of the spiritual validity of the image—the truth to the unconscious content of the ancient world inside each of us moving up through the images and into the poem. And once this is embodied in the poem, then it is possible that through the noises, the line breaks, the rhythms—which are *always* talking—and through the mysterious content of the image—that one inside can communicate with another.

Q: I think you are the only member of your generation to have known Eliot, Pound, Frost, and Dylan Thomas.

A: Maybe so.

Q: Would you comment on the experience of having known these men— their influence if any and your reaction?

A: So much of the world around us, whether we're in school, or with our families, or whatever, tries to tell us, "Don't take yourself so seriously." This is the standard protective device of most of humanity most of the time. We are born bored; we die bored; what difference does it make? If you're going to struggle to try to make an art, you know perfectly well that you may spend your whole life working at something and ultimately failing. *But*, you have the example of the people who have made the struggle anyway, and who in your mind have done something good. This in itself is a force opposite that bourgeois force that says, "Don't take yourself so seriously." The example of the poets says, "It's all right. Try it. You may make it, you may not. What matters is the doing."

When you grow up, you tend to think of life as a slope, up a hill, at the top of which there is a plateau; there is some point at which you have made it in whatever you are trying to do. Then you know that you are good and you walk on a horizontal plane thereafter. Well, I know the name of that horizontal plane. It is death. It's the end. The only possible way to stay alive, the only possible name of being alive, is "continue the struggle." I remember Dylan Thomas telling me when he was thirty-eight, a year before he died, that he didn't think he was very good—that he had written maybe three poems that he liked. One was the poem on his thirtieth birthday, one was the poem on his thirty-fifth birthday, and one he called "an early Hardyish piece," "This Bread I Break." That's the way he felt that night. Another time, there might have been no poems, or twenty-five poems, or three entirely different poems.

All of these men felt that their lives were a matter of their daily consideration, that their life's work was, at each point in time, breaking against the shore of the moment. It is always possible to change it all, suddenly to make the breakthrough, suddenly to be *really good.*

Q: You saw T. S. Eliot when you went to England for the first time. What was the conversation like?

A: I had actually met him first in America, briefly, at a party. He asked me to drop around and see him at Faber and Faber when I got to England. Of course I was spooked out of my mind. He also suggested that I might show him some of my poems. He spoke about them a bit, rather kindly, pointing out one or two places where the poems were bad. He was a generous man.

We also talked about our literary generations in a way that makes me feel very pompous in retrospect. I was twenty-three. I was frightened of him and didn't really realize his humor, which was constant. He was *always* playful in talk, and frequently in his most serious poems, for that matter.

Q: What about your experience with Ezra Pound?

A: My experience with Pound was limited in time. I went down to Rome in 1960 (he was staying in Rome at the apartment of friends), in order to do an interview for the *Paris Review.* I'd been planning to go to see him in Washington when he was at Saint Elizabeth's, but I never got around to it. I was frightened of him too—as someone who had ideas which I didn't like and whom I thought would be unfriendly. What I found was, in fact, an extraordinarily lonely man. He wanted companionship. My wife and I went out to dinner with him several times. He wanted us around all the time: he wanted to talk. He was cordial, friendly, and extremely worried about his own mental state—not about insanity so much as loss of power, loss of creativity. When we were doing the interview, he constantly feared that he sounded too tired, that he could not finish the sentences that he'd begun. He eventually did finish them. Sometimes a sentence would begin one day and conclude two days later. It was a strange time. When I wasn't interviewing him and we were just talking, he felt more energetic. There was less demand on him.

On the last day of the interview, he jumbled around in some suitcases at the end of the room and took out drafts of cantos on which he was working and sat down on the sofa with me and said, "Are they any good? Tell me. Do you think I should go on?" I read them and tried to tell him what I thought of them, just as straight as I could, because I wouldn't lie to that man or try to tell him anything about his poems that I didn't believe. The fragments were superb. But I did not know if he could go on, because of his health.

Once I was waiting for him in a cafe across from the apartment where he was staying. I had been there before and the waiter knew me. The waiter knew him separately. Pound came in and sat with me. The waiter came over and made the connection and said a sentence in Italian which ended with the word "figlio." Pound looked over at me and then back at the waiter and said, "Si, si."

Well, I felt like that temporarily—like his son. He felt at that time that he'd been, for so much of his life, mistaken. It was sad, but it was also triumphant that he could have the strength *and* the humility to think that, perhaps, he had been mistaken. I'm speaking of mistakes of idea—that's what he was speaking of—mistakes to do with politics, to do with fascism, and also mistakes to do with the intellectual structure of the *Cantos.* He used to say—he said it several times—that perhaps he had been mistaken in putting Confucius at the top of Paradise; it should have been Agassiz. He was, of course, greatly troubled by these doubts. Here was his life's work, incomplete and perhaps wrong . . . and he questioned his strength about going on.

Is that possibility—the possibility of these great poets in any era when poetry was so volatile, so changing—is it possible now for that to happen again in poetry? It seems to me that the external circumstances have so altered with the incredible political messes we're in, the sense of prevailing disaster, the wars . . .

Art still exists by itself, aside from social change. We know that a language can cease to exist and that any poetry which survives will be part of a dead language. We know, as Yeats says in "Lapis Lazuli," that sculpture and art are destroyed. We have not only the sense of our own death, which men have always had, but the sense of the death, even the death of our civilization, even the death of our species. And although it is reasonable to acknowledge that with the death of the species, all art is dead, I think that to many of us art is the bulwark against this extinction. Art is created against death.

It's a bulwark, but it's not a conservative thing. It preserves the spirit of a person who created and wrote it to an extent that his times, his people, his language are preserved. However, it is radical in the sense that it will represent the values of the world being born, if there will be a new birth.

And if there will be a new birth in the world, now, I believe that what is happening in the world of poetry will be a leading part of that birth. That birth will come from the dark spirit which moves inside us. We will survive by going beyond the rational, not by suppressing it, not by destroying the machine, which is childishness, but by going beyond this in the wholeness of our lives towards the mystery at the center. Some people have always known about it. Priests and poets.

Q: In the first edition of *New Poets of England and America*, why did you leave out the Black Mountain group, Creeley and others? It seems unusual, to say the least, since you indicated earlier that you take a serious interest in promoting poetry.

A: It's ridiculous, but we did not acknowledge that they existed, and we weren't reading them. I speak for myself anyway. They were printing; the magazines were there. I know that I avoided looking at the magazines because I had decided that the stuff was really no good without opening up my mind to it.

Obviously I wanted to keep my mind closed. I thought I *knew* how to write poetry; I *knew* what to do; I didn't want anybody upsetting me. This was silly and cowardly, but it's how I acted. I had met Robert Creeley when I was an undergraduate and we had one long and good talk. Then I'd read some of his stuff in a magazine (I can't remember which magazine) and it was like e. e. cummings. I remember thinking, "Oh, Creeley's just a Cummings imitator." Later, when his style changed, I didn't read him. He was in magazines, the pamphlets were around, but I didn't read them. So, I think that the parochialism of the first edition of *New Poets of England and America* was a result of a kind of *careful* ignorance.

Q: I want to come back to some of your early assessments of poetry in America. You talked of your failure to see the Black Mountain group. If I read correctly, you had a deep distrust of the Beats also.

A: Sure. You see, two things are going on in any failure to recognize excellence when it first happens. One of them is that you have an idea of what poetry is; this is true whether you are being a critic or being a poet or both. You're *set*; when something new comes along, instead of having the imagination or the energy to accommodate yourself to it, the easier thing is to deny it and to say that it's not poetry, it's no good. This is what happened to Wordsworth when he published *Lyrical Ballads*. This accounts for some of my planned ignorance when new things began to happen in the late 1950s.

But there was also another thing; my own fear of poetry, my own fear of the looseness of the imagination, my fear of fantasy. Most of this new poetry was not fantastic, but a lot of it was considerably more loose and less conventional than mine, especially in intellectual and spiritual ways. So I feared the poetry not only because it attacked my stylistic set but also because it was a danger to my *emotional* set. Learning to read some of this poetry has been a liberation to me.

I think of Allen Ginsberg, among others, although as my own writing has changed, I don't think it has come to resemble Allen's.

Q: In 1961, while reviewing for the *Nation*, you wrote that the most disconcerting thing about modernism had been its discontinuity. Using Olson's essay on "Projective Verse," you alluded to his comment that the time has come to pick "the fruits of the experiments of Cummings, Pound, Williams." Has American poetry been harvesting these fruits lately?

A: Not these fruits. I didn't know so much about modernism then as I do now. The strange thing in English and American poetry, with exceptions that are hardly worth noticing, is that it was separate from international modernism. In international modernism there was a continuity in style among painters, sculptors, poets, playwrights from Latin America to Cuba to Spain to Germany to Russia (around the time of the revolution) to France, Greece, and Scandinavia.

English and American modern poetry, while some of it is excellent, is really quite separate. The movement that Olson was talking about was not a single movement but a series of eccentric acts by people writing alone out of their own reading and experience. It did not have the inwardness that is common to German expressionism and to "modernismo" in the Spanish language and which is also common to expressionist and surrealist painting.

In the last ten years or so, American poetry has joined international modernism. It has not harvested the fruits of Pound and Williams, it has harvested the fruits of the great early painters of this century and of the poets from Spain and France and Germany who had something in common with these painters.

Q: Yes. That's part of what one recognizes in, for example, Bly's *The Sixties* with its emphasis on the poetry of Neruda.

A: Bly is the single, most important innovator—or transmitter of this particular energy. Other people have come to similar positions independently. It had to happen. Even most of the descendants of the Pound and Williams tradition, not just the descendants of Lowell and Wilbur, for instance, seem to me to have moved in a general way toward the poetry of fantasy.

Incidentally, when Robert Bly and I were graduates together at college, we were tremendously iambic. We were poets of the fifties and Bob was writing blank verse narratives and sonnets. When I was at Oxford just after college, Bob sent me a bundle of Shakespearean sonnets that he had been working on for a long time. Even before I could answer him, and tell him what I thought of them, I had a letter from him saying that this was no use; it was too old fashioned; he couldn't write this way now. He had begun to change. We all went through enormous changes. He led the way, for many of us.

At the same time at Harvard when Bob and I were undergraduates (we met when I was a freshman and he was a sophomore), there was John Ashbery, Frank O'Hara, Kenneth Koch. Also there was L. E. Sissman, Adrienne Rich, and Peter Davison. Sissman was in a class with me, and I dated Adrienne a couple of times. Richard Wilbur, a little older, was a Junior Fellow. Robert Creeley had just left Harvard, but he was around the area, and some of us met him. Certainly Creeley was not being iambic! Koch and Ashbery, while seeming a little Audenish then, were beginning to write a poetry of fantasy and strangeness—certainly more than Bly and I were at that time.

Q: How did your poetry change?

A: The old way ran out. I found myself afflicted with a sense of the staleness and glibness of my verse. The forms were predictable, the feelings were superficial, the wit was easy. I had to put it aside. I flailed around. I worked with other techniques, like syllabics and eventually free verse. But it was really a searching for the poetry of spiritual freedom. I discovered that by telling a lie—by telling what is, in outward terms, a lie—we express something which is true inside ourselves. I am speaking of the dream self which is always within us, even when we are awake. In this dream place, things we fear the most are true, and things we desire the most are true. When we express these things, we are telling outward lies. We may say, as I said in a poem that I wrote when I was young, that "the snow hangs still in the middle of the air." You invent such a place because you *want* it to exist, because you dread mutability, because you don't want to die, or grow older, or break up with the girl.

This place has existed in poetry from the beginning. So I wrote a poetry of fantasy, on occasion, when I was in my teens and in my twenties. But for a period in my mid-twenties, I became more aware of what I was doing with fantasy, and I was frightened of it. I courted the poetry of rationality, a poetry in which illusion was defeated, and in which reason asserted its supremacy.

But gradually, from my late twenties on, I have been able to allow the dream self to come up and take its place in my poems. Partly, this came from reading other poems, and partly from accepting parts of myself which I wanted to cover up before. I was able to begin to write poems in which I had no idea of what I was talking about. When I was twenty-five years old, I wouldn't have dreamed of writing a poem in which I didn't know what I was talking about. Or in which I didn't *think* I knew what I was talking about. In the poems from that time which are any good, there is always something going on of which I was not aware. The topside—which I was aware of—is still there, of course; but the underside, which I concealed from myself, is the power that makes the engine go.

In recent years, I have come to accept the beginning of a poem, or even a whole draft, without the slightest clue to the subject matter. Words come to me heavy with emotion, and I accept them even though I have no idea what they are trying to tell me. The first poem I remember writing in this way is my musk-ox poem, "The Long River." In 1958, I remember, I began it with a phrase about a musk-ox. I had no idea where it came from. I trusted it, because it came heavy with feeling. For perhaps two years I lived with these phrases, as the poem began to extend itself down the page. It doesn't extend very long, as a matter of fact. But it took me a long time to write it.

The process of writing a poem is a process of developing and shaping the words which the poem begins with, until finally, upon completion of the poem, you can see what it is that you are expressing. The poem is a vehicle for self-discovery. Of course the premise upon which this kind of poetry is based is that if you discover something that is deep enough inside yourself, it's going to be a part of other people's insides, too, and reveal themselves to themselves.

Many of us, then, went through a movement from a poetry which was formal in its meter and rhyme and which had a rational and external narrative, to poetry which is free verse with improvised forms and improvised resolutions of noise—and which is more intimate, more emotional, and more irrational. I don't see why there should be a necessary connection between free verse and the poetry of fantasy. It seems to me that, in my case, the *associations* of iambic verse were rational. The iambic poem stated a problem and solved it, and tied it up neatly at the end, like a little bundle. It seems to me that I was unable to break through that neatness of content until I was able to move into the form—free verse—where I had no illusion of control. When I am writing a poem now, I don't know, when I am writing the first line, what the next line is going to be like. I don't know what sound it's going to make. I improvise until it sounds right and feels right. Ultimately, for me, the poem has to feel resolved and whole and single and fixed and unmovable. Yeats used to say that the finished poem made a sound like the click of the lid of a perfectly made box. I still hear that click in free verse as well as I ever did in the sonnet. You improvise toward the click.

Q: You have been talking about some of your early poems. That first book, *Exiles and Marriages*, was a huge success. It was in 1955, I think. What do you think accounted for the success?

A: Probably the large quantity of bad verse in it. I was blessed with the praises of *Time*. They printed my picture and did a review of it—something they don't do very often with a first book of poems by a young poet. And, of course, it was a curse.

There are a lot of poems in there that seem to me to come out of the fear of poetry, and which seem to me accommodating to the bourgeoisie. They were mostly poems of the rational period I was talking about. They tell you it's all right to have illusions, but you'd better get over them because, after all, reality is reality. Or they tell you to praise virtue and blame vice, or at least to be nice and guilty over being vicious. Three-quarters of it is without any interest whatsoever. There are a few poems that I like all through. Others are partly OK. Recently I did a selection for *The Alligator Bride*, I was able to revise and improve some of the old ones, and reprint them.

Q: You once wrote that "the true artist refines his feeling and thought in revision until he finds the absolute shape and motion which satisfy him." Do you still revise heavily or do you rely on spontaneous experience to determine the poem's shape?

A: I revise heavily. Usually, it takes a long time. This isn't, of course, a necessity for anybody else. Some friends of mine will work on the same poem steadily for eighteen or twenty hours. I might take two years to finish the poem, and put in eighteen or twenty hours during the two years. I work on the poem for a while, make a few changes, cross out a few things, make a few comments in the margin perhaps, and after a few minutes I can't stand to look at it anymore. I put it away. The next day, the next week, or the next month, I'll come back to it again and get at it. I have never written a poem in one draft which has remained the same. I have had a few experiences where a poem has become *nearly* whole. Very few. However, it still took me six or eight months to make the two tiny changes that made the poems come out right.

You asked in your question, "Do you revise heavily or do you rely on spontaneous experience?" Well, I refuse the question, because I *do* revise a lot and I *do* rely on the spontaneous. The revision is spontaneous. I look at the poem which has seemed fixed to me, and suddenly I see that a part of it is wrong. I quickly cross out what I don't like—I've made something new.

It happens, also, when I'm not looking at the poem. I may be walking down the street and a line will come into my head—not a revision of an old line, perhaps, but a line that is brand new—I recognize that it belongs to a certain poem. I have been working on the poem all the time without knowing it. I'll write it down somewhere and later, back at my house, I'll look at the draft of the poem and see where my new line fits. Or if it fits.

Sometimes when I read a poem aloud at a reading, I find myself making a mistake. If I make a mistake, I listen to it, because my mistake may be what I really should put there. Or it may simply show that I don't really like the line.

I suppose I tend to revise more by deletion than by anything else. I have an original image which develops into a whole draft of the poem— sometimes at one sitting, more often over a period of time. Then the long process of getting it right is often the process of finding out what to omit. Deletion is at least as creative as addition. I tend to explain too much. I tend to go into too much detail. And this over-explaining and this detail are not just technical matters, or ideas about what a poem *ought* to be. These over-statements are a device by which I hold down the feeling, hold it at arm's length through explanation or elaboration. It takes me a long time to come to the clarity and intensity of the single thrust of the feeling. The upper regions of my head, where the words begin to come in from the feelings, are still concerned *not* to see, *not* to understand, *not* to admit.

Q: I was reading this morning an essay of yours called "The Vatic Voice," in which you talk about the way in which a poem surfaces. I wonder if you would talk about that now?

A: Sure. The "Vatic Voice" is not a phrase I'm too fond of, although I made it up. Often, poems begin in a passive way, a phrase comes to me, or some words come to me. I overhear something inside myself. This happens in certain moods. The beginnings come to me in little meteor showers—a day or two, perhaps two weeks—I will have many new ideas. Everything I look at seems to bloom with poetry. During the same period, I make a lot of mistakes when I'm talking. Freudian slips, and so on. I find myself saying weird things in conversation—things I had no idea I was going to say, metaphorical things usually. There seems to be a kind of alleyway down to the unconscious mind. I'm a bit schizoid, I guess, but I feel all right. Mysterious things surface more clearly. During these periods, when I am not with people, I daydream very loosely. Unlike the night dream, I can watch it—I can listen to it. I hear the voice, speaking and delivering sorts of messages. Certain phrases stick with me. They have power—emotional power—and they have intensity. These phrases may become parts of poems or clues to poems or directions toward poems. However, this voice is not always available: laziness and undirected activity sometimes seem to help it to come. But I've had the experience of going through a period like this when I was enormously *busy*. There was one time about a year ago when there was a period of ten days or two weeks before I went into the hospital for an operation. I had to do three poetry readings and meet a deadline on an article early, because I knew I was going to be sick. Also, I was teaching. I was frantic. But during that period ten or twelve poems happened—the first drafts happened. I'm working on them. Some of them are still in notebooks and hardly worked over at all. I remember writing in the backs of books in airport limousines, writing at 30,000 feet, writing in motels. So much was happening. This was the reverse of the usual quietness or laziness. Really, I can't make any rules for the conditions under which I hear this voice.

Q: In your own work, I see a change from the highly optimistic, almost cheerful poetry of *Exiles and Marriages* to a more sober poetry—a poetry, really, of grief. How do you feel about it?

A: In the first place, I think that a lot of the cheerful and optimistic poetry of *Exiles and Marriages* is fakey. Some of it is simply naive. In either case, it is bad.

Of course there is a poetry of high spirits which can be honest and true. I think I've written some of that even recently. A new poem like "Happy Times" in *The Alligator Bride* seems to me to be full of good cheer. That's fine; I've nothing against high spirits as long as a poem is true.

There are a few poems of grief in *Exiles*, like the elegy for my grandfather. But real grief started in *The Dark Houses*, mostly. My father died about the time *Exiles and Marriages* was published. I learned that he was going to die on the day the publisher accepted the book. *Dark Houses* begins with a poem on my father's death. A poem I still like. (I revised it a little for *The Alligator Bride*.) As I look back at *The Dark Houses* as a whole, it seems to me that the whole book is an angry elegy over his death. Though I don't think too much of the book as a whole, it is more honest than *Exiles and Marriages*, partly because it deals openly with unpleasant subject matter. Its failure lies in a muting of these feelings—not a changing or a perversion of them, but a tendency toward gray understatement.

I would like to be able to write poetry out of any mood. I feel that unhappy poetry—poetry that comes out of the situation of grief or loss or anger—tends to be stronger than poetry of the light heart. I think there is a valid reason for this in the nature of the art and in the nature of the poetic process.

This is what I mean. Energy comes from conflict. The sensual body of the poem is pleasure. A poem has a body which gives pleasure—the sounds of it, the weight of it. The poem, no matter what its subject matter—no matter how terrifying or anxious—has its separate existence as a pleasurable object. It has an existence like a stone which a sculptor has worked over. If you are writing a poem out of pleasurable feelings, the theme-pleasure walks hand in hand with the sense-pleasure of the poem. But it can only go a short distance because there is no conflict to give energy. On the other hand, if you are writing a poem out of grief and loss, or out of anger, the side of the poem which is its sensual body moves in conflict with the pain of the content. You move, then, from one thing to the other, consistently. You move from thesis to antithesis, and then the same thing over again. The constant movement, which is so quick as to seem simultaneous, between the pleasure of the body and the pain of the spirit in loss, conflicts and lends energy by this conflict.

Q: In *A Roof of Tiger Lilies* you have several poems on the barrenness of American life. "The Wives," for example. Is your more recent poetry perhaps an attempt to raise the more sensitive garden?

A: Those are terms in which I sometimes think of the new poetry. The second book was called *The Dark Houses* and the third *A Roof of Tiger Lilies*. The color comes into it. If you look through the books, there is a movement from dark colors, which are arid and which represent sterility, to a poetry which looks to an alternative to *The Dark Houses*, which is dark colors and flowers. There is a poem in *A Roof of Tiger Lilies* called "Digging" which is about wanting to become bright flowers.

In that elegy for my father that began *The Dark Houses*, I was talking about darkness and sterility and the grief and loss. I said in that poem "This love is jail; another sets us free." The other love which "sets us free" was only referred to in that book; it didn't happen. I did not plot out my life and say "Now I am going to go after the other side," but, in fact, I think I have been doing it. I prefer pleasure to pain, which doesn't make me very unusual. Bright colors are pleasure. But the search for the yellow flower is a search for a fulfillment of the self and the body which will come to grief both in the idiomatic sense and in the sense of the straight abstraction. Within the poem—within the poet—there is a conflict between the desire to let the impulses free, and the almost continual necessary frustration of these desires. The frustration is partly the punishment we impose upon ourselves for liberating our impulses. It is a self-enclosed circle, and one cannot escape. Still, the search for the yellow flower is the only way.

Q: One of the things that I concerned myself with when I began to read your work was the rendering of image. In some of your earlier poems, the thing that amazed me was the way in which you avoided sensual identifications that can be literally rendered as a "scene." Rather, you tend to excise the literal images out until what remains is an interpreted sensual image. I think particularly of "The Long River." Are you aware of having avoided the literal sensual renderings in your poems—in order to avoid the explicit statement?

A: I try to avoid the literal statement in general, not just in the rendering of scenes. In poems, explicitness is a way of holding experience at arm's length. There are erotic poems in which I originally wrote detail almost with diagrams. I had an impulse early on, in the process of revision, to cut out some of the physiology. But I hesitated, at first, for fear that I was censoring myself, or being merely prudish. Eventually, I came to realize, with a little help from my friends, that the physiological detail had the effect of cutting down the eroticism. The more pornographic they were, the less erotic they were. I have been able, I think, to cut out the specific physiological terms to a great extent, and to retain the action and the spirit, so that the poem is more emotional.

Q: Mr. Hall, two poems have particularly impressed me—one which I mentioned before is "The Long River," and the other is "The Alligator Bride." In both cases these strike me as surrealist poems. In most of your poems, the material is outward, poems like "The Days." But in both "The Long River" and "The Alligator Bride" you seem to go inside or down deeply into an interior world. Do you sense this also?

A: In a poem like "The Days" or "The Table" there is a scene-setting, an outside, but the intensity of the poetry comes from fantasy—after the scene has been established. The movement inward to the emotional situation requires fantasy, or surrealist imagery. But the outside has been a necessary lead towards the inside. The layers of discourse are partially separated in poems like this. It is true that I enjoy and am most excited by poems like "The Long River," "The Alligator Bride," "The Blue Wing," and "Happy Times" in which there *is* no topside—or the topside is nonsensical or absurd or tells a story that makes no sense—and in which all of the coherence and all of the unity is emotional and underneath. This is the kind of poem which excites me the most, from which I learn the most and which pleases me the most, because I feel less control and more discovery. Yet I don't want to make rules for myself and say that this is the only kind of poem that I will write.

Q: Is the surrealist poem for you a comfortable poem? Does it seem to you that the surrealist poem is more suited to the times?

A: I can't say that I'm conscious of what kinds of poems are more suited to the times. Looking at the body of work being done in America right now, it would seem that the surrealist poem is suited to the times, because we are making it so. I don't know.

I find that whatever I write, if I am able to go through with it and complete it there is a comfort in the composition—a comfort in the resolution of the whole. Since there is more anxiety connected with the surrealist poem (we are not aware of the nature of the material as we shape it) there is consequently more comfort in the resolution of that anxiety. You are getting something under control that is hidden and mysterious and sometimes violent. You are able to control it in the sense that you form it—but not in the sense that you take the claws out of its paws.

Q: In many of your selected poems from the previous volumes which you use in *The Alligator Bride*, I sense a dramatic new compression—a tightening to the barest essentials, almost a restriction to a single emotional effect. Does this new work represent a significant new change to you? Does it look forward to your new material?

A: I cannot look forward to my new material. At the point where something is changing, I am aware that there is a change but I don't know what I am doing. Once I understand what I have been doing, it's used up. I must go on to something else. In the process of making a new group of poems, which may be the work of a year or two—I work on families of poems at the same time—only gradually do I become aware of what I am doing. I cannot tell you where I am going to go; I can only tell you where I have been.

In the first part of your question, were you talking about the revisions of the older poems?

Q: Yes.

A: There the compression seems to me, to pick up your word, not a *restriction*, but a *liberation*. I think that when I cut something out, it was something which was restricting the poem either by saying too much or by explaining too much. And the act of cutting, for me, loosens the poem and gets rid of the dead weight so it can fly. I feel this with some of the poems I wrote many years ago, from which I was able simply to excerpt a stanza, like "My Son My Executioner." The first poem in the book is "Wedding Party," a poem I began when I was nineteen. It seems to me vastly improved by omitting a middle stanza which was absolutely worthless. I didn't realize until a year ago when I was finishing the text of the selected poems, with the help of a friend, that the middle stanza was perfectly extra. The poem is more powerful by leaving it out. Sometimes these extra stanzas are simply the results of diffidence. You don't have enough confidence in your images, so you want to explain them.

Q: Much of your work was filled with images of airplanes. Could you comment on the significance of these images?

A: When I was growing up, airplanes were still fairly new. I was born not long after Lindbergh flew the Atlantic and my mother and father were born in the year of Kitty Hawk. I saved pictures of airplanes in scrapbooks. I knew every plane in the sky. I still do. Planes have been terribly important to me as things in themselves. I love to fly. And then, again and again, in my poetry, and even in my conversation when I am reaching around for a metaphor or an analogy, I find myself using flying and airplanes.

I think that at different times these images embody any number of things. Mostly my airplanes—in my poems—are crashed. The first poem which I ever published in the *Harvard Advocate* when I was a freshman (a poem I never reprinted) was about an airplane crash. The most recent airplane poem is the first from which there has been a survivor. Somebody said it was a sign of maturity.

There are other images of stopped machinery, the locomotive lost in the woods, the abandoned automobile, and even the image of empty and decaying houses. There are certainly embodied, in all these images, feelings of loss, death, deprivation, and abandonment.

Q: Do you think this is a common procedure for poets to have fixed symbolic values in a certain sense? David Ignatow, for instance, does it with knives.

A: It's not a procedure. I don't know if they are "fixed symbolic values." They are more likely overdetermined images.

Q: Could you explain what you mean by overdetermined images?

A: I am not sure I am using that phrase correctly. As I understand it, an image is overdetermined when it derives a power, in excess of what you would rationally expect it to have, from being the locus of a number of *different* sources of power in your psyche.

I think many poets, if you look through their work, have certain sets that come up again and again and again. Obviously, in Yeats, there are a certain number of words—like the moon—which recur frequently. And you cannot fix a particular meaning to it, because at one point the moon may be an image for the aging process, for going down towards death—in "Adam's Curse"; yet more frequently it's an image of the imagination and of the world of darkness inside yourself—"Lines Written in Dejection." The word always emerges with power, but the particular association is granted by the particular context.

Q: Some of your airplane poems have skeletons in the cockpits. Today, after we had talked about these poems last night, you showed me an article from the morning paper which reported that a World War II plane had been found in the Philippines in which there were two skeletons. How does this make you feel?

A: The shivers run down my spine again. I read it in the paper after having talked with you about this theme, after having talked about the theme in conversation a thousand times, after having written about it in my poetry—and now when I read it in the paper, it happens all over again. The shivers. There is something more here than I have ever reached. In this particular news item, what struck me and touched me particularly were the dog tags which they found on the skeletons with the names and service numbers—something preserved out of all this time. The plane had crashed there more than twenty-five years ago.

Q: Is this, again, part of the sense of loss you are talking about?

A: I suppose loss—and abandonment. I think that sometimes, at any rate, the sense of the crash of the airplane is associated with an abandonment that has to do with women. (Really, I think I know more than I am telling you. I don't want to tell you.) Certainly this is true in a poem which I like especially, "The Blue Wing." I think that for all of us, in the deepest place, all women are one woman.

Q: What is the loss which the skeleton in the cockpit has experienced?

A: There are two poems—"The Blue Wing" and "The Man in the Dead Machine"—and there are two different losses. I cannot fix the loss any more than the poems fix it. I just talked about "The Blue Wing"'s sense of loss as connected, in some way, with women. In the other poem there is some of that too, because when I was writing about the plane in the jungle I said that it was covered with vines "as thick as arms." Two things happen in that image which are developed throughout the poem, though I was not aware of either one of them at the time of writing the phrase. The feeling is like being caught in a web—like a fly in a spider's web. It is also like being held in the arms . . . of the mother. These senses may be seen as contradictory, but they are two ways of looking at the same thing. You are comforted and cradled in those arms, but at the same time you are stuck and you have to get out. The getting out and the getting away from the arms, which is necessary for your life, leaves many of us perpetually with the sense of the loss of those arms.

Q: But the image which you use, in "The Man in the Dead Machine," is more profound. It is really the skeleton, the body stripped of its flesh. It is death.

A: That is right. When I was writing that poem, I thought of it in a more superficial way than I do now—now that I see what it really does. (A young poet pointed it out to me, in fact.) I thought I was writing about the sense of being stuck or paralyzed (dead) in the midst of life. But really, the poem has that permanent sense of the skull beneath the skin, the potential death in us all. Here the airplane and the skeleton are different. "The Blue Wing" is not at all about the skull beneath the skin. As far as *I* know.

Q: You've already talked about one theme of your work—the longing for sensual pleasure. There are, of course, others. One is the grief for old people who die, and another is an awareness, often frightening, of organic movement inside the body toward death. Poems like "The Repeated Shapes" and "By the Exeter River" are examples of the first. "My Son My Executioner" and "Mount Kearsarge" are examples of the latter.

A: I have felt connected with old people more than any of my friends here. I remember thinking from an early age of the coming deaths of people I loved. I suppose it must go back to something before my grandfather, and I don't understand it. When I was nine years old a great aunt died. I remember lying in bed repeating to myself, insistently, and melodramatically, "Now death has become a reality." I wanted to insist upon it, to know it, and not to turn away from it. I was morbid. I also remember touching the hand of an old great-uncle, a minister in New Hampshire, and realizing that after my fingers pressed into the flesh of his hand, his flesh did not respond immediately, it was not resilient. The flesh very gradually moved out again. I did it over and over again, knowing that what I was touching was dying flesh. I wanted to know that.

I think that I loved them because they were going to die. That sounds simple and direct enough, and yet I am suspicious of it as a whole story. Did I, perhaps, want them to die? Did I, perhaps, in some way love death or want to die myself, and therefore associate myself with them? I really cannot answer. What was the second part of your question?

Q: I mentioned the apparent theme of organic movement inside the body toward death, which you seem partly to be dealing with now. I mentioned the poem "My Son My Executioner."

A: "Sleeping" is an example of that.

"My Son My Executioner" was written when my son was born. I was twenty-five, and I had the sense of his replacing me, and, therefore, of my own necessary death. But this is only the top of the poem. It is *there*, but other things are going on as well. To look upon your son as your executioner is not the friendliest way to look at him. There seems to be anger in the poem.

But why would I be mad at this little baby that I loved to hold and to feed? It was many years before I saw something else about that poem. (I imagine lots of other people have seen it, because they didn't have reasons *not* to *see* it.) A year or two ago when my son was about fourteen, he said to me, "That poem you wrote about me when I was born, that's really about you and your daddy, isn't it?" Of course, he's right. "My Son My Executioner" is much more a memory of my feelings toward my own father than it is, actually about me and my baby son. Having a baby son apparently reminded me of the feelings toward the father which every man must have, the wish to take the father's place with the mother. The poem contains a sense that my body is moving on towards death, but I think it probably takes most of its power from the wish that my father move on toward death. (He died a year and a half later.) Part of me, in a primitive way, wanted him to die, and of course was guilty about it. The energy, I think, comes from this conflict of desire and guilt over desire.

Q: Since we're talking about that early period again, what kind of satisfaction did you get from writing the reminiscences of *String Too Short to Be Saved*? How did it differ from your poetry?

A: Writing that book of prose memoirs of New Hampshire was a tremendous satisfaction, a deep swim into memory. Writing it was relaxing compared to poetry, because I could let the images proliferate. I could go on and on remembering and inventing out of memory. You know the scene, the place, the feel, the smell—and you invent a day. You know the way people talk; so then you make up things for them to say. It is a reenactment of the past by ventriloquism. You drift down into memory and people it, make it talk, feel the sun on your back and the wind in your hair.

Writing it also released things for me, I think. I wrote some poems directly out of it. I'd be writing along in prose and I would get excited about some images, so I'd stop writing the prose, pick up another piece of paper, and begin to write in lines, with tighter control over rhythm, and I suppose more conciseness. But much more important than that, I think the book helped me to open up to feeling, to acknowledge feeling more. Writing that book led to the gradual increase in intensity of feeling that there is in *A Roof of Tiger Lilies*, which I was writing at that time.

The writer's relationship to his own past is fantastically important. Typically, writers have good memories. They are constantly going over things and remembering. People have said that everything truly important in your life happens before you are fifteen or sixteen. We go over this material, reassemble it, put it together again and again. By the act of writing down a part of my life which I seemed able to preserve, and from which I could recall strong feeling, clearly and cleanly—I opened myself to the possibility of writing other feelings from other scenes and parts of my life. *String Too Short to Be Saved* was an exercise in unclogging passages.

Q: So long as we're talking about the shift in emphasis—of being able to deal with other aspects of your experience—would you comment on your new work? Where does it seem to be heading? What new winds are moving it?

A: The new poems in *The Alligator Bride* were written from January of 1966 through April or May of 1969. I began some of them earlier, but I had two years when I couldn't write at all, from the winter of 1964 until January 3rd, 1966. Images came to me which I wrote down in notebooks, but I couldn't put them together. I lacked the quietness, the serenity, where things can combine in your head and grow and move. All I had was little flashes of images. I could take notation in my head, but I couldn't combine things. I was able, in that bad time, to write other things. I wrote some journalism, and put together a play. But I couldn't write poetry—the most important thing to me. I was denying that to myself.

After two years, which were terrible years, I began to be able to combine images again. It seems to me that I was able to get through to a more dangerous and scary feeling than I had before. The example that comes to mind is "The Alligator Bride," which I worked on within the first six months of beginning to write again. To acknowledge these feelings, to bring them out, and to give them shape and form, was something I certainly could not have done ten years before. I don't think I did it so strongly in the poems of *A Roof of Tiger Lilies*, either. A part of me had been holding back, you see, from the acknowledgment of the whole thing. Perhaps there is still some holding back, and I wonder if the humor, or whatever it is, in "The Alligator Bride," is itself a device by which I am trying to palliate the misery in the poem. I don't know.

I am mainly interested in trying to write a poem in which, as Galway Kinnell said to me in conversation last fall, you bring everything that you have done, everything that you know, together all at once. That's not quoting Galway exactly, that's what I got from what he said. That kind of poem involves knowing yourself. You have to be able to get at the truth of your feeling and not to distort it. This is where I want to go now, and where I hope I am going.

An Interview with Donald Hall

David Hamilton / 1983

Conducted in August 1983. From *Iowa Review*, vol. 15, no. 1, article 2, 1985, pp. 1–17.
Reprinted by permission of *Iowa Review*.

Interviewer's note: I interviewed Hall while visiting at Eagle Pond Farm in August 1983; we then shaped the interview further through correspondence.—DH

David Hamilton: In "Poetry and Ambition" you said, "Nothing is learned once that does not need learning again." There's a nice aphoristic ring to that. Could you give an example or two?

Donald Hall: I think that a writer's strengths and weaknesses show early, and usually remain strengths and weaknesses no matter how thoroughly the style alters. If we start, say, with a talent for visual description and for a foot-tapping dance-like rhythm, we retain this ability. And the same, alas, with the ways of failure. I find myself in revision having to teach myself the old saws over and over again: Attend to the verbs; cut the adjectives; don't say the same thing twice; show don't tell. I need to remember: Don't let sound drown sense. I need to remember: Don't write the same poem over again.

Sometimes I learn the old lesson again by reading someone else's poem, admiring it, and thinking: I would not have had the brains to do it that way. Recently I read a brief poem that starts out as the poet tells herself what is *not* to be feared: "A fly wounds the water but the wound / soon heals." ". . . What looks like smoke / floating over the neighbor's barn / is only apple blossoms." Fine. Then she says: "But sometimes what looks like disaster *is* disaster: . . ." Now, after that colon, *I* would have tended to put something abstract and fierce, something about the agony of suffering doubtless. How much better it is the way she does it—to make a scene, like a quick camera shot: "The day comes at last, / and the men struggle with the casket, / just clearing the pews." The poet pretends that the difficulty is maneuvering the coffin out of the church, as if the real difficulty were not: There is somebody inside that thing!

Peripheral vision is where the symbols are.

Hamilton: You've spoken against the notion of workshops. Their main weakness seems clear—a cultivation of haste and of the desire to be admired by one's immediate circle of aspiring writers. What can you say in their favor?

Hall: There is one valid argument for workshops in this country. It's a big country. Suppose you're from northern Maine or west Texas. Poets need other poets to talk with, especially when they're young. They don't need teachers, grades, scholarships, grants, publications, praise, or institutions— but they need each other. In Europe there are capital cities, and a young Frenchman knows where to go. Neither New York nor San Francisco works as a capital, the way Paris or London does. Workshops are all provincial, by their nature, but they remain places where young poets meet and argue, which is good.

Hamilton: You often speak of exchanging your own work with Bly, Snodgrass, Simpson, Kinnell, Wright, perhaps a few others. You speak of going over each other's work line by line. What is the relation of your work to such a circle of friends?

Hall: Ideally a workshop should provide the disinterested, passionate criticism of one's peers. For me, the continual habit of tough criticism from my own generation . . . is the most important thing. With some real exceptions—Jane Kenyon, Gregory Orr, several others—younger poets are not so much use to me. I have known poets in my generation who have relied on the judgment of editors who studied them at college!

Judgment of new art is terrible difficult, always, and when you are impressed by someone older it is easy to kid yourself. But members of the same generation, who have been reading each other for twenty or thirty years, are neither dazzled nor impressed. I remember the note in *A Vision* where Yeats recollects Pound's response to a bundle of manuscripts: "These stink." Of course Pound *was* another generation—I made my own exceptions earlier—but it *was* inferior Yeats. We need people to tell us when things stink. At least I do.

When I begin a poem I work on it alone for at least a year. There is a long patch when I don't want or need anyone else's voice intruding. I can make the poem better on my own—whether it is good or not is another matter. The poem seems to have its own life; it keeps altering on me, moving, making adjustments, sliding in one direction or another, diminishing and enlarging. If I spoke to anyone else about it, the other voice might block some possible direction. The poem must remain loose and unencumbered by others' expectations, strategies, or presuppositions. (I need to rid myself of my own.)

Then the poem slows down, stops moving around on me. Even under the microscope, the bacterial cultures slow almost to stasis. At this point, I show it to Jane; she points out some stupidity or bad habit: I repeat too many words; I fall into abstractions; I say the same thing three times over. Then perhaps I read it aloud at a reading, and discover a soft spot because I lower my voice: *I want to skip over that part.* Rarely, somebody points out an error at the party after the reading. I am grateful. *Resentful*, doubtless, but grateful. Then I make copies, mail the poem off to Bly, Kinnell, Simpson, Snodgrass.

Of course the return mail brings despair! Everything's wrong! Maybe some of them *like* it, but their reservations disassemble the whole thing. They contradict each other. Simpson says I've got a poem here if I just cut half of it. Bly says exactly the same thing, only he cuts the other half. So I decide to chuck the whole thing, to give up poetry and become a travel agent.

A few days later I get back to work. All of them are right, all of them wrong. I correct for the veer of each particular breeze. Bly dislikes this phrase for a reason that I don't accept; he *always* dislikes X or Y. Simpson does best on narrative; A and B are not his territory. I come up with a version, much influenced by my friends—by Kinnell's dexterous cutting; by Snodgrass's meticulous, Johnsonian questioning—and finally have something like "my own" version.

The example is merely typical. Once or twice someone has shown me the whole way. Occasionally someone likes a poem all the way through or, conversely, convinces me the whole thing is a mistake and I chuck the poem.

But I always need help. And I help back. There are phrases in my friends' poems which I wrote. And sometimes when I am reading a poem aloud I remember: I did not write that line.

I'm not going to try to list everyone who has helped. Those you mentioned, of course. Jim Wright not so much. Jim was very sensitive to criticism—and nonetheless usually sought it out—to the point where it seemed difficult for him to be sufficiently negative about one's own poems. Not Bly. He is superb at taking criticism—and good at dishing it out. He and I started reading each other, and working over each other's poems, early in 1948.

Hamilton: Keats, Hardy, and Yeats: these names recur in your criticism and assorted commentary. To what extent do they indicate a tradition of poetry to which you attach yourself?

Hall: There's another circle! It is just as important—doubtless more important—to continue to consult the Old Ones, the original creators of the standards. You learn the Muse's requirements from reading the great poems, from loving them, from knowing them intimately. Of course they shame you—but if you love poetry enough, and if you retain the dumb optimism of ambition, they shame you into crossing out and trying again.

These poets I quote: Keats was early for me and recently came on strong again, one of the stars in the sky. Yeats was the love of my life from about eighteen to twenty-five. (I wrote a senior thesis about him at college, about his printed revisions of "The Rose" over his lifetime; it was before the *Variorum* came out, and I lived in Houghton Library making up my own *Variorum*.) At Michigan, I taught the *Collected Poems* for many years. Hardy came later; I recite him to anyone who will listen. Others I recite, and appeal to, are Wordsworth, Whitman, Frost, and Pound. Very much Ezra Pound. Andrew Marvell!

Hamilton: I know you taught Yeats and Joyce at Michigan. Did you also teach Pound? Can you expand on that "very much," in relation to the others?

Hall: Several times I taught Pound for a term in an undergraduate honors class. Very difficult. Maybe it would have been easier if I had taught graduate seminars but I taught only undergraduates. Once my Honors tutee (it was Tom Clark) wrote a senior thesis on the structure of the *Cantos*. This was in 1963! . . . Brilliant. But I never felt easy teaching Pound. I started reading him when I was fourteen or fifteen, coming to him after H.D. and Eliot; they showed the way. And he was, and is, the greatest craftsman of modern poetry, superb above all for his ear, but also remarkable for the range of his virtuosity. He invented not one but half a dozen styles worth giving a lifetime to. He's like one of his Renaissance heroes. He can strike a medallion, carve or model a figure, engineer a dome, and construct fortifications.

One good thing about *teaching* literature: I taught the introduction to poetry for many years at Michigan, mostly to non-majors, and I kept going back to the old poets. Over seventeen years I wonder how many times I taught "Out of the Cradle" and "The Garden" . . . and each time I found new poems! Marvell is a touchstone. The "Coy Mistress" I read in 1958 is not the "Coy Mistress" I read in 1973.

When I quit teaching, I realized after a while: I have not read Yeats for two years! So I did something about it. Now I tend to read a poet all the way through, finding poems I had forgotten or had never read, instead of rereading the beautiful chestnuts that I used to teach.

Hamilton: Is "tradition" a useful word for those attachments?

Hall: It's a bit professored-over, but that's exactly what it is. Except that I am not so interested in a continuity of literary history as I am in poems one at a time. Doubtless I know more literary history than I pretend to; doubtless it supplies help when I read poems one at a time . . . I worry that many young poets lack the background of older English poetry that my generation had forced on us.

American literature becomes separate and great—but the roots of its syntax and form *include* the great English poets. Nationhood is mysterious. You write American not because you decide to but because of the centuries that make you. Part of what makes the American language and American poetry is the English source. When Americans try to be what they are not— Anglophiles being proper Englishmen, others becoming amateur Navajos— they deny what is genuine in themselves. I think if you cultivate Americanness you may prevent the genuine Americanness from coming through.

Heaven knows, I don't want to *sound* like Yeats, Hardy, or Keats—nor Whitman or Frost, for that matter. You learn from Yeats and company the possibilities of poetry, the notion that something extraordinary can be done, and what it feels and smells and tastes like when it's done. You don't learn—unless you are dumb or unlucky—to use the demonstrative the way Yeats does it. (There are a couple of early poems of mine in which I hear a brogue.) You learn vague things like *shapeliness*—but not how to become shapely in your *own* poems. That part you have to make up.

Hamilton: In *Remembering Poets*, you wrote of Thomas, Frost, Eliot, and Pound. Would it be possible to say which of those poets you learned the most from?

Hall: None of the above! I try to speak to this in *Remembering Poets*, and I don't suppose I have much to add. None of them taught me anything about poetry beyond what I learned from reading their poems. All of them gave me examples of dedication and of shaping the life, for good or for ill, to the art's demands.

For me the most important elder example, and one of the great sources, is not a poet but the sculptor Henry Moore. As I get older—approaching the age he was when I first met him; he was sixty-one, I am fifty-six—I realize how important he was. Is. I started talking with him in 1959. A series of journalistic assignments kept me close—an interview for *Horizon*, a *New Yorker* profile, later another book and another magazine piece. I watched him work, I talked with him; he and Irina came to dinner, he and I played ping-pong. What a man! There he was: a coal miner's son, scholarship boy, decades of poverty as a sculptor, obscurity interrupted by ridicule—and then the immeasurable fame and riches beginning when he was almost fifty, when he won the Venice Biennale after the war. Despite everything he remained gregarious, affectionate, unaffected—and a devil for work. He stayed close to his family, to a few friends, and his eye never wavered from the real task. He worked twelve and fourteen hours a day, enraptured with his medium of shape, form, volume. He competed, magnificently, with the greatest of artists, with Michelangelo, Donatello, with the great primitive nameless carvers he discovered as a young man in the ethnographic exhibits of the British Museum.

I saw him most recently when he turned eighty. He had just managed to find a way to add an hour to his day's work. Just recently I had a letter from him—at eighty-five—telling me to come calling when I was in England. I would love to but I don't. I know he wants to be working even more than he wants to be talking.

His dedication—allowing no distraction, not even fame or riches, to keep him from the task he undertook as a young man—that's the model. A continuing desire to demand the best of himself, to tear down and build up again, never to be satisfied, never to allow discouragement to impede the labor. Or even *en*couragement.

Although my own eye for plastic form is nothing, I could glimpse through his eyes some of his vision—of a mute eloquence of shapes, which by some analogy points me in poetry to the wordless, the under-shape of *art* past words and discourse, the hidden continent . . .

Hamilton: Which in your case must have something to do with Eagle Pond and your memories of boyhood summers here.

Hall: All my life I've written about this place. Prose and poetry both. When I came up here from Connecticut, from the age of twelve when I started writing poems, this was the place of poetry. Although I worked on poems in the suburbs where I spent the school-time of the year, I always felt like a stranger there. Here I was away from other children—I didn't like other children—and with the old people, in a culture of much greater diversity, among great storytellers. My grandfather especially told stories and recited endlessly the poems he had memorized to speak at the Lyceum when he was young. Well, I've told about all that a thousand times: here I wandered through the fields by myself, I daydreamed, I let my soul loose from my body and floated in the air. I wrote poems.

The first summer I spent *away* was 1951, when I graduated from college and spent the summer in Europe before going to Oxford in the fall. For a few weeks at the end of summer I was alone in London, homesick, and I started the prose which became *String Too Short to Be Saved* ten years later. I had already written poetry about this place. The earliest poem I keep in print came from when I was eighteen or nineteen, "Old Home Day," written about this place. At college Robert Bly used to call me "the cellar-hole poet." Then when I was at Oxford my grandfather died and I began the "Elegy for Wesley Wells" that was in my first book. The next year I spent in California, on a fellowship to work with Yvor Winters at Stanford, and I worked more on *String*, and wrote more poems. When I returned to New England for three years I wrote less of it, but coming out to Michigan to teach, I again wrote about what was absent.

Hamilton: *String* could prove a pivotal book for you. You were about thirty when you published it and had already published two books of poems. Do you see it that way or is that just my suspicion?

Hall: A writer's life is such a strangeness! Perhaps it will seem to be the pivotal book. But at the time . . . I wrote most of it in England, in 1959–60, where I spent a year writing in the village of Thaxted. At six in the morning I worked on my poems, for *A Roof of Tiger Lilies* (1963). In the afternoons I took a pad of paper up to a sitting room on the second floor of a 1484 house, and worked at *String* for an hour or two. I used to tell my prose writer friends that I worked on poetry early in the morning, when I felt sharp, and wrote prose in the afternoons, when I was tired. Maybe in the afternoons I was writing the real thing.

It had a history. It began, in a sense, when I was a student at Exeter, and wrote about the wild heifers for a free theme. (I don't suppose that theme exists.) Then in 1951 I spent that first summer away from my grandparents and the farm, but I could not write prose. When I went to the University of Michigan and began teaching, a number of things came together. . . . I was at first discontented with teaching; my desire to write for a living reawakened, and was stimulated by Robert Graves visiting Ann Arbor. I remember sitting with him, having a cup of coffee in the Michigan Union, and telling him that I admired the way he earned his living by writing prose books; I wish I could do that, I told him. "Have you ever tried?" he asked me. I went home from that coffee determined to try, and specifically to try to write a book about the New Hampshire summers.

There was another ingredient. Doing a course in American Literature, I taught Henry James, Hemingway, other prose writers; I also taught freshman English, and began to look on prose as a series of alternatives, as I helped my students revise. Teaching prose literature came together with teaching composition, and for the first time in my life I became interested in prose style. When I was an adolescent I had tried to write stories, and finished two novels, but I wrote them out of contempt for prose, and therefore the prose was terrible. Now I admired the art of prose, the beautiful stylists. In the winter or spring of 1959, I began to write about the wild heifers again, what became the first chapter of *String Too Short to Be Saved*. As I remember, I wrote it a dozen times, revising extensively, learning to write this kind of prose—reminiscent, descriptive—by trying and failing and trying again. When I finished that chapter, I had learned a good bit. By the time I was writing the final chapters of the book, they came in three drafts.

I will never forget sitting in that room, upstairs at the Priory, the day I discovered the ruined locomotive in the woods. I had written about it before, in poetry, in the "Elegy for Wesley Wells."

It was always invented, but I know what it came from. My great-uncle Luther, who could remember the Civil War, told me once about walking in the woods—I think in rural Connecticut, where he had a parish—and feeling under his feet the rails of an abandoned railroad track. No locomotive, just the track. Also, in the woods of New Hampshire there were ruins everyplace—especially cellar-holes, sometimes sheds, abandoned wells, the rusted machinery of a maple syrup operation, the debris of a sawmill . . . and my grandfather told me about the wreck of a railroad spur, up on Kearsarge, where there had been some mining. One afternoon as I was writing about picking blackberries with my grandfather, my hand took off with my pen, and I wrote about my grandfather showing me the old locomotive, and the trestle fraying over the gulch . . . I could not stop! My hand ached, but I could not stop.

When I moved here for good in 1975 I thought—believe it or not—that I would lose this subject. Living in the middle of it, I thought I would no longer write of it. Ha! It was here that I wrote most of the New Hampshire poems of *Kicking the Leaves*. Since that book there are a few more such poems—really, *Kicking the Leaves* poems—but I think that I'm coming to the end of that subject now—the past of the 1930s and 1940s. I continue to write out of the landscape I live in, day by day, but I doubt that I will write much more out of the remembered past; we'll see. Sometimes I have thought I had finished with some familiar obsession, only to return to it.

Hamilton: Sometimes a poem of yours that seems quite set off from *String* really isn't all that distant. I am thinking of "The Man in the Dead Machine" lost in the jungles of New Guinea. Isn't he (and his plane) another version of the old rusted locomotive lost in the New Hampshire hills?

Hall: I noticed that parallel long after writing the poem. In my poems—and in other prose—there is much abandoned and ruined machinery. All my airplanes crash. There is a poem called "New Hampshire" which has a crashed airplane in it. (That poem came out of the prose of *String*, as I was working in England in 1959–60. I wrote it in prose first, then made the poem.) These images continue. When they come into a poem of mine now, I am still not aware that I am repeating an old theme. Something protective in the mind keeps you from knowing it, until it is done.

Hamilton: And isn't "Ox Cart Man" Washington Woodward mythologized?

Hall: I never made that connection! But, yes, it is the dream of self-sufficiency again, Robinson Crusoe and the Swiss Family Robinson. The children's book version is the family and the poem the Crusoe. I eliminated the family from the poem (part of the story as I first heard it) for the sake of economy, trimming the narrative of any detail I could. But maybe I was aware of old Wash.

Hamilton: Your grandfather is the central figure of *String*, and he is a storyteller, reciter of verses, talker, and reader. More than once you praise the fiber of his words. To what extent do you find yourself writing "up to him"?

Hall: Probably a great deal. I admired his character, I loved his love and loved him back, and I did immensely admire his words. He was not literally a poet, so far as I know. He had memorized hundred of poems—the caliber of "Casey at the Bat" and so forth—which he recited. When he told his stories, or when he engaged in wit with his friends visiting, he played with language. This was an example always in front of me, and an example from someone I especially loved. But I do not think that I write *for* him, not literally. Maybe up to him, but not for him. I don't recall that I ever showed him what I wrote. I must have! But it must not have been a big thing, for either of us, because I have no recollections of it. For one thing, the kinds of things I wanted to write—from the earliest times when I can remember wanting to write—were unlike the poems he recited. I loved him reciting them . . . but I did not want to write that way. Why not?

There was a side of me, of course, which was alien to this place and to him. And it was not only Connecticut. I felt alien there myself. I suppose it had to do with learning. My grandmother had studied Latin and Greek in high school, but she didn't even read books anymore. The books my grandfather read were not books that I wanted to read: *David Harum*, Joe Lincoln's novels . . . Early on I found an ambition for learning. I was reading Tolstoy and Flaubert when I was twelve. Exeter and Harvard confirmed and encouraged that side. At the farm, I felt approved of; nobody was critical because I read Shakespeare rather than *David Harum*, or tried to write Shakespeare instead of James Whitcomb Riley.

But while the learning—if that is the right word for it—was something alien to Ragged Mountain, it is also true that Ragged Mountain was something alien to Harvard, and I cherished that difference and that separateness. While I enjoyed my friends on the *Advocate*, while I loved talking poetry all night . . . I had something that they did not have, something that they knew nothing about.

Hamilton: Here, among cousins, living in a community that gathers at church, for the Fourth of July, and so on, you must feel your own relation as a poet to your neighbors somewhat differently from the way you found things at a university.

Hall: Two responses, and the first touches on social things about the country. Being a writer around the university—although it's privileged in many ways—carries annoyances with it. I won't be exhaustive about these annoyances, but there's one that bears on this question. Promotion and eminence in the university derive mostly from publication; the writer at the university publishes, not to be promoted (let us hope!) but because he is a writer: That's what he *does*. But his bibliography is longer than anybody else's; his name is always in print . . . and other professors defer to him and envy him. One gets fed up with ironic deference. It is not just Ann Arbor. After the seventh drink, somebody says, "And how is our famous poet today?"

Everybody want to be admired and maybe if one wants praise very much (I suppose it's a motive, the desire to be loved, that supports artists through difficulties) one may find it especially unpleasant to hear praise when it is dense with ambivalence or when it is phony.

Well, I found displeasure, socially speaking, in the *rôle* of the poet in Ann Arbor. Not unmixed; but much displeasure. But here . . . here it is entirely different. Here there's a convention of eccentricity, and the landscape is full of weird people. If it is weird to be a poet, it is also weird to raise Holstein oxen, or to wear a cowboy outfit to a town meeting, or whatever. People are amused by each other—by "characters," as they inevitably call each other. They are not impressed by each other, but amused. Nobody defers to me because I write books. That is just what I do. Some people are proud of me, as one of the sights of the town. "Fellow over there writes books for a living." One of the wonders is that I can bear to *sit down* all day long; people keep telling me it would drive them nuts . . . and they know I have a hard time driving a nail without breaking my thumb. That's all right. Activities are somehow equal, or they don't exist as a social pecking order. It seems sensible to understand that people do what they can do. And you have to realize, the countryside is full of people who do what they *want* to do. The suburbs are full of people doing what they hate to do, because they need to in order to maintain their debts.

My name's in the paper more than most of my neighbors. (The selectmen beat me out!) When there are interviews with pictures, I know always what people will say, without irony, with politeness: "Nice piece about you in the papuh." I can get back to work without the mosquito buzz of ironic deference around my ears.

I said I had two answers. I'm not certain about the second. Since I moved here, I haven't written a whole lot of surrealism, you might say. My language has been plainer. Someone in a letter suggested that I was writing for the neighbors. It's possible; I don't really *think* so. There might be good things about writing for the neighbors, but as I am writing or revising, it is not their voices I hear in my ears. It is the same old folks, mostly my peers. And I'm not sure it would be a good thing to write for the neighbors. It might be too much of a limitation. We fall into self-limitation, by unconscious habit, and I want to keep my eye out for it. . . .

I should say also: Although I love this community and its characteristic spirit and ethic, and although I work within it, I am aware that I am not exactly *of* it. You are what you were in your first twenty years, and for me that is something mixed: New Hampshire, the farm and the old people, but also the suburbs, prep school, Harvard College. I am a little outside my community. Being outside, I choose it every day, I affirm it, I love it . . . I remain aware of it. It is never as simple as the air I breathe; it will always be more wonderful than that.

Hamilton: More than anyone else I can think of at the moment, you write criticism, textbooks, and journalism as well as poetry, fiction, and now a play, not to mention work as an editor. How do those many activities reinforce each other?

Hall: I take pride in supporting myself as a freelance writer by journalism, Grub Street, without having to write anything that I don't want to write, living by my wits, as Willa Muir said.

While I write a great deal about literature, I write other prose also, for *Playboy, Inside Sports*, a biography of Dock Ellis. I write short stories, juveniles, textbooks, articles about living in the country. I love writing the informal essay. In this country we lack literary journalism. I wish more poets supported themselves this way—like Edwin Muir, like Robert Graves (mostly novels for Graves) or a good many English poets and novelists.

I worked toward this freelancing—not knowing quite what I was doing— by trying first one thing and then another. The first prose I learned to write was reminiscent and descriptive (*String Too Short to Be Saved*). Later I learned a prose for book reviewing, then a more objective, *New Yorker* profile prose. I learned something about writing fiction, something about writing for small children, only by trying and failing, while I was still teaching. I was curious to try all sorts of genres, and wound up learning some competence in a variety of them.

This lends variety to my working day. One kind of writing reinforces another. I cannot concentrate on poetry more than a couple of hours a day, but when I am working on other things—say, something as simple as the headnotes for a textbook—I still work with the medium of language, syntax, rhythm. I take pleasure in simple tasks, where I can manipulate words and rhythms and enjoy *handling* language with small anxiety.

Then, too—I love to do the "same" thing in different forms. "Ox-Cart Man" was first a poem, later a juvenile, still later a magazine essay which will be part of a prose book. I wrote it in lines another way, as a pseudo folk song, when the composer William Bolcom set some of my things. Fascinating, all the differences in diction, sound, grammar—differences necessitated by the genres.

I've written about the old farm days in poems, in the essays of *String*, in fiction, and now in a play. It astonishes me, continually, how the same material alters itself.

Hamilton: You frequently mention the poems themselves going through draft after draft, two or three hundred sometimes. That's another way in which the material alters itself. Is that standard?

Hall: It's always taken me a long time to finish poems. I can remember two exceptions only, when the poem came *almost* right at one sitting, when I changed only a few words. One of them ("The Dump") I still like. When I was in my twenties I found poems taking six months to a year, maybe fifty drafts or so. Now I am going over two hundred drafts regularly, working on things four and five years and longer. Too long! I wish I did not take so long.

Sometimes I wonder: Do I merely wish *not* to finish these poems? Do I want to keep them beside me? What isn't finished is not yet a failure. Yet even after I "finish" these poems, I keep on changing them. I publish in a magazine, see the poem I print—and then I tinker with it some more. When the new book comes in the mail and I look through it, I pick up my pen and make changes in the text. Rereading old poems aloud I discover a bad word, or a cut that enhances the poem; I change it again in the margin.

In the past few years, several times I have learned to cut a poem, not because I dislike a passage, but because something is wrong with a poem's pace—there's an argument between size and the scale; it will be better shorter, no matter what is cut.

The difficulty has increased almost steadily over my life. Not quite. Between the new poems in *The Alligator Bride* in 1969 and *The Town of Hill* in 1975—*The Yellow Room*, which came out in 1972, was mostly written by 1969—I had a strange patch. I floundered, I flipped and flopped. It began with a bad patch in the personal life. I wrote steadily but slowly, with little satisfaction in what I did—trying prose poems, returning to metrics a little, returning to a style I had mostly used up ("The Town of Hill" was such an exercise). I kept writing, conscious that nothing I did was as good as some earlier poems.

Then in the autumn of 1974 "Kicking the Leaves" started something new for me. It was both that long line with pauses in it, a multiple caesura, and the longer poem using a thematic image. Of course when the poem started, I did not know it was a long poem or that I was using a thematic image; I knew I was using a longer line and that it felt right, righter than anything had felt in a long time. I wrote obsessively; everything that I looked at started talking poetry.

And in my excitement I wrote much more rapidly. "Kicking the Leaves" took months rather than years, and so did "Eating the Pig" and "Wolf Knife." By the time I was working on the last two poems in that book—"Traffic" and "Stone Walls"—I had slowed down again; they took a couple of years each. Ever since I've been slowing down more and more. It feels as if growing older slows me down. Maybe not. Maybe if I make another breakthrough—like "Kicking the Leaves"—I will write quickly again.

Hamilton: Are you sometimes confident of having an exception, a poem working out much more quickly?

Hall: Yup. And I'm wrong! It can be embarrassing. A year or so ago I began a new long poem which was the meditation of an aged man, more or less mythical—I don't want to say more about it; who knows what might happen with it?—and it went *swimmingly*, or so I thought. Lots of changes, getting stronger and firmer rather quickly. I read it aloud, then sent it off to friends. One fall in Austin I told Christopher Middleton, "Wait until you hear this new one!" Argh! Another case of self-deception; with the help of a couple of friends, Bly and Kinnell as I remember, I saw through it. Terrible. But something might come of it, someday. Now it's brooding by itself in a dark drawer.

Most of my poems spend time in some dark drawer. One thing I've learned: if a poem is . . . if you think that a poem is going wrong, if you feel something fundamentally awry in it, you cannot cure it by changing the punctuation! You cannot bully it into excellence by staring at it every morning! You have to give it time to change itself deeply, which is accomplished only by not-looking at it. When a poem is in a drawer, that drawer is a kind of metaphor. You are putting the poem back into the sleep-place, so that dream and daydream can work it over. You are "forgetting" it, putting it in the *oubliette*. When I have successfully forgotten a poem, I may wake out of sound sleep with a clear notion of a change for it; I may discover lines for it, popping into my head, while I drive to the butcher's.

Hamilton: Does a poem in a drawer for so long accept major changes?

Hall: Major changes are the rule not the exception. Then it seems, invariably, as if this were the poem I should have known enough to write in the first place.

Other people do not *have* to revise so much as I do, and some people revise even more—Donald Justice, W. D. Snodgrass. Of course others would be better if they would revise even 10 percent as much as I do. (When I edit I see poems dated with one day; once or twice with the clock-time recorded, like 2:10–2:42 A.M., July 2, 1983.) And on the other hand, reading biography, I must admit: Many great poems have come quickly, or with much less obvious effort than I put into my own. Many poets have had the experience, rare but true, of writing good work at one sitting.

The length of time I spend may reflect itself in the kind of poem I make now—and, if there is excellence in the poems, in the kind of excellence. My best work of the last decade is mostly middle-distance, the wonderful ode-length. [Yeats's] "Among School Children" and Keats's odes and [Marvell's] "The Garden" are the shortest [odes]. Then [Whitman's] "Out of the Cradle," [Stevens's] "Sunday Morning," [Wordsworth's] "Intimations Ode," [Milton's] "Lycidas." The work I have hopes for runs from two typed pages to ten or twelve, the product of years, and hundreds of drafts. I don't write them, I *accumulate* them, cell by cell; I grow my poems now the way a reef grows coral. I'm not *much* more conscious than a reef is, either . . . keeping them around in my head, not so much on the page, changing a word a day for six months, then looking away, then changing another word a day for another six months—I find that willy-nilly the internal structure of sound and image builds up a density and interconnectedness; part meshes with part, words with words. I will add a weird word, not knowing why, and discover three weeks later (what other people might have known immediately) that the word picks up and develops another word earlier in the poem, perhaps something that has been there from the first day. Often I discover the interconnectedness only when someone, a year or two later, asks me to explain—and the connection leaps into my head.

I hope that this coral-reef-growth interconnectedness makes a sort of undertone resonance in the poems.

My best lines used to be something else, an intimate resonance of word colliding with word in the lyrical instant. Mostly the best lines came in the first draft, in ecstasy and inspiration, with a rush of language . . . that magical *poetry*-thing. No more. The juices dry up as you get older. Imagination-juice, word-juice. It used to be that four or five poems would start in one day, maybe two days, lyrical messages from the mother ship; then I would have a year's work to get them right. Now, instead, I have five years' work . . . and the inspiration, if that is what to call it, comes at the end and not at the beginning.

Hamilton: That's not learning the same thing over again; that's learning something new! Could we close by speaking of one of these middle-distance, ode-length poems? Say "A Sister by the Pond," which we published. I'm wondering about the effect of the *oubliette* on it. You didn't start with the war picture, did you, but more likely with the ice breaking up on the pond in April.

Hall: Yes, the scene around the pond—the ice breaking up after an open winter—becomes a thematic image.

Hamilton: When did the combination of the New Hampshire setting with the image of the war come together?

Hall: Early. But first I wrote about the photograph independently, as a poem by itself . . . idly, not expecting much. I had seen the photograph as a child, in *Life* I believe, and remembered it when Paul Fussell reprinted it in a *Harper's* article. I worked on the photograph-poem as I began work on the pond-poem, and one day understood how the recollection of the photograph belonged with the pond-feelings, the deaths of children, history and dread. . . . But I don't want to drift into self-interpretation!

Many people helped me with this poem. De Snodgrass helped greatly with the order—it was he who suggested starting with the photograph of the Germans—and with telling me what remained unclear. When I published the short version—intense, but it leaves out too much—Sam Hamill gave me hell. He had heard me read a more inclusive version in an early form; he had the earlier version on tape, listened to it again, and bawled me out. I had cut the parts that were hardest to write. . . . He sent me back to work.

Hamilton: I think I have manuscript evidence of changes in section 5, the shack sinking in water. That's one point where the verbal texture of the poem thickens.

Hall: Thickening is what it needed. Parts were thick early, and I cut the thin parts. This poem needed that slow coral-accumulation, by which the thin parts got thicker.

Hamilton: And the end; you mentioned earlier reading theology and some of your poetry taking up theological ideas. This is an instance?

Hall: Yup. In the last part I quote—*steal* that is—from Meister Eckhart, about what the soul desires, and the nature of that desire.

Hamilton: Thank you very much for speaking with us. And how about that poem? Is it under revision again?

Hall: Seeing it in the *Iowa Review* got me back to it. And also some further comments in letters from friends. I did a *lot* more to it but I didn't alter the big structure. The changes were all clarification and consistency, getting the words right. At this moment I think I've got it. But probably sometime, when I print it in a book or when I read it aloud—damn it—I will want to fiddle with it again.

"Names of Horses": An Interview with Donald Hall

Alberta T. Turner / 1985

From Alberta Turner, ed., *45 Contemporary Poems: The Creative Process* (New York: Longman, 1985), pp. 70–76. The interview and the text of "Names of Horses" are reprinted with permission of Donald Hall and the estate of Donald Hall.

Names of Horses

All winter your brute shoulders strained against collars, padding
and steerhide over the ash hames, to haul
sledges of cordwood for drying through spring and summer,
for the Glenwood stove next winter, and for the simmering range.

In April you pulled cartloads of manure to spread on the fields,
dark manure of Holsteins, and knobs of your own clustered with oats.
All summer you mowed the grass in meadow and hayfield, the mowing
    machine
clacketing beside you, while the sun walked high in the morning;

and after noon's heat, you pulled a clawed rake through the same acres,
gathering stacks, and dragged the wagon from stack to stack,
and the built hayrack back, up hill to the chaffy barn,
three loads of hay a day from standing grass in the morning.

Sundays you trotted the two miles to church with the light load
a leather quartertop buggy, and grazed in the sound of hymns.
Generation on generation, your neck rubbed the windowsill
of the stall, smoothing the wood as the sea smooths glass.

When you were old and lame, when your shoulders hurt bending to graze,
one October the man, who fed you and kept you, and harnessed you
    every morning,
led you through corn stubble to sandy ground above Eagle Pond,
and dug a hole beside you where you stood shuddering in your skin,

and lay the shotgun's muzzle in the boneless hollow behind your ear,
and fired the slug into your brain, and felled you into the grave,
shoveling sand to cover you, setting goldenrod upright above you,
where by next summer a dent in the ground made your monument.

For a hundred and fifty years, in the pasture of dead horses,
roots of pine trees pushed through the pale curves of your ribs,
yellow blossoms flourished above you in autumn, and in winter
frost heaved your bones in the ground—old toilers, soil makers:

O Roger, Mackerel, Riley, Ned, Nellie, Chester, Lady Ghost.

Question: Perhaps because my first memories are of two large, empty
box stalls with the smell of dried manure and the names Billy and Marjorie
Daw, and of our 1922 Apersen car caught coming home from the station
behind a slow team, and of a mildewed buggy harness in the cellar, every
muscle tensed with recognition when I read this poem. But when the poem
was first published, in the *New Yorker* in 1977, how many readers could it
have "happened" to in that way? What sort of experience can readers have
when the experience has become a historical curiosity associated with calendar towels and department store windows at Christmas?

Answer: Exactly. I share the worries that the question entertains, and
not only in connection with *this* poem. Everybody knows about horses—
from a Budweiser ad on television: great manicured Clydesdales pull beer
wagons through landscape reduced to scenery, pretty as a picture. I worry
that in my rural poems I may fabricate calendar art, make postcards of covered bridges, or Norman Rockwell magazine covers. Putting manure into a
poem like this may help to avoid Norman Rockwell, but I suppose there is
such a thing as Norman Rockwell manure.

Obviously if I print the poem I hope that it survives the danger you speak
of. How? Well, if any poem succeeds, its subject matter is only ostensible
(which is why thematic anthologies never work). I question your premise
that the poem is about horses.

Of course it's about horses, but on the other hand two elements in the poem seem to me to point somewhere away from these ostensible dobbins. Half of the poem is about *work*—about muscles, labor, making land, and about the difficulty or harshness of that life. Maybe the other half is a universal *ubi sunt*, an elegy not merely for horses but for people who hayed and cut ice and went to church and spread manure and shot horses, by extension for all the country of the dead. Think of Villon's list of the dead beauties: is his poem about mythology? Is it even about beautiful women? When I had worked on "Names of Horses" for a long time, I came to hope that it was no more about horses than, oh, Keats's ode is about an object among the archeological plunder in the British Museum.

Q: How did you come to determine the nature and sequence of the names of the horses? Are they the name of actual horses you have known, names associated with a single farm, or a composite? Did you invent any of them for their sound or connotation, Lady Ghost, for instance?

A: I wrote the poem over two years or so. As I first worked on it, I did not list the horses' names at the end of the poem. After each stanza I repeated a refrain in which I rhymed the names. Many of the names are remembered. Riley was the first horse of my childhood; then I remember a Ned, a Roger, a Nellie; I remember hearing about a great Chester who ran things before I was born. I made up "Lady Ghost"—you suspected!—not for the sound itself but for a rhyme. The refrain ended with "but Riley the most." "Lady Ghost" was born to rhyme with "most." When I abandoned the refrain idea and went to the one-line list at the end, I kept her around.

Q: How much of the rest of the poem is autobiography? I note that Eagle Pond, for instance, is your present address. Is it the farm where you grew up? Was the stove a Glenwood? Did you have a Holstein herd? Did you yourself help bring in "three loads of hay a day from standing grass in the morning"?

A: This is the farm where I spent my childhood summers. My great-grandfather bought it in 1865 when he was almost forty. He was a sheep farmer, and had worked a hill farm for many years; I suspect that he made money, during the Civil War, selling wool for uniforms. Originally, people farmed up the hill because the frost came later, but when the railway came through, late in the 1840s, the flatter farms in the valley became more valuable. You could raise corn and hay to feed milk cattle, then ship milk by railroad to Manchester and Boston.

My grandmother was born here, and my mother. My mother when she married went to Connecticut, and I lived in a suburb of New Haven during

the schooltime of the year. Summers I spent here haying with my grandfather—what a contrast it was! It set the suburbs of identical families in
identical houses against the farm country where nothing was like anything
else. The suburbs never had a chance.

And I moved into the past, because my grandfather farmed as people
had farmed for a century or so. Farms were poor then—the agricultural depression started early in the '20s—and he farmed with one horse. I worked
here summers, milked a Holstein on occasion, hayed every day with Riley.

We still have the Glenwood stove; the range is also a Glenwood.

But then you ask: "Did you yourself help bring in 'Three loads of hay a
day from standing grass in the morning'?" A sore point. Once or twice a
year, we did that. For the most part, you do *not* load in the afternoon the hay
that you cut in the morning: it is too green; it might burn your barn down.
You leave it to dry for a few days, then bring it in. This line is an exaggera-
tion that I must change. It was early this year at a poetry reading when I
finally understood that I *must* revise this line. (If we do many readings, we
keep examining our old work; we keep finding things to change. I tinker
with old poems continually.) In January when I read my poems in Buffalo,
I saw Wendell Berry sitting in the third row; he was reading elsewhere in
town the same day. When I read this poem aloud I stopped after "Three
loads of hay a day" and left the line short. I couldn't look Wendell in the eye
and say the rest of the line.

Q: What determined your choice of the unusually long lines, the line
breaks, the stanza groupings?

A: I didn't choose the long line; it chose me. On several occasions during the last thirty years, the sound of my poems has altered; it has become
exciting to make a new noise. After years of working with short-lined percussive, enjambed free verse, in the fall of 1974 I found this long line coming. . . . When I began this poem—in 1975, I think—it arrived in a line that
made the new music. Over the many drafts, over years of working, gradually
these stanzas found their present shape.

As I have said before: I intend a thing *after* it happens. It happens first
because one day I write it that way. If I do not change it, then I have intended
it. I am careful indeed. But I am not careful ahead of time; I do not say to myself: "Let me see, I am writing about horses. I guess a long line would be good
because horses are so *big*." I don't write the way Poe said he did, when he told
about writing "The Raven." (I'm not sure Poe did either.) I cannot predict what
I will end up doing. But one thing I *can* do is take a long time; I can make sure
that by the time I print something, I intend most of what is there.

Q: The poem shows signs of a very careful ear, a matching of the sounds to the action, as in the alliteration and the final spondees of the line, "of the stall, smoothing the wood as the sea smooths glass." Could you comment on the strategies and accidents in matching the poem's sounds and rhythms to its sense?

A: I don't believe in spondees; spondees are like the Easter bunny. Another time. . . .

As with the gross matters of line-length and stanza-form, so with the more intimate matters of alliteration and assonance. I don't know ahead of time what I am going to do. When I see what I am doing, I search for ways to do it better. Although I try to understand what I'm up to, *before* I print a poem, it is common for me to keep on noticing things about my poem later, after I have published it and read it aloud many times. Here I have come to notice, for instance, that there are two moments when the sound becomes especially prominent—two separate moments, with quieter patches in between. If you try all the time to make sound that draws attention to itself, you will draw attention to nothing but sound. Wild sound must coincide with a high moment. It will always *make* a high moment anyway, and if it makes a high moment out of low matter there will be disparity.

For me ecstasy signals itself by assonance. In the work-part of this poem, with all its attention to shorts *a*s and to *k*s, there is a *revelry* in the day of haying. This is the first high moment. The second is lamentation and elegy, especially the sentence that ends with the poem's penultimate line. Here I am wholly conscious of *song*. Here I want to belt it out. If I can't make this happen, let the poem collapse in the trash of its phonemes.

I make writing sound like a performance. All right. It is a performance arrived at slowly, in solitude, morning after morning.

There is one other phrase I may change but which I am loathe to revise because I like the sound. Late in the poem I speak of how "Frost heaves their bones in the ground. . . ." Once after a poetry reading somebody asked me if their bones were really so close to the surface. Damn! I doubt it. One buries the bodies deep, or a dog will dig them up. I am afraid that these bones reside below the frost line, despite my poem. Maybe in an *exceptional* winter the frost would sink deep enough?

Q: The genre of the elegy has been used for animals since its beginnings. Did you make any conscious use of or variation from that tradition in writing this poem?

A: I was reading a lot of Thomas Hardy; I think some Hardy comes into the poem. I remember Edwin Muir's wonderful horse-poem, about the strange horses returning after nuclear war. But I was not aware of using animal-elegies as a source, nor was I really conscious of the genre.

Q: What started this poem? What changes did it go through? How long did it take to complete? If you have saved the worksheets, could I see a copy?

A: The poem started when I returned to live here, after years of towns and suburbs. Forty years ago my grandfather met me at the depot with Riley drawing a carriage; he never owned a tractor, much less an automobile. (My wife and I are the first people to live at this place with a car.) I thought about the horse-labor that had gone into this place, to keep it going over many years; to control and maintain the land.

I do not own the worksheets. They are down at the University of New Hampshire with my other papers. I suppose that I took seventy or eighty drafts, and worked at the poem over a couple of years.

I always show poems to my friends—after I have worked on them alone for a year or so. I remember W. D. Snodgrass helping me with this poem, as he has done with many. This time Louis Simpson helped me more than anyone else. He's always so good on narrative—a master. It was he who persuaded me out of the refrain, asking me who did I think I was, Thomas Hardy? (The answer was doubtless yes.) And it was he who suggested that I might save the names of the horses for the end of the poem. I am grateful.

Q: What other questions would you have liked me to ask?

A: "Has anyone set this poem to music?" Some years back the composer William Bolcom set three of my poems. When I knew he wanted to do something with "Names of Horses," I tinkered with it toward the notion of a setting. I piece-cut old stanzas and restored the refrain . . . When he set it (he has performed it with his wife Joan Morris) I called it "Horse Song" to distinguish it from the poem. This is the poem he set:

Horse Song

All winter your brute shoulders strained against collars,
padding and steerhide over the ash hames, to haul
sledges of cordwood for drying through spring and summer.
In April you pulled cartloads of manure to spread on the fields,
dark manure of Holsteins, and knobs of your own clustered with oats . . .
                    O Ned the Elder, Ned the Less,
                    Riley, Chester, and Sister Bess,
                    O Sally-Maggie, Billy Blue,
                    Nebuchadnezzar and Roger too,

O Babe and William, Lady Ghost,
Jesse, Ted—but Riley the most.

All summer you mowed the grass in hayfields, mowing machine
clacketing beside you, while the sun walked high in the morning;
and after noon's heat, you pulled a clawed rake through the same acres,
gathering stacks, and dragged the wagon from stack to stack
and the built hayrack back, up hill to the chaffy barn. . . .

O Ned the Elder, Ned the Less,
Riley, Chester, and Sister Bess,
O Sally-Maggie, Billy Blue,
Nebuchadnezzar and Roger too,
O Babe and William, Lady Ghost,
Jesse, Ted—but Riley the most.

When you were old and lame, one October the man who kept you
dug a hole beside you in sandy ground above Eagle Pond
and lay the shotgun's muzzle in the boneless hollow behind your ear,
and shoveled sand to cover you, setting goldenrod upright above you,
where by next summer a dent in the ground made your monument. . . .

O Ned the Elder, Ned the Less,
Riley, Chester, and Sister Bess,
O Sally-Maggie, Billy Blue,
Nebuchadnezzar and Roger too,
O Babe and William, Lady Ghost,
Jesse, Ted—but Riley the most.

I like "Names of Horses" better as a poem—whatever that means. But with
Bolcom's setting and the voice of Joan Morris, the song is gorgeous.

Donald Hall: An Interview

Liam Rector / 1989

From *American Poetry Review*, vol. 18, no. 1, January/February 1989, pp. 39–46.
Reprinted by permission of the estate of Liam Rector.

Question: You've written poignantly about time and generation. Jose Ortega y Gasset had a scheme for generation:

Ages: 1–15   Childhood
15–30   Youth
30–45   Initiation
45–60   Dominance
60–75   Old Age, "Outside of Life"

How have these moments moved in consort with the time of your life, your work, and the scheme of literary generations as you've experienced them?

Answer: Schemes irritate me. Maybe this scheme annoys me because I'm supposed to move "outside of life" in a few months and I'm damned if I'm ready to. Rigidities, separations get my back up. Maybe I left childhood at fourteen and remained adolescent until forty-three. I like the word "dominance"—and I suppose I felt it first about fifty, though I think I was looking for it from the age of fifteen. So I respond, not by generality on the schemer's level, but autobiographically or egotistically. Chronological skeletons—like somatic or psychological types, like classes, like historical determinism: hell, like the god-damned horoscope!—provide things to talk about, frameworks for discussion. . . . But if you accept them, if you do not rebel against them, you actively desire the comfort of prison! Everything's done for you; relax: prison . . . or *tenure.*

Q: In the essay "Rusticus," you said you grew up in Hamden, Connecticut, a suburb of New Haven, in a "massclass" neighborhood wherein everyone more or less shared four convictions: 1) I will do better than my father and mother; 2) My children will do better than I do; 3) "Better" includes "education," and education provides the things of this world; 4) The things of this world are good. *String Too Short to Be Saved* speaks powerfully for the summer life in New Hampshire you experienced as a boy, but could you say more about the culture and class in which you grew up in Hamden? Have you done better?

A: In the suburban neighborhood where I grew up in Connecticut, the houses were like each other; the cars that belonged to the houses resembled each other; the fathers, working at their different jobs, had incomes roughly similar; the mothers weren't supposed to work, and their leisure or volunteer-work decorated the fathers. In school, there were rewards for conformity and punishments for difference. In the culture of the country, where I spent my summers, there was fantastic diversity—in education, aspiration, income, appearance; what you wore, what you ate, what you did for fun—from house to house along the roads and lanes. Eccentricity was a *value*; a major ethical notion was everybody's right to be different. I belonged to the Connecticut culture and longed for the other. I live in the other now—it's not greatly changed—and live by it, observe it, write about it—but of course I will never be truly *of* it. My whole life comes out of the conflict of these cultures—and my choice to love and inhabit the one rather than the other.

Q: You went to the Phillips Exeter Academy and then to Harvard, Oxford, and Stanford. Did the students at these schools share the cultural and class background you outlined in the essay "Rusticus"? You then went on to the public, sprawling world of the University of Michigan to teach. What led you to attend these schools as a student, and what went into the decision to teach at Michigan?

A: The class structure in England is unlike ours, and I won't try to describe it. Sure, other students at Exeter were mostly from the same suburbs, where people try to resemble each other, but most came from more money than I did. My parents sent me there because they knew it was a good school, I don't think for social reasons at all. They weren't social people. At Exeter the best teachers all came from Harvard; the best students were going there. Quickly I knew I wanted to go there. Some Exeter kids came from money that had been around in the family longer. At Harvard I felt less of this. There was more diversity there, at least among the people I knew. Even at that time, Harvard was more high school than prep school, trying to get the best high school students from all over the country. They were a bunch of tigers locked in a small cage; I liked that. I tried for a fellowship to Oxford because it was a plum and because it sounded like fun to travel and live in another country. While I was there England was in a bad way economically. I never saw my English friends on the continent during holiday because they were only allowed to take twenty-five pounds out of the country that year. There were already lots of scholarship boys at Oxford, but I was so separate culturally—older, from another nation. Being an outsider gave me privileges which I enjoyed, privileges to be weird.

One of the reasons I went to the University of Michigan was to get away from the Harvard I liked so much. After I did the B.A. I spent only three years away at first—Oxford and Stanford—then returned for three more years in the Society of Fellows. There were pathetic sorts around the Square who would take any sort of rotten job in order not to leave Cambridge, or—perish the thought!—go to the *Middle West*. (America's geographical snobbery is repulsive.) I wanted to get away, to try another kind of institution, and Michigan made a good offer. Ironically—probably predictably!—I went to an institution that, within Michigan and nearby states, is considered rather snobbish, rather old school tie. Some students' grandparents and parents had belonged to the same fraternities and sororities—but there were children of lineworkers. I liked that variety, that looseness.

Q: We both grew up spending our summers with our grandparents on farms, you in New Hampshire and I in Virginia. In *String* you wrote of how this shaped your imagination and that residence where imagination and memory commingle. Living now on the same farm where you spent summers, what is your memory, your imagination of the large cities?

A: I've never lived in a great city. For me, large cities are excitement, energy, vitality, almost mania. When I go to New York I never sleep. Oh, I've lived for a month or two at a time in London, Paris, Rome. Because Cambridge is virtually Boston, and I went to school there, I suppose I *did* live in a big city—but living in a college isn't the same. I contrast the country not to the city but to the suburbs; Ann Arbor is a suburb without an urb. (Technically it's a city.)

This place is no longer a farm but the rural culture remains amazingly intact, although thirty years ago I thought it was vanishing. I love the landscape more deeply all the time; I am content sitting on the porch and gazing at Kearsarge; or walking in the woods. Carol Bly speaks somewhere of writers who are "mindless nature describers." Maybe I'm a mindless nature lover, but I love also the independence and solitude of the country, which is by no means only a matter of population density. I don't suffer from the deference, mostly ironic, that hangs around writers in universities; here, I'm the "fellow over there who writes books for a living" and that's a freedom.

Q: Your work has been haunted not only by the grandfather but the father. Did your father encourage you to become a writer?

A: My father was soft and volatile, a businessman who hated being a businessman and daydreamed for himself a life in the academy—probably prep school rather than college—where everybody would be *kind* to everybody else. He read books; mostly he read contemporary historical fiction like Hervey Allen and Kenneth Roberts. Politically he was conservative and not very thoughtful. He wept frequently and showed feelings which other men would hold back. He desperately wanted people to like him and many did. He was nervous, continually shaking; quick, alert, sensitive, unintellectual. When he was forty-two he hemorrhaged with a bad bleeding ulcer and remained sickly until he got lung cancer at fifty-one and died at fifty-two. As an adolescent I needed to feel superior to him; when I was about twenty-five, when my son was born, I felt reconciled. I don't think we talked about matters of great substance but we could love each other. He read my things and mostly praised them, but I don't think either of us wanted to talk about them. He tried to encourage me in one direction, constantly, by telling me that my poetry was just fine but my prose was really great. Some of this at least was his desire that I might possibly be able to make a living. When he realized that I was going into teaching, it pleased him because of his imaginary academy.

Q: Your new book, *The One Day*, is in many ways a departure from *Kicking the Leaves* and *The Happy Man*, both in its elliptical form, its being a book-length shoring of fragments, and its engagement with the very old and the very new, aside from your personal remembered past, which sets much of the tone in the two books before. How do you account for this shift? One section of *The One Day*, "Shrubs Burnt Away," was printed in *The Happy Man*. What made you decide to foreshadow the long poem by printing it there? Had you yet seen the shape that *The One Day* would assume?

A: If you look at my poems from the beginning in 1955, there is lot of moving about and shifting. Surely you're right that the form of *The One Day* is modernist, with its multiple protagonist—but I guess I don't want to . . . Really, I don't want to talk about the form of it. It's new; I'm still finding out what I did.

The poem began with an onslaught of language back in 1971. Over a period of weeks I kept receiving messages; I filled page after page of notebooks. If I drove to the supermarket, I had to bring the book and pull over three or four times in a few miles to transcribe what was coming. It was inchoate, sloppy, but full of *material*: verbal, imaginative, recollected. And it was frightening. After a while the barrage ceased, but from time to time over the years more would come—with a little label on it, telling me that it belonged to this *thing*. (In my head for a long time I called it *Building the House of Dying*.) The first part was there in inchoate form, much of the first two of "Four Classic Texts," much of the "one day" theme in the third part. Every now and then, over the years, I would look at these notebooks, and feel excitement and fear. In 1980 I began to *work* on it; to try to do something with these words. First I set it out as a series of twenty-five or thirty linked free verse poems: Nothing marched. I worked on it for a year or two; I remember reading it aloud to Jane one time, and when I finished I was full of *shame*. Shame over what I revealed, shame over bad poetry; after that, I couldn't look at it for a year.

At some point early in the 1980s, Robert Mazzocco suggested casually in a letter that I ought sometime to write a book of linked poems. Thinking of this notion I developed my ten-line stanza, making some into almost discrete ten-line poems, using others as stanzas. I thought of Keats's ode stanza, developed out of the sonnet and the desire to write the longer ode form. This notion helped me get to work: bricks—cement blocks?—for the house. I worked with these stanzas for a couple of years, then maybe in 1984 developed a three-part idea that *somewhat* resembles the present version, except that the middle part is totally different. I showed a draft to a few people. I remember Bly saying, with his usual diffidence, that the first part was the *best* thing I had ever done and the second part was the *worst* thing I had ever done. The second part was a problem until I worked out the notion that turned into "Four Classic Texts"; I stole "Eclogue" from Virgil, which always helps. Even after I had the "Classic Texts," I thought the third part was my real problem, and sometimes doubted that I would ever finish the whole— because I wouldn't be able to make the third part.

When I put *The Happy Man* together I had "Shrubs Burnt Away" more or less finished, "Four Classic Texts" beginning, and "In the One Day" lying about in pieces. I thought it would be ten years before I would be able to finish the poem as a whole, if I ever did. I had no notion that I might finish it within a couple of years. But I think that printing "Shrubs" in *The Happy Man* allowed me to finish the whole poem. Response was encouraging . . . and some reviews helped me understand what I was doing, like David Shapiro's in *Poetry*, with his reference to Freud and the movement from hysterical misery to ordinary unhappiness!

Q: What about your work in children's books?

A: I've worked on children's books for twenty-five years, starting when Andrew was a little boy, and I've written many—but only published four.

The first was *Andrew the Lion Farmer*, which I may rewrite and reissue. That one came out of storytelling with Andrew when he was four years old. I made up lots of stories. Then one day he said he had a great, scary idea: He was going to go the lion store and buy a lion seed and grow a lion from a pot! . . . Wow! I was *off!* Now I don't have four-year-olds around anymore— maybe I'll make up stories for grandchildren one day—but there's a perma- nent four-year-old in my head, to whom I tell my stories. I've worked on three in the last year, but none is any good. If you have the proper shape, the *fable*, maybe they're not so hard to write—economy, limits of diction, right details . . . but finding the fable is hard! For each of my juveniles, the publisher found the illustrator, asking my approval; then the illustrator has asked me questions, maybe shown me samples. I've been fortunate: Barbara Cooney, Mary Azarian.

Q: Does the war of the anthologies (yours, and Pack's, and Simpson's versus Donald Allen's anthology) stay with you to this day (even though you included the work of Ginsberg, Snyder, and others in a later anthology you edited for Penguin)? What young Turks have you lived to see become old deacons?

A: The war of the anthologies was real enough, back at the end of the fifties. For some nostalgic and sentimental people it still goes on. *Ah, the barricades!* These aging Beatniks remind me of people in my parents' gen- eration, who lived out their lives in nostalgia over Prohibition. Bathtub gin! Speakeasies! . . . I speak without disinterest, because I am still loathed here and there as a leader of the Eastern Establishment, Mr. Hallpack Simpson, Enemy, Archbishop of Academic Poetry! . . . People want to relive their youths, when good was good and bad was stanzas.

For the most part good poets want no part of it. Creeley and I, Ginsberg and I, were famous enemies . . . but we stopped that stuff twenty-five years ago. In 1961 Denise Levertov, who was poetry editor at the *Nation*, asked me to review Charles Olson's first volume of *The Maximus Poems*. Ecumenism was with us. In 1962 I did my Penguin with Levertov, Creeley, and Snyder, only five years after Hallpack. (Five years is a long time when it starts in your twenties.) By 1961 I was abashed by the rigidity that defended my cita- del when I was in my mid-twenties.

I don't think that *particular* war endures except for nostalgic diehards— but there will always be outs and ins; and the first shall be last: sometimes. I see geographical complacency and enmity now. What is a Los Angeles poem? (I don't think there's a New Hampshire poem.) For the most part, geographical groups are diffident folk trying to build castles to feel safe in.

To hell with it. I want to be a poet by myself, not a New England poet or a deep image poet or what have you. In my own generation in America, the poet I admire the most is not considered a member of my gang. Robert Creeley.

Q: Those anthologies provided a dialectic for their time. Does such a dialectic exist now, or is it a time of synthesis, revision, mannerism, or utter impasse? Was the aesthetic distance between your and Allen's anthology a real one? Are you ever tempted to edit another anthology of younger poets, at your age?

A: I've been asked to edit an anthology of the young and I have refused. Let the young edit the young. I could do it—but the passion would not be there, and if I made fewer gross mistakes the whole thing would be a big mistake. I don't like recent anthologies of younger poets because they are too damned big. Out of generosity or whatever, probably whatever, they include too many aspirants and contribute to the confusion of numbers.

I don't really think there's a dialectic now, though it seems so to some. Metrical poets against the world. Free-verse plain talk poets against the world. Language poets against the world. Narrative poets against the world. There's a comfort in being *out*, and people warm themselves by that cold fire. But conflict *does* make energy. Maybe it's a time of warring tribes, Balkanization, rather than a time of dueling superpowers. Oh, it wasn't really superpowers ever, not even back then . . . Allen Ginsberg, Frank O'Hara, Robert Duncan, Denise Levertov, and John Ashbery did not resemble each other.

Q: What's good about growing older?

A: What's bad about growing older is the knowledge that you have less *time*, the frustration that you will not live to write the books or the poems; or to read all the books you want to. What is good, paradoxically enough, is patience. With less time I feel or act as if I had more. When I begin a poem of any ambition, I know that I will be working on it five years from now; I *sigh* a little . . . but I get on with it. I feel more energy, need less sleep, feel more excitement about work than I did when I was thirty or forty. I've been lucky in my second marriage, in living where I want to live; these are not inevitable results of aging.

Q: Simpson says he has scolded you for writing so much about the business of poetry—the number of books sold, number of readings, etc. What do you think about that? (Rexroth also wrote of these matters, yes?)

A: Louis and I fight about lots of things. He was outraged when I wrote an article about poetry readings. I write essays in poetic theory, and essays of appreciation, but from time to time I write essays of fact. I am interested, for example, in how writers make their livings; I always liked *New Grub Street*, and biographies. Think of Emerson making his living by traveling around the country, at first by steamer and stagecoach, lecturing week after week—like Robert Bly. As for numbers: It annoys the hell out of me that people generalize, as if facts were common knowledge, when they don't know the facts. One constantly hears how poetry sells less than it ever did; even publishers say so. But the numbers show something different. Now *numbers* don't necessarily have anything to do with quality—I grant Louis that—but let's find out what the facts are before we generalize about them! I'm curious about the sociology of poetry: If poets typically make a living as teachers, is their workday unrelated to the poetry that they write? I used to be fascinated by all the English poets who lived by their wits freelancing. A couple of centuries ago a good many were vicars. The poetry reading must explain a great deal—good and bad—about the kind of poetry that is written today. There is also the phenomenon of the creative writing industry.

Q: What do you think accounts for the dearth of polemics in current writings about poetics? Compared to Pound and Lewis's *Blast*, or Bly's *The Fifties*, why do we see so few picking up the cudgel these days? Is it part of an "I'm okay; you're okay" relativism and "Make Nice" culture, or just a period of exhaustion, politeness, or fear?

A: Compare the reviews in English magazines! Nastiness is a dumb convention over there as our namby-pambyness is a dumb convention here. "Boost Don't Knock," said the Boosters Club. How many poets have you heard say that they don't want to review anything unless they can praise it? Oh, I don't believe in taking a cannon to kill a flea. It's a waste of time to write a savage review of a book that nobody is going to read. But I believe in taking a cannon to kill a flea continually described as an eagle. I've tried to do it once or twice.

Q: What do you think about creative writing programs being separated from English departments and being put under the aegis, say, of a fine arts department, along with dancers, musicians, theater people?

A: Separating creative writing from the regular English department is a disaster. "Here are the people who can read; here are the people who can write. People who can write can't read; people who can read can't write." Wonderful. Specialization is a curse, especially for poets. Separate departments divide old poetry from new. Some places have literature departments *within* creative writing departments, where writers teach reading to would-be writers. But the value of writers to English departments lies not in teaching of creative writing; it's their teaching of literature classes for regular undergraduates or graduates. Of course most PhDs are dopes; so are most poets. Undergraduate English majors—or engineers and nurses taking an elective—suffer because they never get to be taught by a writer. The faculty suffers because separations make for complacency; nobody's challenging you with an alternative. But the teacher of creative writing suffers most. When you teach literature you spend your days with great work—reading it, talking about it, reading papers about it. Great literature rubs off and you *learn* by teaching, by encountering what you don't know well enough, teaching it to people who know it even less.

This separation makes for narcissism, complacency, and ignorance. It's the worst thing that has happened with the creative writing industry. People spend whole lives talking about line-breaks and the *New Yorker*.

Q: But why should poets teach literature rather than conduct writing workshops?

A: If you teach great literature you live among the great models. You make your living reading Moore and Pound and Hardy and Marvell and Yeats! Incredible. Students ask you questions, and when you answer you discover that you knew something you didn't know you knew. Instead of living with half-baked first drafts by narcissistic teenagers, you live with the *greatest art*. What could be a better way to spend your spare time—when you're not competing directly with Wordsworth—than by reading Wordsworth?

Q: The first readers for your poems—Bly, Kinnell, Simpson, Bidart, Orr, and others—how have their readings changed and developed over time?

A: Jane Kenyon is my first reader and has been for fifteen years. Robert Bly has read virtually every poem I've written for forty years. Simpson, Snodgrass, Kinnell . . . these people have helped me enormously through the years. For a while in our twenties Adrienne Rich and I worked on each other's poems. When we lived near each other, Gregory Orr helped me. I haven't known Frank Bidart so long but he has been extremely helpful; Robert Pinsky on occasion; Wendell Berry very often. Bly's reading has changed the most. He used to cut and rewrite; sometimes I took his corrections and put them in print: More often they showed me what was wrong and therefore helped me toward my own changes. More recently he has taken to speaking more about the underneath of the poem, touching the text less. Galway is a marvelous editor, a great cutter. Snodgrass is superb at a Johnsonian reading, following syntax and implication, allowing himself to be puzzled.

Q: What goes into your choosing someone to be such a reader of your work? Their ability to argue their position? You said in an *Iowa Review*

interview with David Hamilton that the criticism of younger writers has not
been of much use to you. Why is that?

A: I don't choose anybody. We choose each other—a mating dance, tentative advances and retreats. Criticism *must* be mutual, a dialogue. It doesn't
work so well when criticism goes in one direction only. And the poetics has
to have something in common; if two people are simply opposed, there's no
common ground where conversation can happen. And it helps to get your
own notions thrown back at you when you violate them. Within a general
agreement, then you should be as different as possible—like Bly and me.

The requirements are more temperamental than generational. Since that
interview with David Hamilton, I have made great use of some young readers (young compared to me). With some young poets, you sense that they
may be frightened, or deferential, or counterdeferential, which is just as
bad—acting nastier than they feel, in order to show that they're not cowed.
When I answered Hamilton, I was thinking of some dreadful examples of
young fans praising elderly slop; the young were sincere but dazzled. I don't
forgive the old for believing what they want to believe.

Q: You're one of the few writers your age I know who still reads and
comments on the work of younger writers, aside from people who formally
teach or are busy writing blurbs. Most writers, once they reach fifty or so,
confine themselves to reading the work of their own generation and work of
the distant past. Why has this been different for you?

A: I keep looking. I'm *curious*: What's happening? What's going to happen? I've seen nothing so extraordinary as the increased *numbers* of poets,
people with at least some ability; the numbers especially of young women,
compared to earlier generations, including mine. Because I was so rigid
when I was young. I try to stay open to kinds of poetry alien to my own; of
course openness can become a mindless relativism or namby-pambyness.
You have to worry: Do I just want them to *like* me? One thing I learned
ten or twenty yeas ago: If you read something that upsets you, that violates
every canon you ever considered . . . look again, look harder. It might be
poetry. This notion helped me read Frank Bidart. I read the Language Poets without great success, but some please me more than others: Perelman,
Palmer, Hejinian, Silliman.

You can't keep up forever. I look into as many as six hundred new books
a year. I'm not telling you that I read every poem; I get tired. Like everybody
else I get tired reading the same poem over and over again, but it's not only
that. When I was in my twenties Richard Eberhart, who was only fifty, told
me that he could no longer tell the young apart. He was not being insulting;

he was complaining, not bragging. I suppose it happens to everyone. Maybe it begins to happen to me; but I remain avid to *keep up*. I suppose the feeling is more acquisitive than altruistic, but from time to time I can help someone. On the other hand, I continually get book-length manuscripts by mail from strangers, usually wanting me to find them a publisher. I cannot even read them all. Too much!

Q: Could you speak a bit about your processes of revision?

A: I'm not quick. So many things have looked good and in retrospect were awful! I need to keep things around a long time; if I keep staring, I find out what's wrong. Or I think I do. Usually it takes years of staring, until I take them inside me; sometimes I wake up at night with a problem about a poem, or a solution to a problem, when I have not seen the poem for a year or more. Mostly I work on poems every day for months; then I get fed up and put them away; then I find myself obsessing about them again and drag them out and get to work.

I must say, I enjoy revising! It's the best kind of work. The initial inspiration is over quickly, scary and manic; then I love the daily work, the struggle with language and the sweet difficulty of the struggle!

Q: Your work as an editor for the *Harvard Advocate*, the *Paris Review*, the Wesleyan poetry series, Harper and Row, the University of Michigan series, and *Harvard Magazine*—how has this affected your life? What advice might you have for editors, for a long life spent tending to the work of other poets?

A: When you edit you impose your own taste. Especially when I was younger and passionate about the work of my own generation, I wanted to impose my taste on *everybody*. Of course at this point I no longer agree with my old taste; but I don't disavow the motive. Other editors worked with a countertaste. Conflict makes energy, and I'm all for it. I started the Poets on Poetry series with the University of Michigan Press because I wanted to be able to read the books. I'd read an article here and there by this poet or that, but when I wanted to lay my hands on an essay I couldn't find it. I made the series in order to preserve fugitive and miscellaneous pieces—interviews, book reviews, full-dress articles, what have you.

Advice: Never edit by committee! Advocate, disparage, make public what you love and what you hate! When you stop loving and hating, stop editing.

Q: The Michigan Series, Poets on Poetry—Robert McDowell said in a review of the series that "The Mum Was Always Talking." I have the suspicion, along with McDowell, that if this series were not done we would have precious little record of the poetics of your generation. Did growing up, coming to fruition in the shadow of the New Critics inhibit poets from writing prose about their poetry, from writing any kind of criticism at all? W. S. Merwin once said it had that effect on him.

A: Yes, many of us felt the way Merwin speaks of. You had a feeling that some older poets would *rather* write an essay than a poem! And we reacted. Now there's a further reaction, parallel to and symptomatic of the separation of the English department from creative writing, which says that if you think about poetry—or utter thoughts about it, or allude to any poet born before 1925—you're a pedant. Bah!

Q: How long did you write textbooks before you could count on any royalties from them as a basis for your income as a freelance writer?

A: When I quit teaching I had no confidence that my income was great enough to support my family, with my children going to college. At that time *Writing Well* made more money for me than any other book but I couldn't count on it. Really, it hasn't been textbooks that have supported us. My income derives from such a variety of sources—textbooks, juveniles, trade books (many old things bring in a pittance every year), poetry readings, magazine sales. . . . *Writing Well* doesn't sell so well as it used to; other textbooks help but I don't rely on them. The many sources do a couple of things. They provide extraordinary variety in the work I do; and they have the virtues of a multiple conglomerate: If one sort of writing dwindles—if I lose interest or the market crumbles or my ability diminishes within a genre—there's something else to pick it up. Of course these advantages are accidental; I didn't become so various on purpose. I always take pleasure in trying something new.

Q: Bly looks at the world as a Jungian and you as a Freudian. How has Freud affected your view of things? What have the insights of psychology, and psychoanalysis in particular, meant to you and your generation of poets?

A: I started reading Freud in 1953. Ten years later I started psychotherapy with a Freudian analyst, the only analyst in Ann Arbor who would do therapy. Reading Freud was exciting and gave me ideas. I could have found much the same in Heraclitus: Whenever somebody shows you north, suspect south. Later, the experience of therapy was profound. It touches me every day and it goes *with* poetry rather than *against* it. You learn to release, to allow the ants—and the butterflies—to come out from under the rock; but first you have to know the rock's there! The names of the creatures that scramble out are up to you. Psychotherapy properly is never a matter of the *explanations* of feelings, nor of "Eureka!" as in Hollywood. It is a transforming thing. It makes your skin alert; it builds a system of sensors. Not censors! Jung, on the other hand, seems a mildly interesting literary figure, full of fascinating ideas and disgusting ones mixed together with more regard for color than for truth. Freud is as nasty as the world is, as human life is. Jung is decorative. Freud is the streets and Jung is a Fourth of July parade through the streets, a parade of minor deities escaped from the zoo of polytheism. Freud the atheist has the relentlessness of monotheism.

Q: Will you ever write an autobiography of your adult life?

A: No.

Q: How do you work up a biography?

A: You work on a biography by interviewing everybody and reading everything and taking notes and keeping files and taking a deep breath and plunging in. Of course biography is fiction. Again and again you have to make choices because your information contradicts itself. Did it happen this way or that way? Hell, you have to make the same choices writing out of your own life! You remember something with perfect clarity and you're perfectly wrong. How can we expect that biography be true? Mind you, it is not the same as writing a novel; there are *certain* scruples.

Q: Who, aside from writers, have been you most important teachers?

A: Henry Moore. I spent a good deal of time with him, talking with him, watching him work. He had the most wonderful attitude toward work and his art. He was interested only in being better than Michelangelo, and he knew he never achieved it; so he got up every morning and tried again. He was a gregarious man who learned to forgo companionship for the sake of work. He knew what he had to do. He remained decent to others, although it is difficult; people make it difficult for you when you're that damned famous. He knew the difference between putting in time—you can work sixteen hours a day and remain lazy—and really working as an artist, trying to *break through.*

Q: How would you place your poems among the poems of the past? I'm thinking here of Keats's statement, which you mentioned in "Poetry and Ambition," that "I would sooner fail, than not be among the greatest." You've also wisely said that we are bad at judging our own work—we either think too much of it or too little of it.

A: I can't place my poems among the poems of the past and I doubt the sanity or the intelligence of people who say that they can. When Keats said that he would "sooner fail than not be among the greatest," note that he did not tell us that he *was* among the greatest. He *wishes* to be among the English poets when he is dead; he does not tell us that he already *is.* When I was young I had the illusion that at some point or other you would *know* if you were good. I no longer believe that such knowledge is possible. Some days you feel you're terrific; some days you feel you're crap. So what? Get on with it.

Q: You have said that during the time *The Alligator Bride* and *The Town of Hill* were published, you were floundering as a writer, conscious that nothing you did was as good as some earlier poems. Why did you publish the poems of that period?

A: It was from 1969 to 1975 that I floundered; *The Alligator Bride* came out in 1969 and included "The Man in the Dead Machine," which I thought (and still think) was as good as anything I had done up to then. Also, I liked the title poem and several other new things—but after *The Alligator*, for six years, I felt that nothing that I was doing was as good as what I had done. I didn't think that what I was writing was beneath contempt; it's melancholy enough to think that nothing was as good as "The Man in the Dead Machine." I like the title poem of *The Town of Hill* better than anything else out of that patch. I published these poems because I thought that they were good. . . . (I've often been wrong; I've published many poems in magazines that I later left out of books; in the old *New Yorker* anthology, half my poems weren't good enough to put into a book.) Also I published to cheer myself up in a bad time, an ignoble reason but maybe effective. *The Town of Hill* is not my best work, but when Godine bought it I was released into the long line of "Kicking the Leaves." If I had not rid the house of those floundering poems, I'm not sure I could have written the new ones.

Q: *The One Day* works with the kind of "multiple protagonist" voice we find in "The Waste Land." Why did you make this choice, rather than stay in the fairly monolyrical voice which has characterized much of your work?

A: Picasso said that every human being is a colony. An old friend of mine said that she was not a person but ran a boarding house. One of the many problems with the "monolyrical" is that it pretends that each of us is singular.

Q: Your work is your church. Have you always been Christian? How does being a Christian enter into your work? Isn't the absence of a god (or gods) or an agnosticism an important part of much contemporary poetry? How do you see your work amidst that? If it is something you shy from speaking of, why do you shy from it? Better left unsaid, bad manners, or just refusing to talk about politics and religion at the dinner table?

A: I was brought up a Christian, suburban Protestant variety. When I was twelve I converted myself to atheism. During the years I spent in the English village of Thaxted, I used to go to church every Sunday, telling myself that I went because the carving and architecture were so beautiful, because I loved the vicar (high church and a Communist), because the ceremony was beautiful. . . . Now I think I was kidding myself in saying that my feelings were aesthetic. Yes, I am shy of speaking about it. The figure of Jesus is incredibly important, the astonishing figure from the Gospels. I used to think that people who went to church were either swallowing everything or pretending to, hypocritically. Now I know that intelligent practicing Christians often feel total spiritual drought and disbelief; still, even in such moments, ancient ritual and story can be entered, practiced, listened to, considered. . . .

Q: Not too long ago you did a review of small literary presses for *Iowa Review*. John Hollander has said that when he was first publishing you could count on a few of the elders to let you know what kind of noises your work was making. Very few older writers now review the work of younger writers, or emerging presses, except to write blurbs for them. Why is this? What is your "policy" about writing blurbs, and why?

A: Thirty years ago I was asked to write blurbs for a few books. I was flattered to be asked, and wrote the blurbs. When the books came out I looked like an ass. Then I looked at other peoples' blurbs; *they* looked like asses. There are some *honorable* people's blurbs, and even *they* looked like asses. There are exceptions, but almost every blurb is foolish. The formula for a blurb is an adjective, an adverb, and a verb that usually combine opposites. X is both free-swinging and utterly orderly; Y is classic and romantic; Z is high and at the same time, amazingly, low. Many book reviewers review blurbs rather than the poetry. Blurbs are the Good Housekeeping Seal of Approval. I think it's far worse in poetry than it is in fiction. Although doubtless many poets write blurbs out of generosity, it doesn't look that way; it gives vent to the widespread notion that poets live by taking each other's laundry. Blurbs hurts poetry. They are done because publishers are too lazy to name what they're printing. Almost always, it would be better to print a poem or an excerpt from a poem . . . but, oh, these terrible blurbs. I refuse to do it.

Although I've refused 12,457 times, although I've written essays against the practice, I still receive two hundred and fifty or three hundred requests a year to write blurbs. How could I add three hundred books and three hundred mini-essays to my life every year? This is *not* my reason for refusing to do them, but it would be reason enough. When publishers quote from reviews, excerpts from journalistic occasions, nobody can stop them. Blurbs are *pseudo*-reviews, and they appear to be used in lieu of dinner invitations, thank-you letters, and gold stars. They're repellent, fulsome, and rebarbative.

Reviewing is in terrible shape. There's more poetry than ever—more readings, more books, more *sales* of books—and less reviewing. And worse reviewing. Literary journalists like Malcolm Cowley, Louise Bogan, and Edmund Wilson made their living, in large part, by writing book reviews. Their descendants have tenure instead and teach Linebreaks 101. The *New Yorker* by appointing Helen Vendler resigned from reviewing poetry. *Atlantic* and *Harper's* and the old *Saturday Review* reviewed poetry; no more. The *New York Review of Books* isn't interested in poetry and becomes stupid when it pretends to. The *New York Times* is at its worst on poetry. What's left? The *New Republic* and the *Nation* are honorable; there are the quarterlies, each of them read by twelve people. *APR* reviews little. We suffer from a lack of intelligent *talk* about poetry. I don't know why. Maybe it's the same cultural separatism that splits creative writing and literature in the university, an epidemic of ignorance, willful know-nothingism. When Vendler is the leading critic of contemporary poetry we're in a bad way. She can write a sentence but she has *no taste*. She's a bobbysoxer for poets she swoons over: some good, some bad, she can't tell the difference.

Q: You went to Harvard with Ashbery, Bly, O'Hara, Koch, Rich, Davison, and others. You said you dated Adrienne Rich. More to say on the Poet's Theatre, as it started there?

A: Harvard 1947–51 was a lively place. There was a wonderful independent theater group, down at the Brattle. We started the Poet's Theater out of the coincidence of theatrical and poetic activity, and the momentary ascendancy of poor old Christopher Fry; of course Eliot worked at poetic drama. The Poet's Theater never produced anything memorable, but it was another center where energy gathered.

At the *Advocate* we sat around and argued all night. Koch, Ashbery, Bly. O'Hara was around, and Rich. Bly became my best friend. He and I double dated, with Rich my date. I think Adrienne and I went out twice. At least once I was *awful*: I got pissed and argued with Bly, showing off. Adrienne was *polite*. Much later, when I was married and at Oxford and she was living there as a Guggenheim Fellow, we got to be friends, very close. I feel gratitude to her, and affection . . . Bly remains my best friend. O'Hara and I were friends for a while, then we quarreled over something or other. He was wonderfully funny and alert and lively, a nifty spirit. Ashbery was intelligent and quiet and smart and talented. It was a good time. We competed, you might say.

Q: You've championed the work of poets as different as Robert Creeley and Geoffrey Hill. What accounts for the catholicity of your taste?

A: Sometimes I fear that my catholicity is another name for mindlessness. . . but I don't *really* think so. I like to say things like, "If you can't admire both Hill and Creeley, you can't read poetry." (That isn't true either.) Hell, Creeley resembles nobody so much as Henry James. Hill makes the tensest language in the universe, with more sparks flying between adjacent words than any other poet since Andrew Marvell. Both are geniuses. Of course they can't read each other. Vendler can't read either of them.

Q: Who do you think of now as the most interesting men or women of letters? Do you think the person of letters is a kind of vanishing beast?

A: People have been talking about the disappearance of the Man of Letters ever since Uncle Matthew died. People resurrect the phrase when they want to praise somebody who writes more than one thing: Edmund Wilson, Lionel Trilling. But we have candidates even now: Sven Birkerts writes essays about reading, writes essays about poetry . . . Lately, many younger poets in America, male and female, spread out by doing other writing as well as poetry—fiction, essays, criticism. *Good!* You learn about your primary art by practicing or investigating other arts—especially others that use language. Now "man of letters" is a fine phrase but it would be a pompous label to put on yourself. Instead, you can call yourself a literary journalist. (Maybe when you're eighty you can call yourself a man or woman of letters.) Let writers come out from under the Rock of University of America! Let them stick their noses under the rock of the buggy world! Let them make a living by writing.

Q: How do you avoid the whining and the bitterness?

A: Well, to start with, I whine bitterly a whole lot. . . . Whining and bitterness *are* a waste of time and spirit, and they hurt—reason enough to avoid them. You feel bitter about trivial things: *They* have left you out of the Final Anthology—the last bus to the Immortality Graveyard. Or: Everybody *else* gets this prize.

There are things I try to remember, things that help: *All prizes are rubber medals.* All grapes are sour as soon as you taste them. I haven't won the Pulitzer; if I ever win it, within five minutes I will recollect all the dopes, idiots, time-servers, and class-presidents of poetry who have won the Pulitzer; I will know that getting the Pulitzer means that I'm no damned good. Needless to say, I still want to undergo this humiliation!

Also, it matters to remember: *You're never going to know whether you're good.* Nothing in the inside world stays secure. Nothing in the outside world—like three Nobels for Literature in a row, retiring the trophy; like the sale of one million copies of your collected poems in two weeks; like effigies of your person selling in Walmarts from coast to coast—will convince you that you're any damned good. So: Give up the notion. What's left? What's left is work.

Of course you'll still feel annoyance and anger when you're abused. When somebody says something nasty, you can't get the tune out of your head. Words burn themselves into your brain the way an electric needle burns a slogan onto pine; you etch-a-sketch the unforgiveable words onto your skull. It would be good not to read reviews but it's impossible, because if a critic gets nasty there's someone out there who'll xerox the worst parts and mail them to you. The emperor was right to execute the messenger.

But . . . I know so many aging poets, who ream their brains out with rage over mistreatment, neglect, slights both imagined and true. A terrible thing to watch! Because I've seen it so much, I extend energy fending rage off— whining and bitterness—within myself, explaining to myself, over and over again, how the reputation stock market rises and falls as irrationally as Wall Street does; remembering literary history and all the *famous* poets no one has heard of: reminding myself: *Get back to the desk.*

Donald Hall, The Art of Poetry No. 43

Peter A. Stitt / 1991

Conducted in parts: first at Eagle Pond in 1983, then at Eagle Pond in 1988, and later at the YM-YWHA in New York City. "Donald Hall, The Art of Poetry No. 43" interview by Peter Stitt, originally published in the *Paris Review*, Issue 122, Fall 1991. Copyright © 1991 *The Paris Review*, used by permission of the Wylie Agency LLC.

Donald Hall was born in New Haven and raised in Hamden, Connecticut, but spent summers, holidays, and school vacations on a farm owned by his maternal grandparents in Wilmot, New Hampshire. He took his bachelor's degree at Harvard, then studied at Oxford for two years, earning the B.Litt in 1953. After holding fellowships at Stanford and at Harvard, Hall moved to Ann Arbor, where he was professor of English at the University of Michigan for seventeen years. His first book of poems, *Exiles and Marriages*, published in 1955, was followed by *The Dark Houses* (1958), *A Roof of Tiger Lilies* (1964), *The Alligator Bride: New and Selected Poems* (1969), *The Yellow Room* (1971), *The Town of Hill* (1975), *Kicking the Leaves* (1978), *The Happy Man* (1986), *The One Day* (1988), and *Old and New Poems* (1990).

He is also the author of several books of prose, some written for students, some for children, some for sports fans. They include biographies of Henry Moore and Dock Ellis, a reminiscence called *Remembering Poets* (about Frost, Pound, Thomas, and Eliot), and four collections of literary essays: *Goatfoot Milktongue Twinbird* (1978), *To Keep Moving* (1980), *The Weather for Poetry* (1982), and *Poetry and Ambition* (1988). Two of the anthologies he has compiled have become classics: *New Poets of England and America* (with Robert Pack and Louis Simpson) and *Contemporary American Poetry*. Among other honors, he has received the Lamont Poetry Selection Award (for *Exiles and Marriages*) and two Guggenheim Foundation fellowships (1963, 1972). His children's book, *Ox-Cart Man* (1980), illustrated by Barbara Cooney, won the Caldecott Award. He was the first poetry editor of the *Paris Review*, from 1953 to 1961, as well as the first person to interview a poet for this magazine.

In 1975, after the death of his grandmother, Hall gave up his tenured professorship at Michigan and moved, with his wife Jane Kenyon, to the old family farm in New Hampshire. Since then he has supported himself through freelance writing. Sixteen years later, he continues to feel that he never made a better decision. It was at Eagle Pond Farm that the first two sittings of this interview were conducted, in the summers of 1983 and 1988. A third session was held on the stage of the YM-YWHA in New York.

Donald Hall likes to get to work early, and so both interview sessions at the farm began at about 6:00 A.M. Interviewer and interviewee sat in easy chairs with the tape recorder on a coffee table between them.

Interviewer: I would like to begin by asking how you started. How did you become a writer? What was the first thing that you ever wrote and when?

Donald Hall: Everything important always begins from something trivial. When I was about twelve I loved horror movies. I used to go down to New Haven from my suburb and watch films like *Frankenstein, The Wolf Man, The Wolf Man Meets Abbott and Costello.* So the boy next door said, "Well, if you like that stuff, you've got to read Edgar Allan Poe." I had never heard of Edgar Allan Poe, but when I read him I fell in love. I wanted to grow up and *be* Edgar Allan Poe. The first poem that I wrote doesn't really *sound* like Poe, but it's morbid enough. Of course I have friends who say it's the best thing I ever did:

> Have you ever thought
> Of the nearness of death to you?
> It reeks through each corner,
> It shrieks through the night,
> It follows you through the day
> Until that moment when,
> In monotones loud,
> Death calls your name.
> Then, then, comes the end of all.

The end of Hall, maybe. That started me writing poems and stories. For a couple of years I wrote them in a desultory fashion because I wasn't sure whether I wanted to be a great actor or a great poet.

Then when I was fourteen I had a conversation at a Boy Scout meeting with a fellow who seemed ancient to me; he was sixteen. I was bragging and told him that I had written a poem during study hall at high school that day. He asked—I can see him standing there—"You write poems?" and I said, "Yes, do you?" and he said, in the most solemn voice imaginable, "It is my profession." He had just quit high school to devote himself to writing poetry full time! I thought that was the coolest thing I'd ever heard. It was like that scene in *Bonnie and Clyde* where Clyde says, "We rob banks." Poetry *is* like robbing banks. It turned out that my friend knew some eighteen-year-old Yale freshmen, sophisticated about literature, and so at the age of fourteen I hung around Yale students who talked about T. S. Eliot. I saved up my allowance and bought the little blue, cloth-covered collected Eliot for two dollars and fifty cents, and I was off. I decided that I would be a poet for the rest of my life, and started by working at poems for an hour or two every day after school. I never stopped.

Interviewer: What about at your high school? I believe you attended Exeter—was anyone there helpful to you?

Hall: After a couple of years of public high school, I went to Exeter—an insane conglomeration of adolescent males in the wilderness, all of whom claimed to hate poetry. There was support from the faculty—I dedicated *A Roof of Tiger Lilies* to one teacher and his wife, Leonard and Mary Stevens—but of course there was also discouragement. One English teacher made it his announced purpose to rid me of the habit of writing poetry. This was in an English Special, for the brightest students, and he spent a fifty-minute class reading aloud some poetry I'd handed him, making sarcastic comments. For the first ten minutes, the other students laughed—but then they shut up. They may not have liked poetry but they were shocked by what he did. When I came back to Exeter ten years later to read my poems, after publishing my first book, the other teachers asked my old teacher-enemy to introduce me, and my mind filled up with possibilities for revenge. I did nothing, of course, but another ten years after that apparently my unconscious mind did exact its revenge—and because I didn't intend it, I could enjoy revenge without guilt. I wrote an essay for the *New York Times Book Review* which offered a bizarre interpretation of Wordsworth's poem about daffodils. At the end, I said that if anyone felt that my interpretation hurt their enjoyment of the poem, they'd never really admired the poem anyway—but just some picture postcard of Wordsworth's countryside that a teacher handed around in a classroom. When I wrote it, I thought I made the teacher and his classroom up—but a few days after the piece appeared, I received the postcard in an envelope from my enemy-teacher at Exeter together with a note: "I suppose your fingerprints are still on it."

Interviewer: Was there anyone else when you were young who encouraged you to be a writer?

Hall: Not really. My parents were willing to let me follow my nose, do what I wanted to do, and they supported my interest by buying the books that I wanted for birthdays and Christmas, almost always poetry books. When I was sixteen years old I published in some little magazines, and my parents paid for me to go to Bread Loaf.

I remember the first time I saw Robert Frost. It was opening night, and Theodore Morrison, the director, was giving an introductory talk. I felt excited and exalted. Nobody was anywhere near me in age; the next youngest contributor was probably in her mid-twenties. As I was sitting there, I looked out the big French windows and saw Frost approaching. He was coming up a hill, and as he walked toward the windows first his head appeared and then his shoulders, as if he were rising out of the ground. Later, I talked with him a couple of times and I heard him read. He ran the poetry workshop in the afternoon on a couple of occasions, though not when my poems were read, thank God; he could be nasty. I sat with him one time on the porch as he talked with two women and me. He delivered his characteristic monologue—witty, sharp, acerb on the subject of his friends. He wasn't hideously unkind, the way he looks in Thomson's biography, but also he was not Mortimer Snerd; he was not the farmer miraculously gifted with rhyme, the way he seemed if you read about him in *Time* or *Life*. He was a sophisticated fellow, you might say.

We played softball. This was in 1945, and Frost was born in 1874, so he was seventy-one years old. He played a vigorous game of softball but he was also something of a spoiled brat. His team had to win, and it was well known that the pitcher should serve Frost a fat pitch. I remember him hitting a double. He fought hard for his team to win, and he was willing to change the rules. He had to win at everything. Including poetry.

Interviewer: What was the last occasion on which you saw him?

Hall: The last time I saw him was in Vermont, within seven or eight months of his death. He visited Ann Arbor that spring and invited me to call on him in the summer. We talked about writing, about literature, though of course mostly he monologued. He was deaf, but even when he was younger he tended to make long speeches. Anyway, after we had been talking for hours, my daughter Philippa, who was three years old, asked him if he had a TV. He looked down at her and smiled and said, "You've seen me on TV?"

Also we talked about a man who was writing a book about Frost, another poet I knew. Frost hadn't read his poetry, and he asked me, "Is he any good?"

I told him what I thought. Then, as we were driving away, I looked into the rearview mirror and saw the old man, eighty-eight, running after the car— literally running. I stopped and he came up to the window and asked me please, when I saw my friend again, not to mention that Frost had asked me if his poetry was any good, because he didn't want my friend to know that he had not read his poetry. Frost was a political animal in the literary world. So are many of the best poets I run into, and it doesn't seem to hurt their poetry.

Interviewer: Our meeting is an occasion of sorts since you are the original interviewer of poets for the *Paris Review*. Whom did you interview?

Hall: T. S. Eliot, Ezra Pound and Marianne Moore. I had already known Eliot for a number of years. At the time of the interview, he was returning from a winter vacation in someplace like the Bahamas, and we did the interview in New York. He looked tan and lean and wonderful, which surprised me. I had not seen him then for two or three years, and in the meantime he had married Valerie Fletcher. What a change in the man! When I *first* met him, in 1950, he looked like a corpse. He was pale and bent over; he moved stiffly and slowly and coughed a continual, hacking cough. This ancient character was full of kindness and generosity, but he looked ready for the grave, as he did the next several times I saw him. Then, when I met him for the interview after his happy second marriage, he looked twenty years younger. He was happy; he giggled; he held hands with his young wife whenever they were together. Oh, he was an entirely different person, lighter and more forthcoming. Pound I interviewed in the spring of 1960. I was apprehensive, driving to see him in Rome, because I was afraid of what I'd run into. I had loved his poetry from early on, but his politics revolted me, as they did everybody. The *Paris Review* had scheduled an interview with him once before, when he was at St. Elizabeth's, but he canceled at the last minute because he determined that the *Paris Review* was part of the "pinko usury fringe." That's the sort of thing I expected, but that's not what I found. He was staying with a friend in Rome, and I drove down from England with my family. After I had knocked on the door and he swung it open and made sure it was me, he said, "Mister Hall, you've come all the way from England—and you find me in fragments!" He spoke with a melody that made him sound like W. C. Fields. There's the famous story—this didn't happen to me but I love it—of a young American poet who was wandering around in Venice, not long before Pound died, and recognized the house where Pound was living with Olga Rudge. Impulsively, he knocked on the door. Maybe he expected the butler to answer, but the door swung open and it was

Ezra Pound. In surprise and confusion the young poet said, "How are you, Mr. Pound?" Pound looked at him and, as he swung the door shut, said, "Senile."

The Pound I interviewed in 1960 had not yet entered the silence, but the silence was beginning to enter him. There were enormous pauses in the middle of his sentences, times when he lost his thread; he would begin to answer, then qualify it, then qualify the qualification, as though he were composing a Henry James sentence. Often he could not find his way back out again, and he would be overcome with despair. He had depended all his life on quickness of wit and sharpness of mind. It was his pride. Now he was talking with me for a *Paris Review* interview, which he took seriously indeed, and he found himself almost incapable. Sometimes after ten minutes of pause, fatigue and despair, he would heave a sigh, sit up, and continue the sentence where he had broken it off. He was already depressed, the depression which later deepened and opened that chasm of silence. But then and there, in 1960, I had a wonderful time with him. He was mild, soft, affectionate, sane. One time he and I went across the street to have a cup of coffee at a café where I had had coffee earlier. The waiter recognized us both, though he had never before seen us together, and thought he made a connection. He spoke a sentence in Italian which I didn't understand, but the last word was *figlio*. Pound looked at me and looked at the waiter and said, "*Sì*."

Interviewer: In the interview with him, your questions are challenging, yet he seems, not evasive exactly, but as though he just did not quite understand what he had done.

Hall: Oh, no, he never really understood. He insisted that there could be no treason without treasonable intent. I'm certain that he had no treasonable intent, but if treason is giving aid and comfort to the enemy in time of war, well . . . he broadcast from Rome to American troops suggesting that they stop fighting. Of course he thought he was aiding and comforting the real America. He wasn't in touch with contemporary America, not for decades. All the time he was at St. Elizabeth's he was in an asylum for the insane, and his visitors were mostly cranks of the right wing. The news he heard was filtered. I think you can chart his political changes right from the end of the First World War and find that they correlate with the growth of paranoia and monomania that connected economics—finally, Jewish bankers—with a plot to control the world. He started out cranky and moved from cranky to crazy.

Interviewer: In *Remembering Poets*, just as now, the one poet you interviewed that you don't talk about is Marianne Moore.

Hall: Back then, I thought I didn't have enough to say—or enough that other writers hadn't already said. Lately, I've come up with some notions about her that I may write up for a new edition of that book. I had lunch with her twice in Brooklyn. The first time she took me up the hill to the little Viennese restaurant where she took everybody. Like everybody else I fought with her for the check and lost. She was tiny and frail and modest, but oh so powerful. I think she must have been a weight lifter in another life—or maybe a middle linebacker. Whenever you're in the presence of extreme modesty or diffidence, *always* look for great degrees of reticent power, or a hugely strong ego. Marianne Moore as editor of the *Dial* was made of steel. To wrestle with her over a check was to be pinned to the mat.

Another time when I came to visit, her teeth were being repaired so she made lunch at her apartment. She thought she looked dreadful and wouldn't go outside the house without a complete set of teeth. Lunch was extraordinary! On a tray she placed three tiny paper cups and a plate. One of the cups contained about two teaspoons of V-8 juice. Another had about eight raisins in it, and the other five and a half Spanish peanuts. On the plate was a mound of Fritos, and when she passed them to me she said, "I like Fritos. They're so good for you, you know." She was eating health foods at the time, and I'm quite sure she wasn't being ironic. She entertained some notion that Fritos were a health food. What else did she serve? Half a cupcake for dessert, maybe? She prepared a magnificent small cafeteria for birds.

Interviewer: Marianne Moore went to school and she wrote poetry, but she did not study creative writing in school. Do you think the institution of the creative writing program has helped the cause of poetry?

Hall: Well, not really, no. I've said some nasty things about these programs. The Creative Writing Industry invites us to use poetry to achieve other ends—a job, a promotion, a bibliography, money, notoriety. I loathe the trivialization of poetry that happens in creative writing classes. Teachers set exercises to stimulate subject matter: "Write a poem about an imaginary landscape with real people in it." "Write about a place your parents lived in before you were born." We have enough terrible poetry around without encouraging more of it. Workshops make workshop-poems. Also, workshops encourage a kind of local competition, being better than the poet who sits next to you—in place of the useful competition of trying to be better than Dante. Also, they encourage a groupishness, an old-boy and -girl network which often endures for decades.

The good thing about workshops is that they provide a place where young poets can gather and argue—the artificial café. We're a big country, without a literary capital. Young poets from different isolated areas all over the country can gather with others of their kind.

And I suppose that workshops have contributed to all the attention that poetry's been getting in the last decades. Newspaper people and essayists always whine about how we don't read poetry the way we used to, in the twenties for example. Bullshit! Just compare the numbers of books of poems sold then and now. Even in the fifties, a book of poems published by some eminent poet was printed in an edition of one thousand hardback copies. If it sold out everyone was cheerful. In 1923 *Harmonium* didn't sell out—Stevens was remaindered, for heaven's sake! A book of poetry today, by a poet who's been around, will be published in an edition of five to seven thousand copies and often reprinted.

But it's not the Creative Writing Industry itself that sells books; it's the poetry readings. Practically nobody in the twenties and thirties and forties did readings. Vachel Lindsay, early, then Carl Sandburg, then Robert Frost—nobody else. If you look at biographies of Stevens and Williams and Moore, you see that they read their poems once every two years if they were lucky. Poetry readings started to grow when Dylan Thomas came over in the late forties and fifties. By this time there are three million poetry readings a year in the United States. Oh, no one knows how many there are. Sometimes I think *I* do three million a year.

In the sixties, when the poetry reading boom got going, people went to their state universities and heard poets read. When they went back to their towns, they got the community college to bring poets in, or they set up their own series through an arts group. Readings have proliferated enormously and spread sideways from universities to community colleges, prep schools, and arts associations. I used to think, "Well, this is nice while it lasts, but it'll go away." It hasn't gone away. There are more than ever.

Interviewer: We were talking about your *Paris Review* interviews. You also edited poetry for the *Paris Review* for nine years, at the beginning of the magazine. Why did you want to edit?

Hall: At the time I was a fierce advocate of the contemporary, with huge dislikes and admirations, and I wanted to impose my taste. That's why I did the *Advocate* at Harvard, why I did the *Paris Review*, why I did anthologies. When I was at Oxford, besides choosing poetry for the *Paris Review*, I edited a mimeo'd sheet for the Poetry Society, another magazine called *New Poems*, the poetry in the weekly, *Isis*, and *Fantasy Poets*—a pamphlet series which was started by a surrealist painter who did printing on the side. Michael Shanks edited the first four *Fantasy* pamphlets—including mine—and when Shanks went down to London, I chose the second bunch, which included Geoffrey Hill and Thom Gunn.

Oxford was a good time—though I felt rather elderly at Oxford. At Harvard I was a year younger than John Ashbery even, but at Oxford I was older than everybody. I'd been through college, while most of them were just out of boarding school. I had fun being dogmatic and bossy. Over at Cambridge, where there hadn't been any poets for years, Thom Gunn turned up writing those wonderful early poems. When we heard him on the BBC, we invited him over to Oxford. My greatest time as an editor was with Geoffrey Hill. Just before the end of my first year at Oxford, he published a poem in *Isis*—a poem he's never reprinted. Meeting him, I asked him casually if he'd submit a manuscript to the *Fantasy* series. Then I came back to the States for the summer; I was here in New Hampshire when Geoffrey's manuscript arrived. I couldn't believe my eyes: "Genesis," "God's Little Mountain," "Holy Thursday." Extraordinary! In the middle of the night I woke up dreaming about it; I turned on the light and read it again.

I accepted the manuscript for the pamphlet series. Later I put "Genesis" in the second issue of the *Paris Review*. Geoffrey was twenty years old.

Interviewer: I believe you were known, for a period in the sixties, as James Dickey's editor or even as his discoverer.

Hall: Oh, I was not his discoverer—but I did publish him early. When I was editing for the *Paris Review* I got poems from an address in Atlanta—long, garrulous poems with good touches. After a while I started writing notes, maybe "sorry" on a printed slip, then "thank you," then a letter saying, "I don't like the middle part." Finally he sent a poem I liked and I took it. We began to correspond, and I discovered that he was in advertising. He sent me a fifteen-second radio ad for Coca-Cola, saying, "This is my latest work."

When I was on the poetry board at Wesleyan, he sent us a book, I think at Robert Bly's urging. But we took two other books ahead of him—we could only do two every season—and one of them was going to be James Wright's third book, which he was calling *Amenities of Stone*. These two books crowded James Dickey out, which was a pity because it was *Drowning with Others*—his best work, I still think. Maybe two months later, my phone rang one morning at about seven A.M. It was Willard Lockwood, director of the Wesleyan University Press, saying that Jim Wright had withdrawn his book. Wesleyan was about to go to press; there was no time for the committee to meet again. Would it be all right to substitute the runner-up book, which was James Dickey's? I called Dickey in Atlanta, then and there, seven-thirty in the morning, and asked, "Has your book been taken by another publisher? Can we still have it?" He said to go right ahead. So Wesleyan published James Dickey because James Wright withdrew his book.

Interviewer: Did you get to know James Dickey?

Hall: I think I first met him out at Reed College, when he was teaching there for a semester. Poetry got him out of advertising and for a while he traveled from school to school, one year here and another year there. I'm not sure which year he spent at Reed—early sixties—but we had a good visit out there. Carolyn Kizer came down from Seattle. Jim and I drove around in his MG, talking. He was friendly, and flattering about my work, but I began to notice—because of things he said about other people—that loyalty might not be his strong point. So I asked him straight out, "Don't you think loyalty's a great quality?" He knew what I was up to; he said, "No, I think it's a terrible quality. I think it's the worst quality there is."

Interviewer: Let's move away from editing other people to editing yourself. Could you talk about how you work? I gather that you revise a lot.

Hall: First drafts of anything are difficult for me. I prefer revising, rewriting. I'm not the kind of writer, like Richard Wilbur or Thomas Mann, who finishes one segment before going on to another. Wilbur finishes the first line before he starts the second. I lack the ability to judge myself except over many drafts, and usually over years. Revising, I go through a whole manuscript over and over and over. Some short prose pieces I've rewritten fifteen or twenty times; poems get up to two hundred fifty or three hundred drafts. I don't recommend it—but for me it seems necessary. And I do more drafts as I get older.

Or maybe I just like it. Even with prose, I love the late stage in rewriting. I *play* with sentences, revise their organization, work with the rhythms, work with punctuation as though I were handling line-breaks in poetry. In poetry I play with punctuation, line-breaks, internal sounds, interconnections among images. I tinker with little things, and it's my greatest pleasure in writing.

Interviewer: Do you generally have several things going at once?

Hall: I'm not good at working on one thing straight through. When I work more than an hour on one project, I get irritated. Or sometimes I get too high. I spend my day working on many different things, never so long as an hour. When I get stuck, I put it down. Maybe I go haul some wood or have a drink of water; then I come back and pick up something else—an essay I'm working on, a book that's due in six months . . . I work on poems usually in one block of time for an hour or two hours—recently sometimes three hours; things have been hotting up—almost always on several poems.

It isn't just alternating projects; I switch around among genres, and I work in many: children's books, magazine pieces, short stories, textbooks. Obviously I care about poetry the most. But I love working with various kinds of prose also, even something as mundane as headnotes for an anthology. After all, I am working with the same material—language, syntax, rhythms and vowels—as if I were a sculptor who worked at carving in stone all morning, then in the afternoon built drywalls or fieldstone houses.

There's pleasure in doing the same thing in different forms. When I heard the story of the ox-cart man from my cousin Paul Fenton, I started work on a poem. It's a wonderful story, passed on orally for generations until I stole it out of the air: a farmer fills up his ox cart in October with everything that the farm has produced in a year that he doesn't need—honey, wool, deerskin—and walks by his ox to Portsmouth market where he sells everything in the cart. Then he sells the cart, then the ox, and walks home to start everything over again.

The best stories come out of the air. I worked on that ox-cart man poem, brief as it is, for about two years. Just as I was finishing it, I suddenly thought that I could make a children's book out of the same story. The children's book took me a couple of hours to write, hours not years, and the wage was somewhat better. When the book won the Caldecott, we were able to tear off the dingy old bathroom and put a new bathroom into an old bedroom and add a new bedroom; over the new bathroom I have a plaque: CALDECOTT ROOM.

Later I used the same ox-cart story as part of an essay, and as a song that Bill Bolcom set for Joan Morris to sing. Now I've used it again, here in an interview! Every time I tell the story it's different. The form makes it different, also the audience and therefore the tone, therefore the diction—which makes the whole process fascinating. In working on a play I used material from all over the place: from one prose book in particular, from other essays, from fiction, from poems. When I put these things into bodily action, and into dialogue on a stage—material that I had already *used up*, you might have thought—they take on new life, thanks to the collision with a different genre.

Interviewer: You mentioned sculpture a few minutes ago. What is it about Henry Moore that so fascinates you?

Hall: I had admired his work for a long time before I had the chance to interview him for *Horizon*. When I was an undergraduate I pinned a Penguin print of Henry Moore's sculpture on my wall. When I first got to England in 1951, I saw his sculpture at the Festival of Britain. It was 1959 when

I met him and interviewed him; three years later I came back and hung around him for a whole year—watching, listening—to do a *New Yorker* profile, which later became a book. Of all the older artists I've known, he's made the most difference for my own writing. He helped me get past a childish form of ambition: the mere striving to be foremost. He wasn't interested in being the best sculptor in England, or even the best sculptor of his generation. He wanted to be as good as Michelangelo or Donatello. He was in his early sixties when I met him first—my age now—and oh, he loved to work! At the same time he was a gentle, humorous, gregarious man. He got up early every morning—and he *got on with it*. I think of a story from the time when he and Irina were first married. They were going off into the country for a holiday, and Irina tried to lift one of the suitcases that Henry had brought but she couldn't get it off the ground. He'd packed a piece of alabaster. I am sure they paid lots of attention to each other—but from time to time Henry went outside and tap-tapped with chisel and mallet.

I loved hearing him talk about sculpture, and everything he said about sculpture I turned to poetry. He quoted Rodin quoting a craftsman: "Never think of a surface except as the extension of a volume." I did a lot with that one.

Interviewer: Did you envy him for the physicality of his materials?

Hall: The physical activity of the painter and the sculptor keeps them in touch with the *nature* of their art more than writing does for writers. Handwriting or typing or word processing—they're not like sticking your hands into clay.

Yet a poem has a body, just as sculpture and painting have bodies. When you write a poem, you're not hammering out the sounds with a chisel or spreading them with a brush, but you've got to feel it in your mouth. The act of writing a poem is a bodily act as well as a mental and imaginative act, and the act of reading a poem—even silently—must be bodily before it's intellectual. In talking or writing about poetry, too often people never get to the work of art. Instead they talk about some statement they abstract from the work of art, a paraphrase of it. Everybody derides paraphrase and everybody does it. It's the fallacy of content—the philosophical heresy.

Interviewer: You were talking about writing prose. Tell us more about the relationship between your poetry and your prose.

Hall: When I was young I wrote prose but I didn't take it seriously; it was terrible. I began to write real prose when I wrote *String Too Short to Be Saved*, mostly in 1959 and 1960; with that book I learned how to write descriptive and narrative reminiscence. Over the years, I've learned how to write other prose—to write for five-year-olds, stories for picture books; to write articles or reviews about poetry; to write prose for popular magazines, some of it objective or biographical—like my profile of Henry Moore; and to write about sports. Also I've written short stories, combining narrative prose with some of the shapeliness of poems. Writing prose for a living—freelance writing—does another thing I like: it opens doors. Sir Kenneth Clark had me to lunch at his castle in Kent—because I was writing about Moore for the *New Yorker*. By sportswriting I made the major leagues, talking with Pete Rose and sitting up half the night with Willie Crawford. I've listened to the free association of Kevin McHale of the Boston Celtics.

Interviewer: How did the baseball players accept you? As I remember when you tried out for the Pirates you were bearded and, shall we say, a touch overweight?

Hall: I was bearded and weighed about two hundred fifty pounds when I tried out for second base with the Pittsburgh Pirates. Willie Randolph and Rennie Stennett *both* beat me out. (I was cut for not being able to bend over, which wasn't fair: Richie Hebner made the team at third base and he couldn't bend over either.) The players had nicknames for me, like "Abraham" and "Poet," and they treated me like a mascot. When I took batting practice, the whole team stopped whatever it was doing to watch—the comedy act of the decade. The players looked at me as some sort of respite from their ordinary chores; they were curious, and they were kind enough as they teased me. Mostly, athletes are quick-witted and funny, with maybe a ten-second attention span.

Back to the question: there are several relationships between my prose and my poetry. Prose is mostly the breadwinner. Poetry supplies bread through the poetry reading, but prose makes the steady income. I get paid for an essay once when it comes out in a magazine, then again when I collect it in a book. But also, I think that prose takes some of the pressure off my poetry. Maybe I am able to be more patient with my poetry—taking years and years to finish poems—because I continue to finish and publish short prose pieces.

Prose is tentative and exploratory and not so intense; in prose I can dwell on something longer, not just pick out the *one* thing to notice or say. Poetry is the top of the mountain. I like the foothills just fine—as long as I keep access to the top of the mountain.

Interviewer: Have you ever learned from critics?

Hall: Sure. When I was young, critics helped teach me to read poems. Then critics or poets-being-critics have—in person and by letter—led me to discard poems or to rip them up and start over again. I seek their abrasiveness out. I've even been helped by book reviews, mostly by some general dissatisfaction with my work. But if a book review is a personal attack—someone obviously *hates* you—it doesn't do any good. You just walk up and down feeling the burden of this death-ray aimed at you. The critics who help have been annoyed with my work, and make it clear why, without actually wanting to kill me. They give me new occasions for scrutiny, for crossing out.

Interviewer: Another subject. You're notorious for answering letters. Is your heavy correspondence related to your art? Doesn't it get in the way?

Hall: Sometimes I wonder: do I write a letter because it's easier than writing a poem? I don't think so. Letters take less time than parties or lunches. How do people in New York get anything done? My letters are my society. I carry on a dense correspondence with poets of my generation and younger. Letters are my café, my club, my city. I am fond of my neighbors up here, but for the most part they keep as busy as I do. We meet in church, we meet at the store, we gossip a little. We don't stand around in a living room and *chat*—like the parties I used to go to in Ann Arbor. I write letters instead, and mostly I write about the work of writing. There are poets with whom I regularly exchange poems, soliciting criticism. I don't think that either Robert Bly or I has ever published a poem without talking it over with the other. Also, I work out ideas in letters that will later be parts of essays. I dictate; it takes too much time to type and no one can read my handwriting.

Interviewer: Let me ask a typical *Paris Review* question. Do you write your poems in longhand? On a typewriter? Or a word processor? Do you use a pen? A pencil?

Hall: For thirty or thirty-five years, I've written in longhand—pencil, ballpoint, felt tip, fountain pen: the magic moves around. I used to work at poetry on a typewriter, but I tended to race on, to be glib, not to pause enough. Thirty years ago I gave up the keyboard, began writing in longhand, and hired other people to type for me. At the moment four typists help me out, and one right down the road has a word processor. It's marvelous because I can tinker without worrying about the time and labor of retyping. I make little changes in ongoing poems every day, and start with clean copies every morning.

I dictate letters but nothing else. It irritates me that Henry James was able to dictate *The Ambassadors* but I can't dictate the first draft of a book review.

Interviewer: Were you ever part of a group of poets? Did you visit Robert Bly's farm in the early sixties in Madison, Minnesota?

Hall: There wasn't anything I would call a group. I did get out to the Blys' a couple of times. The summer of 1961 I was there for two weeks along with the Simpsons. Jim Wright came out from Minneapolis for the two weekends. We four males spent hours together looking at each other's poetry. Of course we had some notions in common, and we learned from each other, so maybe we *were* a group. I remember how one poem of mine got changed then, "In the Kitchen of the Old House." I'd been fiddling with it for two years. It began with an imagined dream—which just didn't go—and I said in frustration something like, "I remember when this started. I was sitting in the kitchen of this old house late at night, thinking about . . ." Three voices interrupted me: "Write it down! Write it down!" This poem needed a way *in*.

We worked together and we played competitive games like badminton and swimming, but poetry was the most competitive game. We were friendly and fought like hell. Louis was the best swimmer, and Robert always won the foolhardiness prize. There was a big town swimming pool in Madison where we went every day, and Robert would climb to the highest diving platform and jump off, making faces and noises and gyrating his body all the way down. I won at badminton.

Robert and I—he was Bob then, and I feel stiff saying "Robert"—met at Harvard in February of 1948, when I tried out for the *Advocate*. He had joined the previous fall, when he first got to Harvard, but I waited until my second term. After school was out that summer, he came down to Connecticut and stayed at my house for a day or two. I was nervous having my poet friend there, afraid of confrontation between Robert and my father. At lunch Robert said, "Well Mr. Hall, what do you think of having a poet for a son?" As I feared, my father didn't know *what* to say; poetry was embarrassing, somehow. So I said, "Too bad your father doesn't have the same problem," and my father laughed and laughed, off the hook.

Robert and I have written thousands of letters back and forth, and we've visited whenever we could. You know these people who hate Robert and write about how clever he has been at his literary politicking? They don't know anything about it. For years and years he was a solitary. I remember a time before I moved to Ann Arbor, when Robert came back from Norway and stopped to visit while I lived outside Boston. He was talking about going back to the Madison farm and starting a magazine. He had discovered modernism in Norway and wanted to *tell* everybody—but also he wanted to remain independent. Knowing literary people would only make it harder for him, so he did not want to *know* anybody besides me. Then he said, "I don't want to know James Wright. How can I write about James Wright if I know

James Wright?" He wasn't being nasty about Jim; he brought up Jim's name because Jim had just taken a job at the University of Minnesota—three or four hours away from Madison. They didn't get to know each other until a couple of years later, when Jim wrote him an anguished letter. Jim read Robert's attacks on fifties poetry in *The Fifties* and decided that everything Robert said was right and everything Jim was doing was wrong. Jim was always deciding that he was *wrong*.

Robert wanted solitude and independence. He was going to lecture everybody, as he always has done and still does, but from a distance. If he wanted eminence he wanted a lonely eminence. He came out of his isolation, I think, at that conference in Texas when he took the floor away from the professors. Do you know about that?

Interviewer: No. This is something I haven't heard about.

Hall: It was a moment. The National Council of Teachers of English invited young poets, as they called us, to a conference in Houston in 1966. They brought Robert Graves over to lecture, and they brought in Richard Eberhart, calling him dean of the younger poets. Dick was fifty-two; that made him dean. Most of the young poets were forty or close to it. There was W. S. Merwin, Robert Creeley, Robert Duncan, Gary Snyder, Carolyn Kizer, Robert, I . . . And also: Reed Whittemore, Josephine Miles, William Stafford, May Swenson. Young poets! Several of us flew down from Chicago together. We stood in the aisle of a 707 singing "Yellow Submarine"—Bly, Snyder, Creeley and I. We stayed up all night in somebody's room at the Houston hotel talking about poetry. Creeley had an over-the-shoulder cassette recorder, and every time Duncan spoke he turned it on, and every time Duncan finished speaking he turned it off. We stayed up until six in the morning and Eberhart's talk was at eight-thirty, so we didn't get a whole lot of sleep.

We met in a huge hall filled with thousands of English teachers. Eberhart talked about how the Peace Corps sent him to Africa; he observed a tribe of primitive people and told us that civilization lacked spontaneity. Dick discovers Rousseau! Someone else got up, a respondent, and said something silly. Then Laurence Perrine, who edited the textbook *Sound and Sense*, stood up as another respondent. He talked conservatively about poetic form, saying something in praise of villanelles—in 1966!—which made it sound as if all poems were really the same; as if nothing mattered, not what you said or how you said it. I'm unfair, but all of us were tired, some of us were hung over, and everything we heard sounded fatuous after the energizing talk of the night before. So Robert stood up in the front row—turning around to face these thousands of people, interrupting the program—and said: "He's *wrong*. We care about poetry. Poetry *matters* and one thing is better than something else . . ." He went on; I can't remember . . . Whatever Bly said, it was passionate. It woke everybody up, I'll tell you. Thousands of teachers applauded mightily. As Robert sat down and the program was about to proceed, somebody in the audience said, "Let's hear from all the poets." So we took over, to hell with the program, and one by one each of us read a poem and talked. It was Vietnam time and a lot of us talked about politics. Robert gave the rest of us courage, and his platform life began at that moment: he found his public antinomian *presence.*

Interviewer: Somehow one doesn't think of Robert Bly as having graduated from Harvard—but there were many poets there at the time, weren't there?

Hall: Robert went one year to St. Olaf in Minnesota and then transferred to Harvard. He and I overlapped for three years, becoming closest friends, always opposites. The two of us are Don Quixote and Sancho Panza. On the *Advocate* with us were Kenneth Koch and John Ashbery. Frank O'Hara was never on the *Advocate*, but he was a member of the first class I took in writing, taught by John Ciardi, who was a wonderful teacher. I remember John coming into class one day and saying something like, "I just sold eight poems to the *New Yorker*, I bought my first car, and next election I'll probably vote Republican." John supported Henry Wallace in 1948, very progressive. Be wary of what you joke about. O'Hara was writing poems then, but I didn't know it; I saw his short stories. Frank gave the best parties at Harvard: incongruous, outrageous bunches of people. I remember Maurice Bowra, visiting from Oxford as he bounced and burbled on Frank's sofa. Frank was in Eliot House, as I was, and his roommate was the artist Ted Gorey—Edward St. John Gorey. Frank was the funniest man I ever met, utterly quick-witted and sharp with his sarcasm. Once in his presence I made some sort of joshing reference, comparing him to Oscar Wilde. Being gay was relatively open, even light, in the Harvard of those years. One of Frank's givens was that *everybody* was gay, either in or out of the closet. He answered me with a swoop of emphasis: "*You're* the type that would *sue.*"

I admired Ashbery; we *all* admired John, although in general we were not a mutual admiration society. In general we were murderous. John was at the time reticent, shy, precocious. He had published in *Poetry* while he was still at Deerfield Academy. On the *Advocate*, we were terribly serious about the poems we published. We would stay up until two or three in the morning arguing about whether a poem was good enough to be in the magazine. One time we had a half-page gap and asked John to come up with a poem.

After some prodding he conceded that *maybe* he had a poem. He went back to his room to get it, and it took him forty minutes. We didn't know it then, but of course—he later admitted—he went home and wrote the poem. In 1989 I told John this story—wondering if he remembered it as I did—and he even remembered the *poem*, which began, "Fortunate Alphonse, the shy homosexual . . . " He told me, with a sigh, "Yes, I took longer then."

One night Bly came back from a dance at Radcliffe saying he had met a girl from Baltimore, a doctor's daughter who knew all about modern poetry. Adrienne Rich! I met her and we dated, though we didn't get to know each other until a couple of years later. She published her first book, which Auden chose for the Yale Series of Younger Poets, when we were seniors. My second year at Oxford, she won a Guggenheim (at the age of twenty-two) and chose to spend her time in Oxford—not studying, just in town. That's when we became friends, and for several years we worked closely together. In 1954 and 1955 Adrienne and I were back in Cambridge at the same time. I baby-sat every morning while my wife went back to school, and one day a week Adrienne, pregnant with her first child, dropped by from eight in the morning until one o'clock. We talked poetry while I fed and bathed my son Andrew. Many years later, Adrienne and I were talking about those times, early marriages and casserole cookery, and we talked about the sex roles we played. "Don," Adrienne told me, "you taught me how to bathe a baby."

At Harvard, I also knew Peter Davison, L. E. Sissman, Kenward Elmslie. Bob Creeley left the term before I arrived. He was chicken farming in New Hampshire but I met him and talked poetry with him at the Grolier Book Shop, where you met everybody. Creeley and I got along famously, but a couple of years later I insulted him in a magazine piece and we were enemies for a while. A little while ago, Bob sent me a book which included a stick-figure account of his life, and he put a check mark by one item: he had quit a publishing venture, on Majorca with Martin Seymour-Smith, because Seymour-Smith wanted to print my poems.

Richard Wilbur was older—he was born in 1921, and at that time, seven years' difference was something. While I was an undergraduate, he was a Junior Fellow, with a young family at home, so he had a room at Adams House to work in. He was such a generous man. I brought him poems to look at, and he showed me what he was up to. I remember him working on *Ceremony*. Archibald MacLeish came to Harvard as Boylston Professor when I was a junior. Dick Eberhart lived in Cambridge. Frost lived there fall and spring, and when I was a Junior Fellow Robert Lowell came to Boston. Quite a bunch.

Interviewer: Did you know Lowell?

Hall: A little. *Lord Weary's Castle* was my favorite book of the time—which it still is—and I loved "Mother Marie Therese" and "Falling Asleep Over the Aeneid" from the next book. When the *Life Studies* poems started in magazines, a little later, it was totally shocking; but some were great. I can't remember how we met. He and Elizabeth Hardwick came to dinner and we went to their place. There was a bunch that met for a workshop a few times at John Holmes's house—Phil Booth and Lowell and me with Holmes. Lowell was gentle and soft-spoken—I never saw him when he was in trouble—but candid. These get-togethers were fine, but they never flew. Maybe I was too much in awe. For a while Lowell wrote me some of those postcards he was famous for. He wrote about an essay I did in which I said that every time I learned to make a new noise in poetry I found something new to say. He said he'd heard me say the same thing at a Harvard reading, and that it helped him toward *Life Studies*. A few years later, out in Ann Arbor, he came to my house and we spent an evening together drinking and reading poems out loud. He read me most of *Near the Ocean*. I was surprised by how much he wanted my approval—but of course, like anybody, he wanted *everybody's*. Then when he started doing self-imitations with the *Notebook* stuff, I was disappointed. Hell, I was furious—he let me down, as it were—and I attacked him in print. He quoted from one of my attacks in one of those little sonnets—and he rewrote my words a little, so that they sounded more pompous—but he didn't say whom he quoted. We never saw each other after that.

Interviewer: After your time at Oxford, you spent a year at Stanford studying with Yvor Winters, whose name is not generally associated with yours. What came out of that experience?

Hall: I learned more about poetry in a year, working with Winters, than I did in the rest of my education. Also, I was fond of him—we even stayed in his house during Christmas vacation while he went off to visit relatives—but one incident in the spring gave me pause. At a party at his house, he said to me, "Would you get some more ice, son?" When he called me son it was as if he breathed in my ear; I'd follow him anywhere. I thought: *It's good I'm getting out of here.*

When I went to Stanford, I had already spent years working in a conservative poetic. In those days, most of us worked in a rhymed iambic line. I did it—James Wright, Louis Simpson, Galway Kinnell, Adrienne Rich, Robert Bly, W. D. Snodgrass, W. S. Merwin. When I applied for the fellowship, my work didn't depart greatly from the structure and metrics that Winters advocated. He thought I had some technical competence, or I wouldn't have had the fellowship. The best poem I wrote at Stanford was "My Son My Executioner," which could almost have come out of the seventeenth century—the abstract diction, the way it looks reasonable treating the irrational. For that one year I became briefly more conservative than ever, and it became known that I was the poetry editor for the *Paris Review*. Some old acquaintances sent me poems, including Frank O'Hara. Frank hadn't discovered himself, quite—but he wasn't writing rhymed iambic pentameter either. I rejected his poems and wrote a supercilious note. Stupid! Not long ago I came across Frank's answer, in which he accused me of writing second-rate Yeats, which was perfectly true. The letter is snippy, funny, outraged, but *cool*.

I regret I didn't have the brains to take his poems, but I couldn't read them then. I *did* do early work by Hill, Gunn, Bly, Dickey, Wright, Rich, Merwin . . . lots of people. But, also I rejected a good poem by Allen Ginsberg, who wrote George Plimpton saying that I wouldn't recognize a poem if it buggered me in broad daylight.

Interviewer: Back to the way you write. Has it changed over the years?

Hall: When I was younger, poems arrived in a rush, maybe six or eight new things begun in two days, four days. I'd be in a crazy mood, inspired; I'd walk into furniture and not recognize my children. After the initial bursts, I would have my task set out before me—to bring out what was best, to get rid of the bad stuff, to work them over until I was pleased or satisfied. Then, for nine years or so—late thirties into forties—I was unable to write anything that was up to what I'd done earlier. I thought I'd lost it. After all, if you read biography, you know: *people lose it*. Then in the autumn of 1974 I started *Kicking the Leaves*, and most people think that's when I finally got started as a poet. I was forty-six.

With these new poems, I began to follow a different process of composition, one I've stuck with ever since. Usually now I begin with a loose association of images, a scene, and a sense that somewhere in this material is something I don't yet understand that *wants* to become a poem. I write out first drafts in prosaic language—flat, no excitement. Then very slowly, over hundreds of drafts, I begin to discover and exploit connections—between words, between images. Looking at the poem on the five-hundredth day, I will take out one word and put in another. Three days later I will discover that the new word connects with another word that joined the manuscript a year back.

Now inspiration doesn't come at once, several poems starting in a few days; it comes in the discovery of a single word after three years of work.

This process never stops. When a new book of mine arrives in the mail, I dread reading it—because I know I will find words I want to change. I revise when I read my poems out loud to an audience. I change them when they appear in magazines or anthologies. I can't keep my hand off poems. I wrote "The Man in the Dead Machine" in 1965, published it in 1966, and I read it aloud a *thousand* times. Then in April of 1984, driving to the Scranton airport after a reading, I saw how to make it better. So I did.

The kind of poem I've taken to writing is something you could call the discursive ode. I call it an ode because although it's lyrical it tries for a certain length and inclusiveness. I call it discursive because it appears to wander, to move from one particular to another by association, though if it succeeds it finds a unity. It tries to connect things difficult to connect, things that at first seem diverse; often the images make a structural glue. I suppose it's largely a romantic form but one can find classical sources for it, in the satires, maybe in some of Horace's odes, maybe even in neoclassic poems by Johnson and Pope. But it flowers in the ode, even in something as short as the "Ode to a Nightingale" or later "Among School Children."

Interviewer: You seemed, with *Kicking the Leaves*, to enter a third phase of your career. Somewhere, in an essay or interview, I believe you described the first two phases. In the first, you wrote a poetry of the top of the mind, where consciousness was very much in control. In the second phase, you reversed that, letting the unconscious mind rule, letting all sorts of unexpected and unsettling things into the poem. Now in the third phase it may be that you are combining the two.

Hall: That's a goal. Even when I was in the second phase, dredging things from the dark places, I wanted to bring them into the light. Freud said, "Where Id was, let there Ego be." I wanted to subject things—even subterranean things—to the light of consciousness. During the first phase, I had a dream of conscious control, *libido sciendi*; unconscious materials only occurred when I hid them from myself, as in "The Sleeping Giant," where I wrote an Oedipal poem without any idea of what I was doing. Today when I begin writing I'm aware: *something that I don't understand drives this engine.* Why do I pick *this* scene or image? Within the action of kicking the leaves something was weighted, freighted, heavy with feeling—and because I kept writing, kept going back to the poem, eventually the under-feeling that unified the detail came forward in the poem. The process is discovering by revision, uncovering by persistence.

Interviewer: Was your recent long poem, *The One Day*, written in this way?

Hall: This material started to arrive during my years of flailing about. It came in great volcanic eruptions of language. I couldn't drive to the supermarket without taking a note pad with me. I kept accumulating fragments without reading them or rewriting; it was as if I was finding the stone that I would eventually carve sculpture from. Then when it stopped coming, I went back and read it. It was chaotic, full of inadequate language—and it was also scary. There was spooky stuff out of childhood; there was denunciation and mockery that years later went into "Prophecy" and "Pastoral." Something let me loose into this material, something that I was scared to revisit. So I let it rest, waiting until the lava cooled down and hardened. That took years. Finally, in 1979 or 1980, I took a deep breath and began to try to make it into poetry. And I added new material; half of the poem—or more— came during the later writing. There were false starts; at one point, maybe 1982, I had a long asymmetric free verse poem in thirty or forty sections, each several pages long and with its own title. No good. Later I discovered the ten-line blocks that I could build with. I could keep them discrete or I could bridge from one to the next.

Interviewer: When you describe your process of discovery, in conversation, you seem almost to be describing the process of free association that a psychoanalyst asks for. Is this parallel valid?

Hall: It's no accident. I spent seven years in therapy, up to three times a week, with a Freudian analyst. He was an old man with a light Austrian accent and athletic eyebrows; I would explain, carefully and reasonably, why I had done something cruel or stupid; his eyebrows would do the high jump. We fell into the habit of treating poems as dreams. When you bring a dream to a therapist or analyst, he or she isn't likely to pay attention to the manifest content, but if you have a table in that dream he may ask, "What does the table look like?" The table might be the key to what the dream—or the poem—is actually about. In "The Alligator Bride" there's an Empire table. Freudian analysis is a word cure, and it resembles the way we read or write poems. Poems that I wrote in my frenzy were *like* dreams, because they allowed something unconscious to loosen forth. Those years allowed me to overcome fears of hidden things and let them out. Coming into my doctor's office, I learned how to tap instantly into the on-flowing current inside my head. That essential step took me about a year, but once you learn it you don't lose it. I learned to listen for the vatic voice, to watch images running over the mind-screen, to give a telegraphic account of what I heard and saw. It was good for me as a creature and good for me as a poet. Even now I talk with my doctor every day of my life and he explains the sources of feeling—although he's dead. Eventually it was psychotherapy that allowed me to recover my life. And to write *The One Day*.

Interviewer: So there is a sense in which you are touching a deeper Donald Hall in this material.

Hall: I hope so, yes. Not in any boring autobiographical way. In *The Happy Man* I have a poem in which somebody talks about his time in the detox center. A friend asked me what I was in detox for. Well, I never was. For the poem I made up a character; I talked through a mask I invented, which I do all the time. I love to fool people, even with fake epigraphs—but also I wish they weren't fooled. Of course my poems use things that have happened to me—but they go beyond the facts. Even when I write about my grandfather, I lie. I don't believe poets when they say "I," and I wish people wouldn't believe me. Poetic material starts by being personal but the deeper we go inside the more we become everybody.

Interviewer: Has the passage of time, the coming of age if you will, caused any other changes in your notions about your poetry, your career as a poet?

Hall: I'm more patient now. When I was in my twenties, I wanted to write many poems. I had goals; when I reached them, they turned out to be not worth reaching. When you begin, you think that if you could just publish a few poems, you'd reach your desire; then if you could publish in a good magazine; then if you could publish a book; then . . . When you've done these things you haven't done anything. The desire must be, not to write another dozen poems, but to write something as good as the poems that originally brought you to love the art. It's the only sensible reason for writing poems. You've got to keep your eye on what you care about: to write a poem that stands up with Walt Whitman or Andrew Marvell.

Another thing that's changed is my sense of daily time. I spent years of my life daydreaming about a future, I suppose in order to avoid a present that was painful. Teaching in Ann Arbor I daydreamed about a year in England. Mentally I lived always a step ahead of myself, so that the day I lived in was something to get through, on the way to something else. Pitiful! After I left teaching, when Jane and I had lived at Eagle Pond for a year, I realized: I'm aware of the hour I live in; I'm not daydreaming ahead to a future time; I know which direction the wind blows from, and where the sun is; I'm alive in the present moment, in what I do *now*, and in where I'm doing it. This present includes layers of the past—there's so much past here at Eagle Pond—but it doesn't depend on a daydream future which may never arrive.

Interviewer: You've always written a lot about Eagle Pond, things like how your grandmother used to stand at the kitchen window in the morning and check the mountain. Well, it's the same window today and the same mountain. The profound presence of the past in a place like this, even the felt presence of those who have lived here but are now dead, the cows and other animals in your poems—does all this have anything to do with the general elegiac cast to your poetry?

Hall: My grandmother's father, who was born in 1826 and who died fifteen years before I was born, looked out that same window to check the same mountain. I stand in the footprints of people long gone—which I find an inspiriting connection; it belittles the notion of one's own death; it says: "That's all right. Everybody who has looked at this mountain has died or will die. *Then others will look at it.*" A sense of continuity makes for an elegiac poetry. One of my first published poems, when I was sixteen, was about a New Hampshire graveyard. When we were at Harvard, Robert Bly used to call me the cellar-hole poet—like a graveyard poet in the eighteenth century. When I spent my childhood summers here, among the old people, *absence* was everywhere. Walking in the woods I found cellar holes, old wells, old walls. Even now you can sometimes feel under your feet, in dense woods, the ruts that plows made long ago.

Interviewer: As you talk about his, I hear almost a sacred sense of place. You have written about attending church here as primarily a social experience—but you are also a deacon, and I am wondering about the more serious implications of this activity.

Hall: It began from a social feeling, but moved on—from community to communion. When I was a child I went to church every Sunday simply because that was what we did. Uncle Luther, my grandmother's older brother, who grew up in this house, was our preacher. He'd retired from a Connecticut parish and at eighty delivered lucid fifteen-minute sermons without a note in front of him. He was born in 1856 and could remember the Civil War. I used to sit on the porch and get him to tell me stories about the Civil War.

I enjoyed church as a child—sitting beside my grandfather, all dressed up, who fed me Canada mints. But I can't say that I was taken with Christian thought or theology. When I was about twelve I had the atheist experience. I suddenly realized, with absolute clarity, that there was no God. With this knowledge, I felt superior to other people. Twenty years later, when I was living in an English village called Thaxted, I fell into the habit of attending church every Sunday. I *thought* without religious feeling; I loved the ceremony, and the wonderful old communist vicar, Jack Putterill. His church used a pre-prayer book service that was so high only dogs could hear it, and his sermon, after incense and holy water, was a fifteen-minute communist homily. I thought I attended these services out of aesthetic and social motives; now I suspect that I harbored religious feelings I feared to acknowledge.

In Ann Arbor I never went to church. When Jane and I moved back here, I must have been ready. On that first Sunday, I thought, "They will expect us to go to church." We decided to go just that once. In the middle of his ser- mon, our minister quoted Rilke. I'd never heard Rilke quoted in the South Danbury Church! We were already fond of the people—mostly cousins— and we went back next Sunday, and the next. Slowly, we started reading the Gospels, and some Christian thought—like "The Cloud of Unknowing," Meister Eckhart, Julian of Norwich. At one point that winter Jane was sick and couldn't go. I said, "I'll stay home with you." Five minutes before church, I said, "I can't stand it," and off I went. These feelings amazed me . . . and they were accompanied by thoughts: our minister ranged all over the place in his sermons. He loved Dietrich Bonhoffer, the German Protestant theo- logian who plotted against Hitler and was executed, a modern saint and martyr.

By this time, I would like to call myself a Christian, though I feel shy about it. We have many visitors whom Christianity makes nervous; they seem *embarrassed* for us. So many people expend their spirituality piece- meal on old superstitions like astrology that they entertain but don't believe in—like the imperial Romans and their gods. I dislike contemporary poly- theism, that nervous searching which provides itself with so many alterna- tives that it doesn't stick itself with belief: the God-of-the-Month-Club.

The minister who loved Bonhoffer and mentioned Rilke was Jack Jensen, who died of cancer in 1990. We feel terrible grief over him. He taught at Colby-Sawyer College, nearby, and had a divinity degree from Yale as well as a PhD in philosophy from Boston University, a man of spirit and brains to- gether. Watching him, listening to him, I became aware that it was possible to be a Christian although subject to skepticism and spiritual dryness. I use to think that Christians believed *everything*, and *all the time*, which is non- sense. If you have no dry spells, I doubt your spirit. We watched Jack live through the deserts, when he would give sermons that were historical or philosophical. After a while he would liven up, go spiritually green again. He was a great one for Advent, the annual birth or rebirth of everything pos- sible. Although the history of the church is often horrible—I always think of Servetus, the Spanish humanist condemned to the stake by the Italian in- quisition, who escaped to Zurich, where Calvin's people burned him—still, there's power in two thousand years of worship and ritual coded into our Sundays. In China we went to an Easter service and heard the choir belt out "Up from the Grave He Arose" in Chinese. So much culture and geography collapses into the figure of Christ. That's what remains, after all, at the bottom of the two thousand years—this extraordinary figure in Palestine, the figure of Christ.

Interviewer: I haven't asked you about Jane Kenyon. There are after all two poets of Eagle Pond Farm.

Hall: I know. Everything that my life has come to—coming here, the church, my poems of the last fifteen years—derives from my marriage to Jane in 1972. And I've watched her grow into a *poet.* Amazing. Of course we work together, show each other what we're doing, occasionally getting a little huffy with each other but helping each other all the same. But it's living with her that's made all the difference for me. We have the church together as well as the poetry and baseball. But I don't want to go on about it. I don't want to sound like someone making an acknowledgment in a book. Some day she'll do her own *Paris Review* interview.

Interviewer: Let's end with one more historical question. Since we are talking just now on the stage at the Y in New York City, I wonder if you would tell me the story of the first reading you gave here.

Hall: I think it was in 1956, thirty-four years ago, that I read here for the first time. I was on a program with May Swenson and Alastair Reid, and I read third. In those days, instead of all three of us sitting out here and listening to each other we waited in the green room until it was our turn. I was nervous. This reading might have been my second or third ever, certainly my first in New York City—and this was the Y. I nipped at the Scotch that Betty Kray provided in the green room. Then I thought about where I was and I nipped some more. When I came out here to read, I was still able to see the pages of my book, and I didn't fall down, but I was horrible. I was at a stage of drunkenness that allowed me to think that I was George Sanders. I felt wonderful sophistication and coolness, sure that everything I said was utterly witty and wonderful. I was a horse's ass.

"Ox Cart Man"

Jay Woodruff / 1992

Conducted by mail during February–June 1992. From Jay Woodruff, ed., *A Piece of Work: Five Writers Discuss Their Revisions* (University of Iowa Press, 1993). Interview reprinted by permission of the University of Iowa Press; text of "Ox Cart Man," from *Kicking the Leaves* (1978), reprinted with permission of the estate of Donald Hall. *A Piece of Work* originally printed facsimiles of many of Donald Hall's drafts of the poem as well letters from the *New Yorker* about the poem. The drafts and letters are omitted here; but color facsimiles of the drafts may be viewed at https://www.library.unh.edu/exhibits/eagle-pond/drafts-donald -halls-ox-cart. The interview is included in its entirety.

Ox Cart Man

In October of the year,
he counts potatoes dug from the brown field,
counting the seed, counting
the cellar's portion out,
and bags the rest on the cart's floor.

He packs wool sheared in April, honey
in combs, linen, leather
tanned from deerhide,
and vinegar in a barrel
hooped by hand at the forge's fire.

He walks by his ox's head, ten days
to Portsmouth Market, and sells potatoes,
and the bag that carried potatoes,
flaxseed, birch brooms, maple sugar, goose
feathers, yarn.

When the cart is empty he sells the cart.
When the cart is sold he sells the ox,
harness and yoke, and walks
home, his pockets heavy
with the year's coin for salt and taxes,

and at home by fire's light in November cold
stitches new harness
for next year's ox in the barn,
and carves the yoke, and saws planks
building the cart again.

Donald Hall's first book of poetry, *Exiles and Marriages* (New York: Viking, 1955), earned him the Edna St. Vincent Millay Award of the Poetry Society of America. Since then, he has written or edited dozens of other books, including a biography of the sculptor Henry Moore, a collection of short stories, two plays, and numerous anthologies. His poetry and prose appear frequently in the *New Yorker*, the *Atlantic, Esquire, American Scholar, Yankee*, and many other periodicals. One of the founding editors of the *Paris Review*, Hall served as poetry editor during the early years of that quarterly, conducting some of the early *Paris Review* interviews with such notable poets as T. S. Eliot, Marianne Moore, and Ezra Pound. His many awards include a Lamont poetry prize and a Guggenheim fellowship.

Educated at Harvard, Oxford, and Stanford, Hall became professor of English at the University of Michigan. In 1975, he moved with his wife, the poet Jane Kenyon, to his old family farm in rural New Hampshire, where the couple has remained ever since.

We conducted this interview through the mail between February and June of 1992. Hall began "Ox Cart Man" in the fall of 1975, producing nearly twenty drafts before submitting the poem to the *New Yorker* in May 1976. "Ox Cart Man" appeared in the October 3, 1977, issue of that magazine; then again, slightly revised, in Hall's volume *Kicking the Leaves* (New York: Harper and Row, 1978) and again later in Hall's tenth volume of poetry, *Old and New Poems* (New York: Ticknor and Fields, 1990). The poem was also expanded to provide the text for the children's book *Ox-Cart Man* (New York: Viking, 1979), which received the American Library Association's Caldecott Medal in 1980.

Jay Woodruff: In your interview with the *Paris Review*, you describe hearing the story of the ox-cart man from your cousin Paul Fenton. Were you attracted immediately to this as a subject for a poem?

Donald Hall: When my cousin Paul Fenton told the ox-cart man's story, it thrilled me—I felt an electric tingle along my spine—and I did not know why. I did not immediately know that I would write out of it, but maybe the next morning I began to draft the poem. The turn in the story is the selling of the ox, which emphasizes Total Dispersal—a phrase I found later at the auction of Paul's son Dennis's cattle farm: the thrilling notion of emptying out, getting rid of absolutely everything. It is thrilling because: *Only if you empty the well will the water return to the well.*

JW: What else about this story appealed to you?

DH: Surely the subject appealed to me also because I love work and ideas of work. Also there was something immortal about the story—as if a person could come back again and again, having died, like a perennial plant. Perennial, not immortal.

JW: Also in the *PR* interview, you say that "sense of continuity makes for an elegiac poetry." You also once asked Ezra Pound if the artist needs to keep moving. Your life has taken you from Connecticut and New Hampshire to Boston, Europe, the Midwest, and finally back to New Hampshire. I wondered if this return home made you especially receptive to the pattern of the ox-cart man's life; whether your having returned to your family's farm in New Hampshire somehow provided a sense of connection with this story.

DH: Oh I have wandered, like many people. I heard this story from Paul shortly after returning to New Hampshire, knowing for the first time that I had come someplace to stay. Perhaps, yes, it struck me so much because of the notion of return.

JW: You've described what has become your usual process of composing a poem—beginning with a flat, prosaic language to search, over the course of many drafts, for discoveries and connections to exploit. With "Ox Cart Man," you began already knowing the story the poem was to tell. How did this influence your approach to the poem and its development?

DH: Many poems begin for me without any sense of where they will go; then the voyage of revision is pure discovery. But, even when you know where you are going to go, there are things to discover along the way. There are the matters of cadence, and coherence. With this poem, I had a narrative, an external coherence, but I had no idea how I would get to the end of the travel. As you see in the draft, originally I tried a grander or more general conclusion—rather than allowing it to remain implicit. Eventually it became implicit—and then *more* implicit. But all along, maybe the ox-cart's story was connected with my own work as a poet—Total Dispersal, so that the well can fill again. If so, I never knew it as I was writing. This kind of discovery—when you find out years later something about a poem, the fuel that may have fired the poem's engine all along, without your knowledge— it's an excitement.

With this poem I had a lot handed to me. Old stories are wonderful: You gather them from the air. With this poem, I had nothing to invent but strategy and language.

JW: And you didn't feel constrained by what you already knew?

DH: I would have felt free to alter the story if I had wanted to. The received plot was not a constraint.

JW: Do you generally prefer to know less than you did in this case about a poem you're beginning?

DH: I cannot say. I wish more people told me such stories! So I guess I wouldn't prefer to know less. Often I've felt great excitement in starting something because I knew nothing—except a phrase, a cadence, and the desire to explore. But even when you know a lot you don't know everything; if you knew *everything* ahead of time you would not write the poem. If we sense, sometimes, that an author knew the poem before the poem began, this sense may define or describe a failed poem.

JW: You've discussed and written about your interest in Henry Moore, and quoted Moore as saying, "Never think of a surface except as the extension of a volume." The great number of drafts you do sort of resembles a sculptor chipping away to discover the form that exists within the material. In the case of this poem, I wondered whether knowing the story made you even more aware from the beginning of that form within.

DH: Ever since I heard Henry Moore making that sentence, I have looked at words for the pressure at their surface. If the ox-cart man's Total Dispersal, in order to fill up again—his dying into the ground in order to rise up again in the spring—relates to poetry, the relation happens underneath the surface of the words, a volume pressing up from underneath.

The story is the surface. Against this surface a volume extends its pressure, my own psyche forcing itself up to the surface or through it—and into the story, by the language I use and the cadences.

JW: You once asked T. S. Eliot, "Would you have chosen the form before you knew quite what you were going to write in it?" How did knowing this story influence your thinking at the very beginning about the prospective poem's form?

DH: Form is meaning. When you decide on a form before you know what the poem is about, it's no problem. What a poem's *about* is the least of the matter. With this poem, I have no recollection of thinking ahead of time about its form—length of line, composition into stanzas, length of stanza. I suppose I improvised. In this case my improvisations reached fairly early something like the final look of the poem.

JW: Moving now to the actual drafts, I see that the first draft's initial words come quite close to those of the final version. Did you sense initially that these first *two* lines of the early drafts were closer than others to what you were after? How important is it to you to get those first words nearly right before you can go on?

DH: When I answer your questions about composition, you will understand that I am guessing. I cannot really remember what was exactly on my mind, sixteen years ago. I look at a draft and guess—and sometimes it almost seems as if I remember.

Surely my notions governing language (and in one matter the form—the narrowness of it, the relative paucity of detail) came from the impress of laconic New England speech.

The first two lines of the second draft at any rate come close to what I eventually arrived at. I was lucky. Sometimes I fumble for a long time before I find the beginning. The beginning of a poem is of the utmost importance, the *real* beginning—though it may happen halfway through the drafts of a poem. By the real beginning I mean the moment at which you catch the tone; tone proscribes the limits of the vocabulary, the possibilities of diction; in the real beginning, you catch the cadence you are stuck with—length or variety of line, general degree of line break, not to mention degrees of attention to consonance and assonance. At first these limits are not conscious, but they exist in practice; revision makes them conscious. Once you set these limits in your mind, it is like knowing the story ahead of time. You have the guidance of chosen limitations. Of course these choices limit your opportunities; but these choices give you a path to follow.

JW: The initial two drafts also seem to reveal that you're not terribly concerned at that point with stanzas or lining strategies. What occupies your attention most at this stage?

DH: At the beginning I search for characteristic diction and characteristic cadence, for the defining words and tone. I *listen* for it. When I get something like it, I refine it, and during the rest of the drafts I keep on refining it. My first drafts show me fumbling toward it.

JW: The title of these first two drafts is also "*The* Ox Cart Man." Why did you decide to eliminate the article?

DH: I don't know. I eliminate articles when I can—maybe sometimes when I can't? I want to get rid of all the little words, and "load every rift with ore."

JW: You also seem at times to write on legal-size paper, at other times on regular-size.

DH: The size of the page has no significance. I was writing then on yellow legal pads—I still do, from time to time. I used ordinary typing paper when I typed it up.

JW: The third draft includes the final title and also shows you've nailed down the first line. Except for the use of the first person, the second line is also in its final form here. In fact, except for alterations in lining, the first stanza is basically complete. What about this early idea you're pursuing here in the final stanza—the idea of the vessel?

DH: By the third version I had the cadence. Note that I cut out an article at the beginning of the second line, reaching for that percussive rhythm that characterizes the poem—a rhythm emphasized by noisy consonants—c, p, d, g, c, c.

So: "cellar" is more particular and local and intimate than "winter." I've always had trouble *saying* "cellar" out loud; listeners may hear "seller." I decided to let the printed version assert itself, even though the spoken version might contain an ambiguity. In some poems, when the spoken version is ambiguous because of a homonym, I print it one way and say it another; here I could say "rootcellar" and print "cellar"—but "rootcellar" on the page would make the line too long.

The vessel. I always tend to think of this poem in terms of liquids. "Only if you empty the well will the water return to the well." But why a liquid? I don't know. I like the image—the analogy works—but in this poem I let the story tell itself rather than explaining it in an analogy—or writing an editorial about it.

JW: The next draft, number four, shows the five-line stanzas. How did you decide on this form?

DH: The form is improvised. Say, I found myself making a first stanza that did its job in five lines, with cadence and length of utterance that pleased me—and so I set out to follow the template that I arrived at. Sometimes it won't work—and I must go back and change the template.

JW: You seem in this draft also to be searching for the right details, the objects he loads into his cart and carries to market. What was your primary concern at this stage?

DH: I wanted details, the right details. I read about "birch brooms" in a book about colonial times. Some things I knew already. Then I must set the objects in the right order. Heaven knows the sounds of the words—sometimes their percussiveness, as with "flaxseed"—determine them *together* with their accuracy. I could have found seventy-five other things for him to put in the cart.

JW: What guided you as you searched for the right details, the right objects for him to carry?

DH: Probability and the sound of the word.

JW: In the fifth draft, the second stanza seems to begin to take shape, though in the third stanza you've eliminated something you'd later include again: "and the bag that carried potatoes." The fourth stanza is close to the final version. This draft seems to include an interesting shift in your thinking, a movement away from the vessel idea toward something to suggest continuity and repetition. Was this a breakthrough?

DH: I think that "continuity and repetition" was always there. They were the shape and attraction of the story to begin with, but the cutting away of other things—like the metaphor of a vessel—allowed this shape to show more clearly. Remove the feathers and you see the bird's shape.

I suppose I eliminated "the bag that carried potatoes" to keep to my stanza-shape. You will see what I eliminated, in the next draft, in order to bring the bag of potatoes *back*. When he sells not only the thing contained but also the container, I foreshadow the sale of the ox-cart after he emptied it.

JW: The next draft is the first typewritten one. Does this signal that you've taken a poem to a certain stage of its development?

DH: Yes, a typewritten draft. At this time in the history of my writing habits, when I arrived at a stage where the poem stopped moving around on me, I typed a draft. I never liked to type, and held off typing as long as I could, but then I needed to type it up in order to see it. (My handwriting never showed me the poem, as the poem came to finish itself.) The typed draft showed me the visual shape of the poem.

JW: Here again, you've eliminated the final stanza about the vessel, and in fact this draft ends where the final version would, although here the comma (as well as the partial typed stanza at the bottom of the page) indicates you're still searching for something more. At this point *were* you beginning to sense that you might combine the second and third stanzas?

DH: I had been cutting down the final editorial comment even in the draft before this one. Here, I almost get the notion of ending it, as I finally did, with building the cart again . . . but not quite. I reckon I wanted at this time to end with something obviously—too obviously—beautiful.

I don't remember whether at this point I was thinking about combining the second and third stanzas.

JW: In the seventh draft, you've put an *X* through stanzas two to four, even though your revisions within those stanzas seem to be moving rapidly toward the poem's final version. What did that *X* signify?

DH: In the seventh draft, where I make the big X, I wrote a note to myself on the right-hand side of the page, virtually illegible: "Cut to two?" I think I had the notion that my listing was simply too heavy, too many objects, went on too long. . . . I wanted to cut down the numbers of things and let the story tell itself more quickly.

Note also that I cut out "my" four times and substituted the definite article—which I think springs the tone loose, maybe from the particular toward the general, or from the self-regarding toward the fabulous.

JW: You've also included a new final stanza.

DH: The last stanza of this seventh draft is the one hinted at in the typing at the bottom of the sixth draft. I suspect that we miss some scratch sheets of handwritten revision here.

JW: In the eighth draft, you seem concerned mostly with the second and third stanzas. Each draft, in fact, seems to reveal that you focus on discrete challenges in a poem. Is this your usual way of working?

DH: In the eighth draft I cut the second draft down in order to make the stanzas more *integral*, finishing cider in the second stanza. This cut allowed me to return "the bag that carried potatoes" to the third stanza.

I don't believe I *chose* to work on one part of the poem at a time. I saw problems and possible solutions in a localized way, first here and then there.

JW: The next draft seems to represent a significant leap forward: the note indicating your decision to use the third person, present tense. What made you decide to switch to the third person?

DH: Sometimes I will look at the poem not during my work hours but later in the day. I don't want to work on it then, so I make notes for future work—thus the "he" and "but present tense" notes toward the top of the ninth draft. Later—probably the next morning after making the note at night—I followed my own suggestions.

Some of the details like "linen" had been there earlier in earlier drafts. Typical: to put words in and take them out and put them back again—as with the potato bag.

The switch to the third person resembled the switch from "my" to "the." Sometimes the proper tone for a poem *steps back*, making the subject something seen from a distance, as through the wrong end of a telescope. Local particulars diminish; general features become clear.

JW: After experimenting in one draft [draft 9] with the past tense, you appear to have decided against it right away. Is this because the past tense undermines the perennial aspect of the narrative—that sense of repetition and continuity?

DH: Exactly. The present tense should be luminous here, or even fabulous.

JW: The next version shows continued work on the second and third stanzas. What was the hardest part about getting them right?

DH: My problem in the order of details had nothing to do with meaning, nothing semantic in the sequence, but with the cadence and the voice of detail.

JW: Apart from the slight revision, changing "scent" to "cry," you seem to have continued to leave the final stanza untouched. Did this represent an ambivalence about the ending?

DH: It's interesting that later Howard Moss wanted me to turn "cry" back into "scent." By the time I was arguing with him, I didn't remember that I had ever thought of "scent." (I scorned his suggestion!) I wrote "cry" not only for noisy synaesthesia but for assonance with the first syllable of the last word.

I didn't feel ambivalent about that ending—later rejected. At the time, I thought it was the best thing in the poem! Watch out for what you think is best.

JW: In the thirteenth draft, you exchange "linen" and "yarn," and except for the inclusion of the final stanza, the poem is virtually complete. Does your signature at the bottom of the poem indicate that you sensed the poem was nearly complete at this point?

DH: In the thirteenth draft, I changed the positions of "linen" and "yarn" because—saying the poem aloud—I could *hold* the last three letters of "yarn," almost singing it.

The signature at the bottom means I was showing it to someone, or even thinking of sending it to a magazine.

JW: The next draft is another clean draft—another break from the poem? If so, how long will you generally let a poem "cure" before returning to it? Or, more to the point, how long did this sit before you went back to it again?

DH: It's a clean draft because I wanted to see it as finished. Every draft is a final draft, after a while. But I know from experience that I will probably keep on tinkering.

I first show my poems to my wife, Jane Kenyon. Then I mail them to friends. At some point—usually after my friends have given me verdicts—I type it up clean again and send it out to a magazine.

I don't know how long I waited on this—or if I waited very long at all. It interests and amuses me to realize that I have been lying about this poem for years. (When I talk about process, I always emphasize how long it takes me, how arduous the process is, and how much I love it—but often I admit that all poets lie about their processes, and add that therefore I must be lying too.) I've said for years that it took me two years to write this poem, and at least fifty or sixty drafts. Well, we have found something like nineteen drafts, and if anything is missing it's not *much*. I began writing the poem no earlier than September of 1975, my first year back in New Hampshire. Paul Fenton told me the story in the autumn, I'm certain, and apparently I mailed the poem to the *New Yorker* the next spring, May of 1976. So it took me eight months at the longest. Well, I did fiddle with it afterwards, partly at the *New Yorker*'s suggestion.

JW: In the fifteenth draft, you decide to omit the final stanza, and you include some notes to yourself about the poem. "I'm pretty sure about omitting the last stanza—it's fidgety. And redundant." How hard was it to reach the point where you could let go of the idea of going beyond the previous stanza?

DH: These are not my comments on the poem. These are Louis Simpson's, and as you can see he helped me a lot. Louis was right about the unnaturalness of "by ox head," and I should have made it "the ox's head" as he suggests, or (as I have it now) "his ox's head." Louis's comments were probably in the summer or early autumn of 1976—because I think he suggested omitting the last stanza *after* Howard Moss told me that there was something wrong with it. I mentioned Louis's suggestion to Moss in our correspondence.

JW: The next [sixteenth] draft shows you trying to find the right rhythm for the last line. What guided you here?

DH: Having decided to eliminate the final stanza, I didn't admire the concluding cadence of "to build the cart again," maybe because it's too solidly iambic trimeter. I needed something to provide a finality. The simple change of an infinitive into a participle seemed to do the trick.

JW: At this point, when the poem was virtually complete, would you have set it aside for a while or sent it to the *New Yorker*? Or do you send things through an agent?

DH: I send my poems out myself. My agent would do it for me, but I know the market better than he does, and I enjoy handling things myself. Frequently

I send poems to the *New Yorker* before I send them elsewhere. Lots of people read a poem there; and they pay a bit more than other people do.

This may have been the draft that I sent the *New Yorker* when I made the final revision after they had bought the poem. As you can see from Howard Moss's letters to me, I sent him a draft of the poem in May of 1976. He was about to go on vacation and asked me to send the poem back again in September.

Which I did, for you see his letter of October 21. I must have asked him in my letter whether I should say "ox head" or "the ox's head." How did I ever lose the article, for *Kicking the Leaves*? I went through an article-destroying phase during the latter portions of work on that book. There are a lot of telegraphic phrases in there. Both Jane Kenyon and Galway Kinnell, I remember distinctly, warned me that I was sounding too damned much like Samuel F. B. Morse.

You will note Howard's "grave doubts" about the last line. Naturally enough he objected to the phrase I liked best in the poem—"cry of lilac." (Incidentally, I have found a place in another poem to say that "bees wake, roused by the cry of lilac." It's in "Daylilies on the Hill," which I've published in a magazine but not yet in a book.) Note how Howard, having taken the poem, now tries yelling and screaming to get me to change this last line.

Maybe it was about now that I received the note from Louis Simpson which we spoke about earlier. When I first read Louis's suggestion about omitting the last stanza, I thought it was ridiculous: "It's the best part, etc., etc." But Louis is a genius about narrative. He was absolutely right. When, in the original final stanza, I completed the circle, I insulted the reader; writing a circle-poem for grown-ups, you do not make the circle complete; you do something like the capital C and you leave it to the reader to make the circle whole by turning a C into an O. People don't literally feel insulted but bored: "I knew this was coming." However, when you write for five-year-olds you are allowed to complete the circle. In the children's book about the ox-cart man, a child can turn from the last page back to the first page and start it all over again.

As you can see, I argued fiercely with Howard about "cry" versus "scent." It seems fairly typical of the *New Yorker* that it would avoid the loud obviousness of synaesthesia and assonance in favor of something more tame and/or tepid like "scent." Of course I had originally written "scent" myself.

In his letter to me dated the tenth of November, taking the new solution, Howard actually goes into literary criticism in his first paragraph. Editors rarely do that.

JW: The final *New Yorker* proof shows that you've decided to change "ox head" to "ox's head." Do the other marks on this version reflect conversations with editors? Someone appears to have been concerned as to whether "deer-hide" is a word—"(not in Web)." Also the question of whether to hyphenate "Ox Cart" in the title, and whether to include a comma after "harness."

DH: The *New Yorker* is writer-friendly. They make suggestions; they even implore you on bended knee to make changes—but finally they will let you do what you want to do.

I have found editorial suggestions useful from time to time over the years: Howard Moss, Alice Quinn, M. L. Rosenthal, Robert Pinsky, Mary Jo Salter.

JW: The only other revision to this poem I'm aware of is the small one that occurred between the time the poem was collected in *Kicking the Leaves* and the time it was included in *Old and New Poems*: you revise "ox's head" to "his ox's head." Is it difficult, if not impossible, for you to reread any of your poems, years after they've been published, without wanting to make changes?

DH: Yes, I keep wanting to tinker. In the margins of the book that I read from, when I do my poetry readings, I write continual small changes. Not long after *Kicking the Leaves* came out, I added "his" to my line about the ox's head. When I did *Old and New Poems* I was able to put this change into print.

JW: The writing of this poem seems to recapitulate the challenge facing the ox-cart man: like his cart, the poem can only hold so much, and only what's absolutely essential. When you first heard the story of the ox-cart man, did it strike you immediately as, among other things, an analogy to writing poems, or was this a sense that developed as the poem did?

DH: No, when I first heard the story it did not strike me as an analogy to writing poetry. Now I believe that it is—and maybe something inside me always knew. For years and years, I have told everybody—including myself— that when you write a poem you should bring everything to it that you know. I've quoted Galway Kinnell, who told me decades ago that he only respected poems to which the poet brought everything that had ever happened. You should never hold anything back. You should let everything go, and put everything that you know into the writing of every single poem. "Only if you empty the well will the water return to the well." I never thought of this analogy until after the poem was finished—and someone else suggested it.

JW: I'm interested in how this idea of emptying the well relates to something you've addressed in your essay on two of your early teachers,

Archibald MacLeish and Yvor Winters. In "Rocks and Whirlpools," you describe the condition of "busy laziness" that sometimes afflicts those who "put in their hours and with[hold] their spirits." How does the young writer who is concerned with craft and form, as well as with what Faulkner called "the eternal verities of the heart," distinguish between effective well-emptying and mere compulsiveness? This seems to me to be one of the hardest things to learn—how to get beyond just scratching at the surface, how to learn to make your revisions dig deeper.

DH: Henry Moore quoted Rodin, advice an old craftsman gave him when Rodin was young; it was, more or less, "When something's not going right, don't keep making little changes in your model; drop it on the floor and see what it looks like then."

Well, in this one I could just keep picking at it. With other poems, I have often dropped them on the floor. Sometimes I begin over again with a new form of line or of stanza; sometimes I change narrative strategy, or point of view, or person, or the sex of the protagonist. Often I switch from history to fiction; or telling a lie sometimes liberates language and imagination.

JW: You said in the *PR* interview that while the poem took you two years to write, the text for the children's book *Ox-Cart Man* took only a couple of hours. Did you see the children's book as an opportunity (finally, after the rigorous process of paring down for the poem) to pursue the impulse you felt to go beyond the rebuilding of the cart?

DH: In that interview I exaggerated; or maybe I *lied* . . . a little. Certainly the children's book was relatively easy—sometimes they take endless drafts—maybe because I had thought so much about the story.

I remember the occasion. My daughter was visiting—not a child, nineteen or twenty years old—but maybe her presence allowed me to think of the story as something for children. I had the sudden notion that if I took Paul's story and treated it differently (adding a whole family, which was there in Paul's version, and completing the circle), it might make a picture book. The solid shape of the circle was good for a kid's book, and for the mythic or archetypal nature of the story.

JW: You once asked Ezra Pound whether he believed a poet's greatest quality was formal or a quality of thinking? Observing how you work, I wonder whether, at this point in your writing life, you see these qualities as distinct.

DH: You're right. It is a *quality* of thinking—to think in formal terms, about wholeness of shape, about resolution, about marching to a particular tune. The tune is the thinker.

JW: You've written about and discussed a number of older poets you had the opportunity to meet and get to know—Pound and Eliot, Dylan Thomas, Marianne Moore, Robert Frost. Am I wrong in thinking that this is a poem that perhaps Frost might have particularly admired?

DH: I can't say that Frost would have liked it. After all, it's written in free verse, like playing tennis without a net.

JW: In your *PR* interview with T. S. Eliot, you and he discussed the importance of common speech in poetry, and how common speech was being influenced by television. How do you think common speech has changed in the years since you spoke with Eliot, and what significance does that hold for poets?

DH: Common speech changes. I have hope now that pockets of locality may resist the onslaught of the airwaves, and maybe ethnic enclaves, maybe the vitality of immigrant speech. Common speech will need to absorb Cambodian habits of thought, Russian, Haitian.

JW: One of the most remarkable things about "Ox Cart Man," I think, is that it somehow manages to suggest a kind of traditional, old-fashioned, Yankee laconism using a language and syntax that seems to consist largely of contemporary common speech. "November cold" seems to me to be the only phrase that even remotely suggests an anachronistic syntax. Was this hard to pull off?

DH: I suppose that "November cold" is a bit poetical. Maybe "November's cold" would improve it. Maybe I should make another note in the margin of my book.

A Conversation with Donald Hall and Jane Kenyon

Marian Blue / 1993

Conducted in April 1993; Wayne Ude contributed one question. The interview originally appeared in *AWP Chronicle*, vol. 27, no. 6, May/Summer 1995, pp. 1-8. The lightly revised version reprinted here appeared in Jane Kenyon's posthumous collection *A Hundred White Daffodils* (Graywolf Press, 1999). Reprinted by permission of Marian Blue.

Marian Blue: The theory of artistic temperament negates the concept of two artists living harmoniously together; yet you two have worked and lived together for twenty-one years. Do either of you perceive in the other, or yourself, an artistic temperament which has required adjustments or pampering?

Jane Kenyon: Whatever an artistic temperament might be.

Blue: Yes. Is there such a thing on a day-to-day basis? Do you have warning signs you watch for in each other?

Kenyon: I think we're well aware of what is happening to each other in terms of whether the work is going well and whether the results are very exciting. We're aware of each other's rhythms. I think Don understands me when work is very absorbing and I just want to be absentminded and not very present.

Donald Hall: We take care not to intrude, as well. It's important to keep a separateness, a privacy, bounds. If Jane is away and I have to go into her study for some reason, I would never read a manuscript on her desk.

Kenyon: No, he wouldn't; and I wouldn't either.

Hall: When one of us is in a dry period or depressed about the work, we may discuss it casually. We don't probe; the worst thing in the world would be for me to say, or for Jane to say, "What are you working on?" or "What's it about?" Our privacy is important and we respect each other's.

Also, I hold back from presenting my work, which is another kind of privacy. I work on a poem for a long, long time without showing it to Jane. I may be desperate to show it to her, desperate for that praise, but I know that once I show it to her, it is no longer something that is absolutely private to me. When a poem, any work, is private to me, its spirit and possibilities are limitless. Once I show it to anyone—Jane is always number one—somebody else's spirit, psyche, tone of voice, has entered that poem. There is something mysterious in the way in which I know when it is all right for another mind to come into this poem. This holding back is essential to me, perhaps more for me than others, but too many people rush to show work to their best friends or spouses.

Kenyon: It works that way for me, as well.

Hall: It varies with the poem. A week or two ago I showed you three poems which I had been working on for a long time. That was a case where I had been saying to myself, for maybe five weeks, "Well, maybe tomorrow."

Kenyon: I have a little bunch in my desk that I've been meaning to show you—

Hall: And at some point, you'll take a deep breath and say, "What the hell, here—"

Kenyon: That's it.

Hall: Normally we'll each save up two or three new poems. When I have a bunch, I think, "Maybe I'll show them to Jane tomorrow," and then I see a word I want to change and think, "Well, maybe one more day." Finally I show them to her and she says, "Perkins . . . ," and she tells me something. She never praises them enough, I can say for sure.

Kenyon: I will have saved up work, too, then Don says, "This is going to be good."

Hall: Then she says, "Going to be?" There have been times, though not lately, when we get a little testy. We don't fight, but we get very polite. "Well, thank you very much," or "Oh, really? Isn't that funny; I thought that was the best part," or "Yes, thank you, I'll think about that." Each of us will say, "I'll think about this"; then we go off and do exactly what the other has suggested.

Kenyon: That is the funny part. Everything in me resists what Don is saying at the moment he's saying it and when I climb the stairs I'm saying, "He's dead wrong, he just doesn't get this." The next day I sit down, look at his suggestions, and think, "Why don't I just type it up that way to see what it looks like?" Sure enough, he's found something.

Blue: So you both are most comfortable commenting orally rather than through written notes?

Kenyon: Yes. We generally sit together with the manuscript and we talk it over—

Hall: "Get a metaphor!"

Kenyon: —then we both start throwing out possible substitutions and he'll say one I like and I'll say "Write that down!" and he'll write it in the margin.

Hall: First, we read the other's work alone. I make little notes in the margin, to remind me what to say. I think you do that, too.

Kenyon: Yes.

Hall: Or I cross out a line or a word. I'll take out all her participles. She isn't allowed to say "was making." I write in "made." That's one of my tics. Talking over a poem helps; I might discover that it's not really the word she dislikes but the one right after it that makes the problem: it's not "purple" but it's "passion." Even when she makes a suggestion I don't accept, her criticism might point out a problem; or maybe a misunderstanding demonstrates that I didn't make clear what I meant to say. This discovery allows me to reenter the poem. This time, a new sensibility helps. When I show poems to Jane, I know from experience that they are probably not finished, but I don't know what's wrong with them.

Kenyon: I reach the point where I just can't see one more thing to do with a poem. I've poked and poked. Yet I sense that it needs more. Even if I think it is finished, I still want Don to confirm my opinion. We can't either of us finish poems without each other's critical opinion. Once I have Don's ideas, and the ideas of my workshop, then I can complete the work. Finally, of course, I must please myself, taking some suggestions and rejecting others.

Blue: Do you hold back your emotional reactions to your work, whether good or bad, as well?

Kenyon: Sometimes that holding back is a way of keeping the work out of other activities. There are times when I don't mention that I've started new poems. If the poems don't turn out to be anything, then I won't have to take back what I've said.

Hall: I can remember mentioning to Jane that "I started a new poem the other day." That was after two or three days when I thought the work was going to stick. I don't say I started one five minutes ago because I don't know if I did; I just think I did.

Blue: These sound like established patterns for mature writers who have shared a long-term relationship. Yet when you first met, Jane was a new writer in a new relationship with an established writer. Did that intimidate you, Jane?

Kenyon: I wouldn't apply the word *intimidated* to it, and yet I used to work more freely when Don was gone.

Hall: The first couple of years after we married, you wouldn't write anything except when I left for poetry readings, so there was something—I don't know if "intimidated" is the right word—but there was some pressure. But consider this: I was nineteen years older than Jane—and still am—and I had published four or five books. I also work sixteen hours a day, which means I'm a living reproach. Finally Jane just said to hell with that, and did her own work. I have always thought it was brave of Jane to put her head down and keep writing.

Kenyon: It didn't seem brave. No.

Blue: Yet you were a new writer?

Kenyon: Well, I was twenty-three years old and hadn't really done anything—

Hall: You were twenty-two when we met.

Blue: So it was brave to continue; but in the process did you feel as though you were damming up work, Jane?

Kenyon: I was never aware of damming up poems. I worked when the spirit moved, at first, which was not often. Certainly I had no patterns to my work at all . . . I had a job at the Early Modern English Project at Michigan, and spent half the day there. We did discuss my work habits, I'm sure. It may be similar to my interest in the piano when I was growing up; I never played when anyone else was in the house. It was difficult to submit poems to editors. It was difficult to publish, and difficult not to publish.

Blue: How did that type of tension affect your ability to critique each other's work?

Hall: Jane and I were student and teacher and friends for some time before anything romantic happened. When we were first married, we had to cope with that earlier relationship. I couldn't criticize her poems, because then I became the teacher. It was psychically confusing; her husband suddenly turns into Professor Hall. The solution—and this is comic—was that we needed a third person. When Gregory Orr would join us, then I could say anything about Jane's poems and she could say everything about mine. Greg's presence made it a workshop in which we were equals.

Kenyon: That was a very felicitous discovery.

Hall: After two and a half years of working with Greg, he went to Virginia and we went to New Hampshire. By then, Jane and I could read each other's work. We didn't need Greg.

Blue: Did you have the same trouble accepting criticism from Jane as you had giving it, Don?

Hall: I don't recall any difficulty, and it would not be likely. When I taught writing, usually once a year toward the end of the term, I brought in some of my own poems. Then my own standards were hurled back at me! I took advice from students.

When Jane was a student, long before there was anything else, I remember once in office hours when something in one of her poems made me think of a poem of mine; I pulled it out and worked on it right in front of her and asked for her help.

Blue: Your authority, confidence, has grown during the time you and Don have been married. How do you perceive Don's influence on your development as a writer, Jane?

Kenyon: You can see for yourself that our poems do not resemble each other at all. But whatever it is that I know about writing poems, I have learned most of it from being with Don, moving to his ancestral farm, keeping my ears open when his peers came to visit. One very important thing I've learned from Don is to be ambitious. Just do it, and take the knocks and praise as they come.

Of course I've had to establish and learn to honor my own habits of work, my own pace, my own areas of interest and struggles. When we married, he had long since established all of these things for himself. My work habits have evolved over time, just as his had. As part of that, my own group of peers has been equally important to my development of skills and nerve.

Blue: In the past, Don, you've mentioned that your work on essays was almost play but that poetry was more of a challenge. Does living with a poet make writing poetry more of a challenge?

Hall: No. Earlier, I lived with someone who was not a poet. Sharing the experience allows us to understand each other's challenges. This is all good; not every single thing about two writers under the same roof is good, but I find it a confirmation to live with someone whose endeavors, whose desires, and whose love of art are similar—and who struggles to make that art. This identity of endeavor is comforting. I know I talked about establishing boundaries and being separate, but you only have to establish boundaries when there is something bringing you closely together. That is mildly paradoxical but no real contradiction.

Blue: What do you think, Jane?

Kenyon: I think it is pleasant not to have to explain what I am doing, or trying to do.

Blue: You've workshopped each other's work a great deal over the past twenty-one years. When you're writing and revising, do you hear the other's voice?

Kenyon: Oh, I've internalized Don's little tics. I work with several other friends very closely and I've internalized their tics, too. I just lay these principles on the poem like a grid when I'm working on it and I try to anticipate their difficulties with it. That's very important to my work.

Hall: I do the same thing, of course. I know what Jane is going to say; I may be wrong sometimes, but I think I know. In my mind I hear her voice telling me not to do something and I get mad at her—this is all in my imagination. I know that when I repeat a word, words repeated close to each other, Jane is always going to object; therefore I watch for this habit of mine, which I suppose is faintly Victorian. Sometimes I get the repetition out before she sees the poem. But then if I really like the repetition, and she criticizes it, I am apt to think, "Oh, that's just one of Jane's things." There are typical stylistic aspects to her poems, like the repetitions in mine, that I am apt to object to and that she can therefore dismiss. Not that she always dismisses them. Often when she makes a joke, I don't like the joke, not in the poem. But of course, in spite of my familiarity with her habits and work, still she often astonishes me with some of her moves.

There is a danger in expecting criticism, that you'll censor yourself and not allow yourself to go in certain directions—

Kenyon: Yes. I always watch for that.

Hall: It's essential for each of us, for anyone, to have more than one reader. We're each other's first reader but not the last. Jane has in particular two female friends. I do my workshops by mail usually.

Kenyon: We need other people to find a balance and to see what we are doing from a variety of perspectives.

Hall: Back to your question about hearing the other's voice, sometimes that shows up in other ways. I had a poem that included the phrase "exhalations of timothy," which was a direct steal from Jane. One day before I showed it to her, I realized I had stolen from her, changed the image, and told her. She said, "Watch your ass."

Kenyon: I count on Don and my other friends, Alice Mattison and Joyce Peseroff, to catch me if I'm unintentionally taking something from another poet. I stole something from Geoffrey Hill once without knowing it, and I just felt sick about it.

Hall: I ended an elegy poem with a quote from scripture shortly after you had written a poem that closed with scripture.

Kenyon: That didn't seem terribly serious to me.

Hall: It did for a moment!

Kenyon: Did it?

Hall: Oh, yes, I remember. You were annoyed.

Blue: As you've worked your way into these established patterns of writing and living together, has there ever been any sense of competition between you, or a temptation to compare quality of work?

Hall: When a magazine prints one of us and rejects the other, at the same time, that can be uncomfortable. No big deal. We used to have a problem based more upon the differences in our ages. That we are of different generations was a help because we were not head on head in rivalry; I belong to the generation of the late 1920s and Jane of the late 1940s, a twenty-year gap. But when we were first married, and for about ten years thereafter, we sometimes had a problem when others would treat me as the poet and her as the little wife who wrote poetry, and isn't that adorable? Nobody said those words, but that was the tone.

Kenyon: That was definitely the tone.

Blue: Did people expect you to promote Jane's career, Don?

Hall: Oh, that was a terror.

Kenyon: We were very scrupulous in our separateness.

Hall: But however scrupulous we were, you'd still worry that people would think I was promoting you. I had to do less for you than I would for another poet. That was difficult for me. Always in the past, when I found a younger poet whom I admired, I tried to push the poet—publications, awards, fellowships—to call other people's attention to the poetry. Of course I am not allowed to push in connection with Jane! Maybe I have not been perfect—certainly in letters and in conversation I have praised her work to other people; but I have tried not to do anything that she would disapprove of. I do a little editing for magazines, and I edit anthologies, but for a long time she would not let me print her.

Now I feel that I can recommend her or praise her work more openly than I could before, because so many other people have praised her, given her prizes and awards.

Kenyon: Yes. We're okay now. But there were many years when I really didn't want to be with Don for readings and festivals.

Hall: It is new that we be together at a festival or a reading. I remember when it changed, about a year and a half ago in Michigan. We did separate readings, then a joint question period with MFA students. Jane got more questions than I did; it was then that Jane said maybe we could read together.

Kenyon: When we sense malice behind comparisons, I become upset. People can be incredibly rude. Differences in our ages have little to do with this. Often I think people make much more of that difference than we do.

I needed a man capable of complexity. I enjoy Don's human wisdom and I admire it. It would be rare indeed in someone younger.

Blue: How do you perceive the differences in your work, your styles?

Kenyon: I think our visions are very different. Don has been writing a long time and he has passed through many shapes and sizes, if you will, for his poems. He is writing large, ambitious, loose-limbed poems these days, poems in which all his wisdom appears. I am working at one thing—the short lyric. It is all I want, at this point: to write short, intense, musical cries of the spirit. I am a miniaturist and he is painting Diego Rivera murals. I'm not being modest when I say that I am a miniaturist. There's nothing remotely modest about trying to write short lyrics in the tradition of Sappho, Keats, and Akhmatova.

Blue: Have you ever collaborated on a work?

Kenyon: In one sense we collaborate on everything.

Hall: I think there are words of Jane's in my poems and words of mine in hers, in the way friends help friends. Of Bly and Simpson and Kinnell, I can say the same; but we don't write collaborative poems. I don't want that.

Kenyon: I don't either. I think it would make a sort of monstrous poem.

Blue: Have you each written a poem in response to a very specific incident that allowed you a chance to immediately compare your work?

Kenyon: Yes. We each wrote about the Gulf War.

Hall: As it happens, Jane's poem is a lot better than mine. That's not modesty, just a fact. But it's funny: these poems are gross exaggerations of the differences in men's and women's characters. Mine could not have been written by a woman. Hers could not have been written by a man. When we do our ABAB readings, we don't deliberately pair poems up. Yet just reading at random, not consulting the other, we constantly refer to the same dog, the same countryside, the same weather—in totally different ways.

Kenyon: Although we don't pair up poems for readings, I often ask Don what he plans to read. I like to construct a reading that is a "voice answering a voice" in Virginia Woolf's phrase. If I know the poet's work well enough, in the case of reading with someone other than Don, I might well ask beforehand what she or he plans to read. There is an improvisational aspect to reading with others, but also a communal one.

Hall: I never knew you were doing that!

Blue: I'm intrigued by the gender differences you've mentioned, since I've read reviews of your works that referred to the feminine awareness in Jane's work and the anima/animus aspect of Don's work, particularly regarding *The One Day*. Could you elaborate on that difference?

Kenyon: I don't know if it has ever been clearer than in these Gulf War poems that Don is talking about. My poem begins with tearing up an old nightgown just out of the dryer to put in the rag bag. The thought moves from that act to dismemberment, thence the war, and what happens to ordinary people in the street during an air war.

Now, *chez nous*, I do the laundry, I'm afraid. Only if my husband had married a woman who refused to do the wash under any circumstances would he a) do the wash, and b) have written this poem. He works long hours, very hard, but he does not do the laundry.

His poem about the Gulf War is all public, declamatory, loud, and outward. But I don't know that such critiques are useful really.

Wayne Ude: Jane, you've most often mentioned female friends who workshop with you. Is that an aspect of gender-specific focus in your work?

Kenyon: That's interesting. I hadn't thought of that, but it's true. Don works with some female poets. I don't work with other men except on certain occasions when they happen to be around. Robert Bly was with us in December for a few days; he flew up to be with Don because he had been ill, which I thought was very sweet. While he was there, he looked over very carefully the new book and made a few suggestions. It was wonderful—really wonderful.

Blue: Certainly both you and Don do write personal material. Are there times when the personal quality in a poem presents problems for discussing each other's work objectively?

Kenyon: That happens; it's something we have to nurture. In the new book, I have a poem about one of Don's first surgeries for cancer and I'm ambivalent about it myself. He says he doesn't mind. When you're living with a writer, as you know, you'd better watch your ass because you might turn up someplace that surprises you.

Blue: Has Don ever returned a poem to you that he couldn't critique because of its personal nature?

Kenyon: Not yet. But I did ask him specifically about this surgery poem. I said, "Do you mind? Does this trouble you?" He said, "No, I not only don't mind, I'm proud." Writing about grief does help to resolve it, because one comes to newer and deeper understanding in the process of writing. Of course there are things I refrain from writing about just as there are things I refrain from saying. Only an idiot says everything!

Blue: On the opposite side, do the daily concerns of a married couple ever intrude into your ability to critique each other's work, or to receive criticism from each other? Might you, for instance, refuse to discuss a new poem until anger over a domestic issue has been resolved?

Hall: No, and one of the reasons is that we practically never have a fight. Therefore, when we do fight, it is terrible. I know that there are times when Jane is distracted, or maybe very depressed, when I would not trouble her with a poem. I think about her feelings or her fatigue or her mood before I show her a poem. Because I tend to hold poems back, perhaps mood or fatigue provides me with an excuse, from time to time, for withholding a poem a bit longer.

Kenyon: There really is very little discord between us. Of course if we have argued about something, we both feel disturbed and it may spill over into our work. I have written about the damage of arguing.

Blue: *From Room to Room* and *Let Evening Come* both seem very meditative, tranquil. *The Boat of Quiet Hours* carries more harsh sounds, more religious overtones. That surprised me since you were in the same tranquil setting, still living in a way that most of us regard as ideal. Were the poems deliberately collected because of that tone or was there a time in New Hampshire when a change occurred?

Kenyon: I think probably the poems that you're referring to in *The Boat of Quiet Hours* are poems I wrote during my father's illness or after his death, in the early 1980s. It took me about five years to write that book and we had entered into a decade in which there was just non-stop trouble, big-time trouble. My father's illness and death. My grandmother's. My aunt's. My own health suffered when I was in my thirties: I had cancer; I had some serious, debilitating infection in one ear which knocked out my sense of balance. I was really very ill for a couple of years and even now I stagger; I had some hearing loss with it. We just had a real bad time of it. The theme is continuing in the 1990s with Don's trouble and his mother's troubles. Life just keeps coming at you. I think all that did make for a loss of self, a loss of self-possession, which was probably good for my work. The new book has a great deal of very painful material in it.

Blue: Is it still tied to nature and landscape?

Kenyon: Yes. It just seems to me that those areas present the perfect area of image. Image is important to me, probably *the* most important thing.

Blue: Your arrival in New Hampshire obviously carried a strong significance in your work. Now you've been there almost twenty years, an amount of time when poets often seek change. Do you ever feel that you can use up that landscape, that place?

Kenyon: Never. I've put down very deep roots there. I can't conceive of being anywhere else.

Blue: The sense of landscape is less prevalent in much of your work, Don; in fact, "Old Roses" is a poem I think of as unusual for you. Did Jane have a strong influence on that work?

Hall: I don't recall that she did. Does it seem—?

Kenyon: I probably contributed some botanical thing.

Hall: Doubtless I was calling them tulips or seagulls or something.

Kenyon: You had them blooming in August.

Hall: Jane keeps me straight on natural terminology.

Blue: You talk of your love of the landscape, the rural scene, Jane. Were you raised in the country?

Kenyon: Yes. I was born in Ann Arbor and lived there until I was twenty-eight when we moved to New Hampshire. I went to a one-room school until I was in fifth grade. At that time, the Ann Arbor township schools were annexed into the city schools, but I continued to live across the road from a working farm. For me the move to New Hampshire was a restoration of something that I love very deeply because Ann Arbor kept creeping outward to the point where the road was paved and the farmer's fields were subdivided and ugly houses were built. The move to New Hampshire was a restoration of a kind of paradise.

Blue: Almost a coming home?

Kenyon: Yes, it was.

Hall: At the same time, Jane was not a farmer's daughter; her father was a musician. Her father and mother made a union of opposites: a sophisticated house and life in a country setting. I think contrast makes energy and the more different things you can subsume, the more interesting your writing.

Blue: Do you think your poetry would have developed similarly without the move to New Hampshire, Jane?

Kenyon: I don't know. It seems to me that the move opened up a whole area of possibilities. Certainly the move was the beginning of my serious work on poetry. I used to work just when I felt like it. When we moved to New Hampshire, I had twenty-four hours a day, seven days a week to structure for myself and I began working more regularly and began to publish in magazines and pull together my first book.

On the other hand, it wasn't easy. I found total freedom daunting. I was making over my world in that move; I was replacing my outer constraints with new, inner ones, establishing new priorities. As I mentioned, I needed time to establish patterns. Now I work every morning; Don's bringing me a cup of coffee in bed is a small but significant kindness that sets the tone for the day. I almost never write in the afternoon unless I have a deadline, or unless I'm really hot. I have a lot of chores and responsibilities to attend to in the afternoon.

Blue: Would you recommend the full-time writing life to others?

Kenyon: The simple act of becoming a full-time writer will not significantly change your work. There are full-time writers who can't push things to their limits—poets who stop when a thing is "good enough." The amount of time has nothing to do with being bold or fearless, telling the whole truth.

Donald Hall: Without and Within

Steven Ratiner / 1997

Conducted in December 1997. From Steven Ratiner, ed., *Giving Their Word: Conversations with Contemporary Poets* (University of Massachusetts Press, 2002), pp. 237–65. With Steven Ratiner's permission, two sections of the interview have been omitted for reasons of space; his original reference to a poet who wrote poems in the form of letters to his dead wife has been corrected to refer to David Ignatow. The locations of omitted material are indicated by the use of three asterisks; ellipses and notes in brackets are in the original. © 2002 by Steven Ratiner and published by the University of Massachusetts Press.

There was a certain symmetry about it. My first visit to Donald Hall's home at Eagle Pond had been in autumn, though in the New Hampshire hills winter announces its approach early on. Hall's wife, the poet Jane Kenyon, had been away that day but as I was given a tour of the house and its surroundings I noticed signs of her presence everywhere I looked. She too was an exceptional writer, someone I hoped eventually to include in my interview series. But I didn't worry; there'd be time.

With Hall, I discussed how rooted to this bit of the earth he and Jane had become over the years, how it was a presence in much of their work. Work, weather, memory, the resonance of place, and of course love—we spoke of how these elemental experiences seemed even more precious now that his cancer may have drawn a boundary line on what he might expect to enjoy. Yet it was a wonderful conversation, one that led to a friendship through correspondence and occasional visits as the years passed.

Now, once again, I drove along the twisting country road and saw the farmhouse and barn come into view, snow-sheathed this time, a dark December afternoon in 1997. Once again, Donald Hall appeared on his porch to greet me—only this man barely resembled his earlier self. He'd grown a scruffy beard and his hair was long and wild. His face seemed marked by his long period of grieving. He wore a sweater with a hole prominent in its side (and I instantly caught myself thinking: if Jane were alive, I wonder if she would have prodded him about that—"You're going to be photographed today; put on a nicer sweater").

As it turned out, he had come out of doors to smoke a cigarette, something Jane preferred he not do in the house. And though it was approaching five years since his last operation, a period after which the doctors had pronounced him cured, and nearly three since leukemia had erupted, claiming Jane Kenyon's life—Donald Hall was in no hurry to reestablish the license of a solitary life. He was acutely aware of what was now absent. After all, the new book of poems detailing the year of his wife's dying and the series of letter poems that followed bore the simple title: *Without*. But he was trying to live with as much of Jane's presence as imagination could bear.

He still had the rooms they shared and their painted bed, the hill paths they walked with Gus, their old dog who still traipsed beside him. He had poems and journals that preserved something of her voice, and a tiny shrine he'd erected in his study: photographs, an old driver's license, a passport, the small intimacies of a shared life. And chiefly, he had the daily routine of a full-time writer, a discipline that had sustained him for decades and something he was now struggling to reclaim.

Later on, it didn't surprise me when I found that both of my interviews, six years apart, had culminated with similar statements (though the tone of the two lines revealed a world of difference). The previous one closed with the poet declaring, "Find what you love, and do it"; this one, with the pronouncement, spoken two times for emphasis, "Get back to work."

Steven Ratiner: One of the reasons I wanted to come back to Eagle Pond to talk with you again is that, of all my interview subjects, your life has changed most dramatically in the intervening years—a change that, as the new book makes clear, has had an equally dramatic effect on your poetry. Our earlier conversation focused on home and place-making, and the role language has in that process. You described the many ways this house, this terrain helped form you as a writer—when you were a young boy visiting your grandparents and especially when you came back to live here with Jane. Before I get into the more crucial changes, I wanted to ask about differences in the way you look—something I remarked upon when you greeted me on your porch. I'm curious whether this was a conscious choice—trying to make the outside match the inside, so to speak.

Donald Hall: Well, I think I'm restless without Jane and perhaps the change in my appearance is part of floundering about, flailing about, trying to find it—and I don't know what "it" is. But I'm traveling more than I used to. At the beginning, after her death, I couldn't leave the house, I couldn't even go away overnight for a couple of months. Now I travel more. I'm very glad to get back because place is very important to me and I wouldn't want to move, to get away. People have counseled that, people make all sorts of suggestions, you know, "Go away, take a trip, get away from Jane." I don't want to. She's more *here* than she is anywhere else. The first year or so she was very present—and I don't mean supernaturally. All her clothes were here, her study was untouched—and still everywhere I look—her handwriting is on all the herbs, in the telephone directory, and so on. I don't want to be away, but I am restless. What I want I do not have.

I haven't let my hair grow by deciding to; I just haven't been going to the barber. And I'm aware that Jane was my barber for twenty years of marriage and more, perhaps that's why. When people ask me, I tell them that. Growing the beard was again something. Life has totally changed, my life has totally changed and it's as if with the beard I've acknowledged this change. I had a beard the first half of our marriage, a different kind of beard, a big bushy one. But I suppose a sort of seeking after change, looking for something, that may satisfy me—as I am not otherwise satisfied—may explain the change in appearance.

SR: I mentioned to you in my letters how pleased I was that you still included Jane in your readings. Just a few months back when you read in Cambridge, you began with a few of her pieces even before you read your own. You weren't hiding your grief or your pain—it was acknowledged as part of all that you were doing.

DH: I tell you, far from wanting to hide from it, I wanted to scream it. In the days and weeks and months after Jane died, I couldn't talk about anything but the last eleven days [of her life]. We knew she was going to die the last eleven days, and then there were the details—of Cheyne-Stokes breathing, of the eyes stuck open, of closing her eyes. People often say, "How courageous of you to speak of it"; well, it wasn't courageous at all, I couldn't *not*. I felt like the Ancient Mariner, who had to tell his story. And I made up a story about myself—not as a truth but as illustrative—that I go into a diner and I have a hamburger and say "Could you pass the ketchup?," and the man passes me the ketchup and I say, "My wife used to like ketchup; she died of leukemia," and I tell him the whole story. . . .

I would meet somebody, an old friend or anybody I hadn't seen for a long time and I couldn't talk about anything else. Or I'd meet somebody for the first time—often this still happens—and I tell it again. For a long time it was, say, the last eleven days that I'd talk about mostly, and then it would go back over the whole illness. There are a million stories, many of which are in the book *Without* that you have read, but there are others as well. There are subsequent poems. . . . I cannot *not* face it; I think it does me good to face it. I don't believe in hiding things and tamping things down—but it's a matter of temperament, not a matter of the right choice. Henry Adams, after Clover's suicide, lived forty or fifty years and never mentioned her name, not in any letters that survive. I don't know that he ever mentioned her name to his dearest friends—but if he did they didn't say so, John Hay, and so on. But that was his way, and it was an enormous grief and an enormous mourning for him that he expressed in silence. I don't think he denied it (I'm an Adams freak). But my way, far from denial, was proclamation. . . .

The worst day was not the day she died, which was April 22nd, but April 11th, which was the day we were told that she was going to die. For fifteen months she struggled to live and had a bone marrow transplant; and suddenly on April 11th—a week earlier her blood work had looked good— the leukemia was back and there was nothing to do. That was the worst day. And a year after her death, I arranged to give a talk on that day. I didn't have to do it that day but I knew that if I could talk that day—and I would talk about her—that would relieve my mind or my heart. It is as if to spread my grief out onto the world is a form of relief for me. I think, *I know*, it makes some people very uncomfortable. I think *Without* will make people uncomfortable, people will find it—some one or two people have—relentless, and insistent upon horror, and that is my way. I don't apologize for it nor do I say it's the only way to be. But it's my way.

SR: Actually, the poems had something of the opposite effect on me. A first reading involved, as you said, a profound welling of sadness. The horror to me centered on the medical technology surrounding the act of dying— having to deal with the hospitals and medical procedures and drugs. But as I went back through the manuscript, I was struck again and again by the ways you were forced to savor the littlest things in life, the sorts of experiences that we squander thoughtlessly.

DH: That sense is common. Of course, I had had cancer twice before Jane had her leukemia, and I was supposed to die. She had cancer first—ten years before she died she had—what in retrospect was a minor thing—she had a genuine cancer totally enclosed within a salivary gland. That was removed and there was no chance, we were told, of metastasis, and it had nothing to do with the leukemia. But of course we faced possible death for one of us then. And then probable death for me when the right half of my liver was removed, which was just two years before Jane took sick, less than two years before Jane took sick. We faced the possibility or even probability of one of us dying over those many years. And then of course in fifteen months we knew. . . . Leukemia is a dreadful disease that kills half of adults who have it. Jane's type, I won't go into it, but because of the particulars of a cancer cell and Jane's type of leukemia, her chances were far fewer than most leukemias, her percentage was lower. We knew that the probability of death was high but we did everything to make her live. Out in Seattle, where she had her bone marrow transplant, Janey was in terrible pain—from the treatment, not from leukemia—and she used to say again and again, "Perkins, am I going to live?" And what she meant, of course, the rest of the sentence was, "Or am I going through all this shit for nothing?" I never answered her cheerfully. She wouldn't want false cheer. I said, "That's what we're here for." And when we knew she was dying, she didn't talk a lot. But I could see her thinking a lot and at one point she said, "It was worth it. I'd do it over again." Despite the earlier thought, she just followed the process toward possible health. Wouldn't you, at this point or at that point, have given up? We did savor things. Her dying was of course the worst thing in my life. Taking care of her, however, was one of the very best things in my life. I'm very happy to say that it's the best thing in my life. I loved taking care of her.

SR: That comes across quite clearly in the poems, even though the imagery may be somewhat frightening to us.

DH: And she loved being taken care of. She was a depressive—had suffered through profound periods of depression—and I don't think that she could always believe I loved her as much as I claimed to, but she finally did. I don't mean it's compensatory, for one moment, but taking care of her was a joy. And when I was sick over a much less extensive time, but possibly mortally ill, she was wonderful taking care of me. She was my model. I didn't have any struggles about taking care of her; it's absolutely what I wanted to do, what I wanted to do every day. When she was in the hospital I was by her bed by six or before every morning and at night she'd get really tired by seven or eight and I would put on a record and leave, but come back in the morning early.

When she was here—she was probably here half the time or more of the early fifteen months, and the other half in one hospital or another—here, I worked by her side most of the time. I was able to do a great deal of work while she was sick. I read to her when I could, I did every errand for her I could do, I brought her blankets or whatever, hot blankets, I fed her when we were home, I learned how to program pumps and deliver material into her bloodstream—but still there was a lot of time left over. The only thing that could take my full attention was writing. And I wrote about her a great deal; the first half of *Without* was all or virtually all drafted while she was alive. I read her some of the things I was writing about her. But I also wrote about other things; I wrote three or four short stories, some poems on other subjects, some children's books—or I'd work on things that I'd already begun.

SR: I'm remembering the time when you were ill, the things Jane and you discussed during the television interview you did with Bill Moyers. It was as if you were talking this out in order to make life ready for your absence, for Jane's sake. It must have been terribly hard to make the switch when suddenly it seemed as if you were given a reprieve from your cancer, but almost as quickly Jane's illness appeared.

DH: I was terrified of course that my cancer might return while she was ill. If I had died before she did, if my cancer had come back early on, God knows who would've taken care of her or taken care of me! I was worried about that a lot. The irony of her death—she was supposed to survive me by twenty-five years—and the loss of someone you love and you've been married to for a long time . . . It's horrible in any case, but I felt outrage as well! It just could not have happened. When we left Ann Arbor and moved here, I was forty-seven years old and most people think that was when I began to be a good poet (if they think I'm a good poet at all). When she died she was forty-seven. It's just outrageous, outrageous. When the Moyers [interview] came out, the *Boston Globe* did a long article—the Moyers show had quite a bit about my cancer, my "imminent death"—and the *Globe* article actually had the title, "Happy For Now." One month later, Jane was diagnosed with leukemia. The irony is with me every day. When I write poems about her now, I cannot help having that thought: *she* should be writing these poems about me, not me about her. A pointless thought, but I cannot get rid of it.

SR: In one of the letter poems after Jane's death, you speak to her saying,

> When you wrote
> about lovemaking or cancer,
> about absences or a quarrel,
> I loved to turn up in your poems.
> I imagined those you'd make
> after I died; I regretted
> I wouldn't be able to read them.

—From "Midwinter Letter"

But the very act of imagining such a thing used poetry to infuse this place with some sense of continuity.

DH: Right, right. When I wrote some of the letters, when I was moving along in the letters, I would consciously think, "If Jane were writing this what would she do?" I wanted to learn from her. In the absence of Jane Kenyon, I wanted to write Jane Kenyon poems. I don't think I did.

SR: In my last letter I asked you about just that. I felt, in various ways, that her influence was there in this manuscript. In some of the clipped rhythms, the simple but striking images, the restrained tone.

DH: Well, I'm glad if it is. I don't think I could really sound like her if I tried. But if I could be influenced, because I admire her so enormously, her work—I'm happy.

SR: But somehow, now that the situation is reversed and *you* are the one left to make these new poems, you don't seem at all comforted by that vision—Jane taking pleasure in your continued work. How do you cope with the burden of the poetry?

DH: I have no choice, if I'm to write at all, but to try to cope with it. These are the thoughts that haunt me as I write.

SR: No sense there must be joy for her, knowing . . .

DH: No, no, not really. I would love it if I thought she could read them and she'd like them. I want her to like them: "Pretty good, Perkins!"

SR: By the way, where did "Perkins" come from?

DH: The story's not particularly interesting. When we were first living here, we drove over to Maine and we went to Perkins Cove and we seemed to see Dr. Perkins and Perkins the lawyer and Perkins' drugstore—and Jane just laughed and said, "This Perkins must be some fellow!" And she started calling me Perkins thereafter. But I thought, why this—and I realized that when she first knew me I was her teacher; I was a poet at Michigan, and Donald Hall was kind of an institution. And this was the sixties and all the students called me "Don," for that matter, and I think Perkins was more comfortable for her probably. I asked her this and she said, "Well, maybe."

Only last April, two years after her death, was I able to begin to work on her archives. When she was dying, one of the first things she said was that she wanted her papers to go to the University of New Hampshire, where mine are. But I couldn't touch them for two years. And I found amazing things—diaries, the journals from when she was fourteen and fifteen—she never threw anything away—and all the drafts of all the poems of all the books, even the ones that weren't extraordinary. But I also found a notebook from the time when she was taking my class. She actually took a big lecture course of mine and I didn't know her. The following term I let her into—not knowing her, not interviewing her or anything—I let her into a small writing class, which was how I really got to know her. I admitted her on the basis of reading her work only. That class would meet for the first time in a classroom that was [listed] in the catalogue. But thereafter we would meet in my living room. We'd find one night a week when we could all get together, and so at the first meeting of the class in the classroom, I told them where I lived. Jane had never known my address. I found a note in her notebook, which must have been written that day: "When I discovered that Donald Hall lived not three doors from me, it was as when I heard that Dublin was a Viking stronghold or when I went to take the goldfish out of the bowl but discovered that the water was too cold to sustain life." It was pretty scary. No wonder she called me Perkins.

SR: The earlier poems in *Without*—they're clearly autobiographical, following the experiences as they came, yet you choose to refer to the characters as "he" and "she" instead, distancing yourself from them. Only later on the "I" appears and . . .

DH: It's "he" and "Jane" or "she." I originally wrote "I"—and it was just a forest of I's, trees of I's. I didn't know what to do about it, I had no idea. And one friend of mine—many people read through this manuscript, several as much as three times, and did me an enormous amount of help—one friend in particular . . . About fifteen months after Jane died, I had a draft, and I knew I was going to change every page, and I did, but I was ready to show it to some people and she was one of the first readers. And she told me change "I" to "he." I thought she must be wrong, but one thing that I've learned to do often is to try something out. With a computer (which I don't use, but I have someone else use it) it is easy to do. So I changed all the I's to he's to see what it would look like, and tried it out on other people. And it turned out right. I would never have thought of it, but she was right. No one is deceived—or is supposed to be deceived. The "I" was not just not egotistical; this intimacy in such dreadful situations was painful. When she's gone, she's dead, and I'm writing her, I feel that the intimacy of address absolutely requires "I." The first poems are not addressed to her or to anyone. They're descriptive; they're narrative. And the use of "he"—no one has actually objected to it. I showed it to ten people the first time and then I rewrote the whole thing entirely, largely based on what people had said to me but also on ideas I had, and showed it to another ten people. . . .

SR: A different . . . ?

DH: A different ten people, yes. So they wouldn't notice the change about a "he"; they would see "he" for the first time, as it were, among other things.

So I would get a clean reaction to it. And nobody objected to "he," nobody was puzzled by it or anything. So I really think that was a good thing. It was Caroline Finklestein who came up with the "he" instead of the "I." Ellen Voight helped me enormously with the structure, and had great effect on the structure of *Without*. Galway Kinnell, Sharon Olds . . . actually, I shouldn't list people because I'll leave some out . . . Alice Mattison, Jane's great friend—these people were enormously important to it, and I've left out two or three names that were as important as them. I won't try to list because it's invidious when you leave people out. Anyway, I always have had a lot of help, beginning with Jane, going on to Robert Bly and old friends, but also younger friends—Liam Rector has helped me and Cynthia Huntington. I call them young—they're in their forties, but that's young compared to me anyway. I had a tremendous amount of help and a sense of validation from these people.

SR: Getting a whole separate reading of the text—ten different responses to the poems—I assume you couldn't simply incorporate other people's readings into one in order to produce a whole? How could you respond . . . ?

DH: Oh, I listen, I listen, I listen. I correct for the veer of particular winds. And always it is true that somebody will say, "This page is wonderful except for that line, take that out of the stanza." And somebody else will say, "Now most of this page isn't very good, but *that line*, that's really good, don't lose that!" Opposites. It's frustrating at first. There are various things that you can do. Sometimes a stanza didn't belong there; it belonged to another letter. I moved parts of letters back and forth. And the little postcard on the nine-month anniversary of her death was part of a letter originally, but it was a false climax, making it an anticlimax in the letter. So I removed it and made it a separate item. There were numerous and enormous changes. There was the Thanksgiving letter which became incorporated in a Christmas letter. The midwinter letter was probably a third again as long originally and I cut it down considerably, so you can never . . . I don't suppose that anybody's reading is represented all the way through there, but everybody is represented in places all the way through.

SR: Some poets resist so strongly incorporating outside influences, other writers' opinions or viewpoints—for Stafford, I remember, it was almost a matter of religion that no one be permitted to look at the poem until it is complete and ready for submission.

DH: I know, I think it's foolish, I think it's self-protective (even though I love Bill Stafford's work). There are some people who simply can't work my way. But I can't really work without it. I've always had a lot of friendly help. And I've given a lot. By and large, it doesn't work unless it's reciprocal.

SR: Like the sort of partnership you've described with Jane.
DH: Oh yeah, yeah.

* * *

SR: Let me ask you a question about the idea of the letter as a form for the poems in the book's second half. After I received the manuscript of *Without*, I began coming across a number of other examples. [David Ignatow] has letter-like poems spoken to his dead wife, some dealing with the anger and shame associated with desire when one survives the loss of a partner. But the ones that reminded me most of yours were [Eugenio] Montale's *Xenia* sequence. They too create an ongoing conversation with the memory of his late wife. I was surprised you weren't familiar with them. In one of the letters, he writes: "But it's possible, you know, to love a shadow, / we ourselves being shadows." And I wonder, in some sense, if the very nature of the letter form was a way of purposely trespassing across the boundary of the grave.

DH: Oh, perhaps not accepting it exactly. I knew she was dead. I think perhaps it took two years for the last cell of my body to admit that she was dead. I stayed with her body a long time, about four hours, before they picked it up. And I kept touching her and kissing her, she got colder and colder. And I knew what I was doing. I wanted to know she was dead. And I had "calling hours," which people don't like so much anymore but they do it in the country.

SR: Calling hours?

DH: That's where the body's displayed in the funeral parlor the night before the funeral. Very few people have the open coffin at a funeral any-more—that used to be common—but I knew that would freak out certain people close to me, so I didn't do that. But I had calling hours the night be-fore. Knowing that she was dead was very important. Still on the day of the funeral, when everybody left—my children volunteered to stay with me, of course, but I wanted to be alone—the minute everybody left, I went down to the graveyard and stood at her grave.

SR: At night?

DH: Yeah. And the next morning I was there by six. I talked to her. I didn't think she was listening, but I talked to her at the grave and it com-forted me to talk to her at the grave. I needed to do it. *Comforted* is much too comfy a word. I talked to the dog about her a lot. But I also talked to her photographs. The letters were the written versions. It was not that I felt re-ally in communication with her; it was a one-way conversation all the time.

But it helped to be able to do it. One of the things that happens as the years go on is that she's no longer "you," she's no longer *y-o-u*: she is "Jane," she is third person. But it took at least a year before that happened. She recedes, she diminishes. I had a dream in which there were, at the end of the room on shelves, like bookshelves, something like 269 small corpses, about the size of dolls—all of Jane. And I realized I had not yet buried them all, that this was a task that was ahead of me. This was a little over a year after she died that I had that dream.

I had some wowser dreams, goodness knows. Everybody believes they're somehow responsible for a death. And I had dreams where Jane had abandoned me, running off with another man—which was not a part of our life together or an anxiety in our life together. Ridiculous, you know, but you can't call a dream ridiculous. My mother died when Jane was two months sick; and then Jane's mother, who was very close to both of us, died three months before Jane did. I had a dream in which Jane had died, and our house was deep in the woods, not right on the road, and l was aware (without seeing them) that the townspeople around where we lived were very saddened for me because Jane had died. But they were also sad because they knew the sheriff was coming to put me in jail. And the sheriff was coming to put me in jail because, in my caring for Jane, I had neglected the old women who lived in the woods in their little cottages and they had all starved to death and died. That one was clear enough.

SR: I wonder if these poems then aren't about trying to bear this huge weight of responsibility, to apply a verbal remedy to the real-life heartsick pain you were experiencing?

DH: In the poems I do talk about taking care of her. She knew it; there was no doubt in her mind that I was taking care of her, but perhaps I need to say so to the world.

SR: Let me ask you a question about your sense of time. In one of your books that was always my favorite, *The One Day*, you talk a lot about this altered sense of time; time is portrayed as being quite fluid, expanding or compressing in response to our activity in the world. And the purest joy is to be wholly immersed in some act of labor, some *now*, to the point of where time seemingly disappears altogether. Here's a passage from the third section of that book:

> Here, among the thirty thousand days of a long life,
> a single day stands still: The sun shines, it is raining;
> we sleep, we make love, we plant a tree, we walk up and down

eating lunch: The day waits at the center when I reached out
to touch the face in the mirror, and never
touched glass, touched neither cheekbone nor eyelid,
touched galaxies instead and the void they hung on.

And there's a parallel to that expressed here in the new poems, though with
a shift in tone. There's the bleak compression in the poem "Without":

no spring no summer no autumn no winter
no rain no peony thunder no woodthrush
the book was a thousand pages without commas

Later, there are the lines that say,

The hour
we lived in, two decades
by the pond, has transformed
into a single unstoppable day,
gray in the dwelling place
of absence.

DH: Now it's transformed, changed because of Jane, yeah. I've also been
working on a poem which is sort of the fourth part of *The One Day*. A year
after Jane died, I went into mania for three months and then I plunged into
the worst depression of my life. I had seen Jane be as bad as I was, but I had
never been so bad. I had been up and down like everybody, a little more so
perhaps, but I went into mania and depression for the first time in my life.
I was not delusional but I'd sleep two hours and roar around like crazy for
twenty-two hours, and this went on for about three months. Then abject
despair, abject despair. At the onset of this abject despair, the movement
between mania and depression was a rapid cycling where I would go from
euphoria to despair to terrific, murderous anger, not directed toward anyone in particular. It was awful. It was just terrible. The murderous anger was
the worst. I read *The One Day* again—and the third part, which seems to
allow that people can be happy together, I hated, I really hated it. Because
it was a lie. Because somebody dies. [*Hall's words were coming slowly, as
though he were struggling with emotion.*] So I wrote at this time, a long time
ago now, of coming out of depression into anger. I wrote something, which
at the moment is called the "The Dead Day" but I think I may call it "Dead

Days," in which I'm repudiating that complacency. I'm saying that "day" that I lived in was an illusion, a complacency, and that really everything about human life is rotten. [Entitled "Kill the Day," this poem eventually appeared in *Gettysburg Review*.]

SR: Well, that's a lie too.

DH: Tell *the poet*. Don't tell me. [*Laughter.*] You know I'm not going to argue with you.

* * *

SR: I think maybe some of the questions I'm posing about *Without* seem to duel with you because I'm still viewing it as a literary document, on the outside as a reader. Your commentary reveals how the making of the poems affected who you were day by day. For example, when you talked about taking on Jane's characteristics I immediately thought about the last poem in the collection, "Weeds and Peonies." When you describe bringing in the flower—"One magnanimous blossom . . . "

DH: " . . . and float it in a glass bowl . . . "

SR: And that image not only recalls your wife, it also takes on a gardener's sense of time. Like the earlier Christ child image, we see a thing that is born to die, yet its beauty is what reaches us.

DH: They "lean their vast heads westward / as if they might topple. Some topple." That was actually the first poem I wrote after Jane died. I put it last. It was Ellen Voight, the structure genius, who suggested that. She was absolutely right. It is not a letter, but it ends the letters. It puts a cap on it. Having all the letters addressed to her, this one—which has a lyric structure, not a letter structure—provides a kind of cap to end the poem. It could've led into it, I mean, I think I originally put it chronologically, then ended with "Letter After a Year"—"not seeing it fade." But I think that this is better because it's less crepuscular than the "fading" ending. I think it's a strong poem, and it's a whole and coherent poem. The letter poems are coherent finally but they appear to wander, and in a sense you need them all rather than one of them. And "Weeds and Peonies" is a single poem. It provides a coda—I keep saying cap, coda might do. . . . Of course, I did change a few words in it after I knew it was going to be at the end. An early draft was in the *New York Times* at the end of '95. The *New York Times Magazine*, in the final issue of the year, writes about the notable dead of the previous year. I was thrilled when they called me up and asked if I could write something about Jane. Could I write a poem? Well, I couldn't sit down and write one, but I had been writing poems about Jane. And I had parts of "Letter with No Address" at that point, but "Weeds," a slightly earlier version, was, I knew, complete enough. I knew I would make it better, but I knew it wasn't bad. So I printed it there and it was printed on Sunday, December 31st, 1995, the year she died.

SR: Let me ask you two more questions.

DH: Absolutely.

SR: There are two questions I thought of immediately when I knew we'd have this chance to talk. But I didn't know if it was fair to ask them—until I read the manuscript and saw the ways you'd already stretched the boundaries. The first question is about place and the second is about the place you've built within your work—books, poems, and stories. We've come to see your life as wholly enmeshed in this place, this farm house. In one of the poems here, you describe attending to your mother's belongings after her death, "preserving / things she had cherished—and in late years dreaded / might go for a nickel at a sale on the lawn." It's both wonderful and somewhat frightening to think of how much of ourselves we invest in mere things, and then to imagine them without us. But then, in another poem, you contemplate setting a fire and burning Eagle Pond to the ground.

DH: Right, I mentioned that. Partly because I didn't want everything dispersed. I didn't say anything to my children, and finally they realized it and got together and said they wanted to keep the house after my death. I know they mean that, and yet it could become financially impossible and so on. There are one or two people who want to keep it as a trust. If my grandchildren want to live here, fine. Otherwise maybe it could be used for artists or something like that. But I don't know where the money would come from to keep up a trust. There might be answers to that too. The notion of it being a museum, as it were, like the Frost place—that's not a pleasant notion. My favorite notion would be that a grandchild, or great-grandchild or great-great-grandchild might continue to live here in the house where Jane and I lived—in the house where my grandparents and great-grandparents lived—and really *live* here. But I cannot control that. I can just imagine that and hope for it. The notion of it being stripped and auctioned off is, of course, a bitter and horrifying notion, but I can't control anything.

Whatever I can control, in the sense of working out contingencies for what to do with the books, the objects, and the photographs, I will do. My children can keep them as long as they want for the grandchildren. Otherwise, UNH has what it wants because UNH has my archives. These are practical matters I work out with my lawyer. I haven't yet done a new estate and will, so I will have to do something new. So I have to do something new. But it requires the cooperation of a lot of different people, all of whom are very busy and it's hard to get going. This was my grandparents' place, it became Jane's and my place; and it's still the old place with the "string too short to be saved" objects around here. Many of my grandchildren are fascinated by it. When my grandchildren come here—they are five, five, seven, nine, nine (that means there're five of them)—they love to explore and see things and so on: "Let's go upstairs!" I take them up to the barn—I've just had the place cleaned out and fixed up—and we explore that. They're not living here the way I did in the summers, but they're enjoying it and knowing about it and hearing stories about it.

The place is very important to me. I can go away from it longer now. I take on more travel than I would if Jane was here because I really didn't like to leave her very much. But I don't want to move somewhere else. It would be very hard to think of another woman moving in here, in Jane's shadow— it would be hard for another woman; I don't mean hard for me to accept.

SR: It would not be a conflict?

DH: Well, I haven't found a woman. I think I really would like to live here with a woman in monogamy and quiet. When I start working on the job description, it sounds a hell of a lot like Jane. It's not as if I'm trying to duplicate her. That's highly unlikely. I know it would be hard on a woman who was a poet, but even on a woman who's not a poet. When I go out with a woman, people will tend to say to her, "Are you a writer? Are you a poet?" That is a complication. And there's the gravestone with my name on it with Jane's. I'm not advertising for a wife. But I am lonely. And I'm lonely for the female. And I *have* many female guests—I'm not speaking of lovers only— old friends and so on, and it's nice to have them come here; it would be nice to live with someone. But I am in my seventieth year; I'm sixty-nine years old. I'm vigorous now and healthy, but how long will I be? And what am I asking someone to put up with?

SR: You've talked about this place as almost a spiritual entity, and I can understand your wish that some grandchild could eventually be like the child you were and take emotional ownership of this house. But, as you said, those decisions aren't of your making. I wonder now whether you think of your own work—maybe even your poems and Jane's together—as another kind of ground, a tangible place? And do you have a hope for what will become of that place and who will visit there in the future?

DH: I hope for it. I feel clearer certainly about the value of Jane's. I also know, with my brain, that I don't know anything about what is going to happen. I've seen literary reputations rise and fall. *Otherwise* sold twenty thousand hardback in the first year; it's remarkable, and there's a remarkable amount of tribute to her since she died. That does not mean that she's going to be read in a hundred years. When I look at the poems, I find it hard to believe they won't remain. I read them aloud to crowds, I read them to myself, I read them to my friends. They seem, if anything, better than they did before she died. From the time of, say the mid-eighties, when she was writing the best of the poems in *The Boat of Quiet Hours*, I have admired her enormously. We were very careful not to compare each other. We didn't like it when other people compared us. When we were first married, she got condescended to—"Isn't it nice that you write poems too." Later on there'd be people who would tell us, when we were together, that she was better than I was. That was sexist too because it was "man bites dog"—"Isn't it weird: she's better than you are, the woman is better than the man, the younger better than the older." She didn't like that, either. Even after her death I don't like to make comparisons. I know that, if you put a gun to my head, I would think I like her poems more than my own. But I also would laugh at anybody who said that, because how the hell would you know? You don't know. I would love to have the poems, as it were, walk hand and hand into the sunset and be together and terrific, and people loving them together.

And I think sometime someone would like to make a book of our work together, write a book about us together, and so on—I don't want it to happen now. If somebody came to me and wanted to write some joint biography or something like that, I think I would run and hide because I wouldn't be able to stand any sentence of it. I'd know ahead of time, no matter what the sentence was, I wouldn't stand it. So let it be after I'm dead and gone!

But I do think of these things. I think this is apropos your question. That's a pleasant thought that we would be remembered together, preserved together, as writers, as makers of poems, and that our poems were thought of in conjunction with each other. There're no parallels; there's Robert Browning, Elizabeth Browning, husband and wife both poets, and we stop there. Sylvia Plath and Ted Hughes—no, it's not quite a good example. Of course there are many poet couples now because of the plethora of poets in the United States, people getting together, meeting each other in MFA programs. We did very well at avoiding bad feeling. One thing, we were different generations—so her first book came out when my sixth book came out. We weren't head on in competition. And we were very good at drawing boundaries. When two people read together, the first one is always the warm-up band. Sometimes with friends we'll flip a coin or draw straws to see who gets first, rather than "*outmodesty*-ing" each other or whatever. Janey and I just alternated. One night in September of '93—'93 was a wonderful year, the last year of health—we read in Trivandrum on the southern tip of India on a Friday night, and the next Monday we read in Hanover, New Hampshire, totally exhausted—and we remembered who had started the reading in Trivandrum!

That's just a little example of the boundary-setting. And we had rooms on the opposite corners of the house. We would knock on each others' doors, not to interrupt each other. And we knew absolutely that we could leave manuscripts around on tables—and it would not be looked at without the invitation of the other. I would *never* read a poem of hers without her asking me to, or any other piece of print . . . I think to live with each other all day long and to do the same thing, as it were, we really needed to be careful.

SR: I think that was one of the vital dynamics of your life together, and I can't help but feel it's affected the work that's been written in this house, written about this landscape. But do you think of this word place as its own territory, something enduring beyond the lives of its makers?

DH: The trouble with thinking of it as a place—this would mean to say that something would remain. It's not that I'm modest. I've read literary history, I've been around a long time; I know that people who seem, at some point in their lives and even at the moment of their deaths, to be a permanent part of American literature—fifty years or thirty years later, are not read. I also know that a hundred years from now they might be read again! I can't say anything about my own work.

There are two books of mine that seem persistent; they're not my favorites among my work. One is *Ox-Cart Man*, the children's book, and another is *String Too Short to Be Saved*, my first book of prose. There are others that have their fan clubs, and there are some poems that get reprinted a lot—but I've known since I was in my late twenties that I would never know how good I was (or how bad I was). I also know that, as opposed to younger people, I translate the word *good* to mean "endurance." By good I mean the poem will be read two hundred years from now. That's a long time. The young, Generation X or something, [don't] think about that. When Shakespeare or Milton talked about immortality they meant lasting *forever*. Well, we can't think of that. But if I say two hundred years, that's just as good. . . . Henry Moore was wonderful to hang around—I wrote about him. Every time he began a sculpture, he wanted it to be better than Michelangelo. Every time he finished he knew that he had failed—but maybe the next one would be. There's something like this in Yeats too. Yeats was constantly saying, "Everything I've written is no good, but *now* I'm going to write what's good!"

I don't feel that way about the work I'm writing right now, but I would still hope a year from now I might. There are times when I think that what I'm writing right now, what I'm working on right now, as with *Without*, might be the best I've ever done. One thing that's really true for a writer, for every writer I know—when you want to write well, you really want to write well *now*; you're not interested in *having* written well, you know? Oh yeah, that was twenty years ago, terrific, thanks a lot. What have I done for myself lately? [*Laughter.*]

SR: I hope you realize, from your audience's reactions when you read these poems, you're achieving some of those precious *nows*.

DH: It's good, the responses. But there are ways to discount praise. I tend to discount it—when I get praised, when I win a prize, I find ways to discount it—and I think that's probably more healthy than not. If you start to believe your good reviews, you're dead already. You can be pleased and feel fine for a moment—but then get skeptical and get back to work. Get back to work.

It's about Orgasm; It's Not about a Musk Ox: Interview with Former US Poet Laureate Donald Hall

Anne Loecher / 2012

From *Numéro Cinq* (online magazine), vol. 3, no. 11, November 2012. Reprinted by permission of Anne Loecher. Accessed January 2018 at http://numerocinqmagazine.com/2012/11/12/its -about-orgasm-its-not-about-a-musk-ox-interview-with-donald-hall-anne-loecher/.

On an early afternoon in early May I arrived at Eagle Pond Farm in Wilmot, New Hampshire, to interview Donald Hall. Hall, born in 1928 in New Haven, Connecticut, and raised in suburban Hamden, summered at Eagle Pond, home of his maternal grandparents and place of his mother's upbringing. Eagle Pond operated as a farm for generations, up until his grandparents' time. Rows of bright daffodils lined the driveway, planted there by Hall's late wife, the poet Jane Kenyon, daffodils being among her favorites.

Hall published his first poem at age sixteen, graduated from Harvard in 1951 and earned a B.Litt. degree from the University of Oxford in 1953. He subsequently served fellowships at Stanford and Harvard, and in 1958 began his teaching career at the University of Michigan, where he met Kenyon, who was a student of his.

In 1975, Hall left his tenured position at Michigan with Kenyon so both could dedicate themselves to writing full-time. After nearly twenty years together on the farm, Kenyon was diagnosed with leukemia, and died in 1995. Hall has remained at Eagle Pond since, continuing to write.

Across his writing career, Hall has published numerous books of poetry, prose, literary essays, sportswriting, and children's fiction, and amassed a lengthy list of honors and awards including the Lamont Poetry Prize, the Edna St. Vincent Millay Award, two Guggenheim fellowships (1963–64, 1972–73), the Caldecott Award (1980), the Sarah Josepha Hale Award (1983),

Poet Laureate of New Hampshire (1984–89), the Lenore Marshall Poetry Prize (1987), the National Book Critics Circle Award for Poetry (1988), the National Book Critics Circle Award (1989), the Los Angeles Times Book Prize in poetry (1989), and the Poetry Society of America's Robert Frost Silver Medal (1990). He has been nominated for the National Book Award on three separate occasions (1956, 1979, and 1993), the Ruth Lilly Poetry Prize for lifetime achievement (1994) and appointed US Library of Congress Poet Laureate (2006). Most recently, Hall was awarded the National Medal of Arts by President Barack Obama for 2010. Writing in a pre-interview e-mail that he might tire out during our chat ("If there is one thing I'm constantly aware of—it is that I am old!"), Hall was energetic and animated as we discussed the topics of posterity, reputation, and the conclusion of his poetry writing career.

Anne Loecher: I've been considering the careers of several poets who have drifted in and out of popularity. I wanted to ask you about posterity, obscurity, popularity, and how you feel about it with regard to your own work and reputation.

Donald Hall: I have seen so many people become famous, and disappear. If I live to be 300, I'll see some of them come back. I mentioned Archie MacLeish, who was my teacher. I have doubt that Archie will come back, although he won three Pulitzers.

There were famous young poets when I was at college—Wilbur, Lowell, and Roethke. Dick Wilbur is alive at ninety-one, and in January he had a wonderful poem in the *New Yorker*.

I wrote Dick about the prosody of his poem. The second line has a caesura, after two syllables, the second after four syllables, then after six syllables, after eight syllables. I asked how many people would recognize that metric.

But, there's William J. Smith, who is older than Dick and lives in the same town as Dick. Back around 1950, Smith was famous as a poet. I don't think I've heard his name out loud since 1970.

Have you ever looked in the list of Pulitzer winners? I think they begin in 1932 or so. See how many names you recognize. There are many I don't recognize, and you won't recognize because of your youth.

AL: I'm not so youthful!

DH: Reputations go up and down.

AL: You've talked about *The Back Chamber* being your last collection of poetry. Did you know it would be, as you were writing it?

DH: Toward the end of the volume, the last two poems that I started for it both began in 2008. I did well over a hundred drafts, and I realized that this was the end. I felt it coming.

AL: *The Back Chamber* does not hold back from addressing sexuality, alongside aging.

DH: Poetry is sex. And the engine of poetry is the mouth. Not the eye, not the ear. The ear and the eye are perfectly fine, but poetry originates in the mouth. Obviously the mouth is used in sex, beginning with the kiss.

The spirit that infuses me in reading a poet of beautiful sounds, like Keats, is sexual feeling. My poems had a lot of personal sexual feeling well into my seventies, but then I think the testosterone diminished. I felt the horniness going away, for two or three years. I rubbed testosterone into my chest, and it came back for awhile. That's when I worked on later poems. But the cream diminished in its powers so I stopped.

There was an early poem that Janey [Kenyon] always liked—"The Long River." I wrote it when she was eight years old. It's the first poem I ever wrote which began without any notion of where it was going to go.

The Long River

The musk ox smells
in his long head
my boat coming. When
I feel him there,
intent, heavy,

the oars make wings
in the white night,
and deep woods are close
on either side
where trees darken.

I rode past towns
in their black sleep
to come here. I passed
the northern grass
and cold mountains.

The musk ox moves
when the boat stops,
in hard thickets. Now
the wood is dark
with old pleasures.

It's about orgasm. It's not about a musk ox. But musk ox is there because it is "SK, KS". Actually, there's a kind of meter to this poem, which
I've never used elsewhere. In English verse, you're counting volume when
you're talking about stress, or you're talking about greater volume. "Con-
tent" is iambic, and "*con*-tent" is trochaic. But in English, rather than Greek
verse, which the Latins learned to imitate, it was the length of the vowel, not
the length of the syllable you counted. In this one, it's—short, long, long,
long/ short, short, long, long/ short, long, long, short, long/ and, short, long,
short, long/ and then short, long, long, short.

There are a few lines when it doesn't really work. I first had "the musk ox
in his long head" and I was captivated, and kept going. And toward the end,
working on it, or even after I'd finished it, I figured out what it was about.
People have not used a sexual word to describe it, but found it sensual.

AL: Was that the first experience you had of moving through a poem
without knowing what it was really going to be about?

DH: When I wrote a poem in my early twenties, I had to know what I
was writing about before I started. Stupid: one of the poems from that time
came from a definite idea, and it's there. What the poem's really about is
something I never understood for years. Five years after I wrote it, somebody wrote an article about me, and explained to me what I really meant.
It's called "The Sleeping Giant," which is the name of a hill, near where I
grew up in Connecticut. I had the thought, that if a little kid believed it really was a sleeping giant, it would be pretty scary. Then he'd grow up and
know it wasn't. It was a poem, I thought in my head, about illusion and
reality.

The Sleeping Giant (A Hill, So Named, in Hamden, Connecticut)

The whole day long, under the walking sun
That poised an eye on me from its high floor,
Holding my toy beside the clapboard house
I looked for him, the summer I was four.

I was afraid the waking arm would break
From the loose earth and rub against his eyes
A fist of trees, and the whole country tremble
In the exultant labor of his rise;

Then he with giant steps in the small streets
Would stagger, cutting off the sky, to seize
The roofs from house and home because we had
Covered his shape with dirt and planted trees;

And then kneel down and rip with fingernails
A trench to pour the enemy Atlantic
Into our basin, and the water rush,
With the streets full and all the voices frantic.

That was the summer I expected him.
Later the high and watchful sun instead
Walked low behind the house, and school began,
And winter pulled a sheet over his head.

People reading the poem in the *New Yorker* liked it best among my poems. I was jealous for my other poems. Then someone wrote an essay, saying that I had written many poems about fathers and sons, but the best one was "The Sleeping Giant." It had not occurred to me. It was classically Freudian. When you are a baby, an enormous figure stands over you, not handing you a breast. It's scary because it's big. When I read the essay, I was stunned, and I agreed. I hadn't known what I was writing about. I think that the people who preferred it to other poems didn't know what it was about any more than I did. It communicated. It's mysterious, how you can communicate by images, to another person. You can't do it on purpose.

But, on purpose, you can write something in which you don't know what's happening. You can always cross out and throw it away. But that part of poetry—the part where you write things down, that feel right, but you don't know why they're right—left me as I got older. I was about eighty. As I said, it's testosterone. (I tell that to a lot of people, and they want to look away.)

AL: I understand that. I write about loss, but I wonder, as I say that, what I would find within my poems if I looked more closely?

DH: A great deal of poetry is about loss, love, and death. Death is loss. My poetry has been called elegiac. I can be praising the old farm life, but then something is gone. The praise is love, the elegy is less, in the same poem.

AL: Regarding the issue of posterity, again, in your new poem "Poetry and Ambition" from *The Back Chamber*, there's a line " . . . If no one will ever read him again, what the fuck?'"

DH: Nobody will ever know about future reputation. I began writing very young, with ambition. I certainly wanted to be a great poet. In my day, or my generation, there were so many of us. At Harvard, weirdly enough, I knew Adrienne Rich. We double dated. We got to be good friends, later, not at that time. Robert Bly, John Ashbery, Frank O'Hara, Kenneth Koch; I'm missing some. We had the notion—and I wrote of it in an essay called "Poetry and Ambition"—that there was no point in writing unless you were going to be a great poet. It took me some time before I realized that nobody ever knows how they will seem in the future.

Ambition begins when you want to publish a poem in a magazine. Well, I did that when I was sixteen. And then, you wish that you could be published in the *New Yorker*. Then, you want a book. Then you want a second book, then you want a selected poems. It could certainly all be called careerism. It can also be called ambition, and an eagerness to get better.

My father was the elder son of a self-made man who went only through the fifth grade, and worked for ten cents an hour, then was successful with his dairy business. And my father, being the elder son, could never do anything right. He was beaten down his whole life, which was short. He could never do anything right, and he was discouraged.

My mother came from this place—New Hampshire, where I live. In rural places, women worked as many hours a day as men did. Good God, my grandmother made soap. She churned butter. There was Monday washing, Tuesday drying, Wednesday baking. And at night time—do you see there, in the middle of the ceiling? In every room, there are lights in the middle of the ceiling. Do you know why? There would be a table in the middle of the room, and a great, big kerosene lamp, and the whole family would be around it at night, the single source of light. My grandfather would read books, not good ones, but books. And as the women talked, they were darning socks, they were tatting, or knitting. They never stopped. That was the way people lived.

So my mother then moved in 1927 to the Connecticut suburbs, where women didn't work. No married woman was allowed to work. She wanted to "pass." Her New Hampshire accent stayed with her—she said "Coker Coler." She wanted to be a suburban wife, like everybody else, she grew up the oldest sister of three girls. She was the oldest sister to the universe. She was full of ambition. None of it had anywhere to go. So it went to me.

I was an only child. She was ambitious for me, and always pushing. When I started sending poems to magazines at fourteen, they would come back with printed slips. My mother would say, "Oh, there's a rejection today, Donnie." That was the beginning of my career.

When my first book came out, it was reviewed everywhere, instantly, reviews that praised it. And it's no good. There are two poems in that book, one called "My Son My Executioner" and "The Sleeping Giant" which I told you about. After the first reviews of praise, there was a second wave, responding to the first wave, that tended to be negative. Some of the negative reviews were certainly right, and they had me walking up and down.

All through my life I have written and published poems which I thought were good and which turned out to be terrible. And it's hard to believe why I thought they were good at all. Some have held up for me.

AL: Is it possible that it's a matter of your tastes having changed?

DH: Oh, it's also being dumb about your stuff! There was one time I remember sending poems to Alice Quinn, who was the editor at the *New Yorker*. I had one poem that I was afraid was no good, and I almost did not send it to her. I decided at the last minute—what did I know? It's called "Affirmation." She took it, and published it about a week later. And people all over the country wrote me about it and told me they'd cut it out and put in on their refrigerators, and so on.

AL: What do you think of that poem now?

DH: I was kind of shocked, and convinced that it must be some good. I think that there are two opinions about the ending of it. I thought that one direction was obvious. And then most people took it the opposite of what I thought I'd said. And so many people took it the opposite of what I thought, that I decided it must have been one of those occasions where I was writing with the wrong idea of what I was writing.

It begins: "To grow old is to lose everything."

I don't think I was seventy when I wrote that. I'm eighty-three! It's funny to read. What did I know?

Affirmation

To grow old is to lose everything.
Aging, everybody knows it.
Even when we are young,

we glimpse it sometimes, and nod our heads
when a grandfather dies.
Then we row for years on the midsummer
pond, ignorant and content. But a marriage,
that began without harm, scatters
into debris on the shore,
and a friend from school drops
cold on a rocky strand.
If a new love carries us
past middle age, our wife will die
at her strongest and most beautiful.
New women come and go. All go.
The pretty lover who announces
that she is temporary
is temporary. The bold woman,
middle-aged against our old age,
sinks under an anxiety she cannot withstand.
Another friend of decades estranges himself
in words that pollute thirty years.
Let us stifle under mud at the pond's edge
and affirm that it is fitting
and delicious to lose everything.

When I wrote it, I thought when I said, "it is fitting and delicious to lose everything" that my sarcasm was obvious, and that it was all in the one direction, of a lamentation. And then I discovered that people took the word "affirm" as a positive, the reversal of what I thought I had said.

AL: That's how I understood it. I didn't understand it as sarcastic at all. So, if you can never know, does it also mean you can never know if your poem is good?

DH: I guess I'm saying so. A friend wrote me about it, believing "affirmation" as positive, and telling me I was all wrong, I was sentimental, to be affirmative, because really, only the negative was true. That's really what I thought I was writing, and that's why I thought it wasn't good. Who knows?

AL: You make some pretty striking points about aging in your recent essay "Out the Window."

DH: In almost any poem that I care for, there has to be a contradiction. If there's "north" in the poem, there has to be "south" in the poem, or it's no good. Oppositions. This was a snowy winter, and I kept sitting in this chair, looking out at the birds. I was writing about looking, thinking ahead to spring and the flowers, and it was all very lyrical. I thought: this essay doesn't have any counter-motion in it, any north to go with its south. Then I went to Washington, and that fucker said, "Did we have a nice din-din?" I'm so grateful to the idiot. It's what I needed. That condescension is totally other than the pleasant lyricism of looking out the window. And I think it made the essay. People say—did you bop him? I didn't get mad. I was grateful. To Linda he says "Did you have a good lunch?" and he leans down to me and says "Did we have a nice din-din?"

AL: Are you working on more essays now?

DH: I'm going to do a book of essays. I've got a wonderful one I've just finished, I think, which is about smoking, when everybody quit. *Playboy* bought it.

The first essay in the book will be "Out the Window" which was all about being old. The others all will *include* aging. There's another one I'm trying to write about poetry readings, where I find it hard to climb up to the stage. I have to sit down when I read now.

AL: When I was driving up here, I noticed the stone fence, and the cemetery down the road. So beautiful. Are there any family members buried there?

DH: No. It is beautiful, this is Wilmot. That graveyard was the beginning of East Wilmot. They were going to build a church—I think it was Methodist—and they started their graveyard before they had built the church. But New Hampshire shrunk. The population was at its greatest about 1855. It went way down, and it's up again, but it's all southern commuters to Boston. Early, it was single farms, every quarter of a mile, and pasture land up the mountain. The population dwindled, and East Wilmot never happened. About a mile farther down, there's another graveyard, and on the right, there's another church, the South Danbury church. In the South Danbury graveyard, I have a great grandfather and great grandmother. He fought in the Civil War and died in 1927.

When Jane and I were first here, we loved our place so much that we knew we'd stay here forever and that's why we bought a graveyard plot. It was a positive, not a negative—love and death, this is where we'll be. She died right in there (motioning to the back bedroom), and I will die in the same bed. My kids and doctor know that.

Five miles the other way, there is another old cemetery right next to the road, where I have great-great-greats. A little farther there's a big cemetery, begun early in the nineteenth century, holding my great grandparents as well as Jane. There's Jane Kenyon, 1947–1995, and then Donald Hall, 1928–__, in a plot at the edge of the cemetery with the great trees above it.

Writing Naked: Donald Hall on Poetry and Metaphor in Journalism

Mike Pride / 2013

Former poet laureate Donald Hall talks to Mike Pride, Nieman Fellow '85, about what journalists can learn from poetry. From *Nieman Reports*, Spring 2013, reprinted by permission of the Nieman Foundation for Journalism. Recorded on March 29, 2013. Accessed at http://niemanreports.org/articles/writing-naked-donald-hall-on-poetry-and-metaphor-in-journalism/.

Donald Hall, former US poet laureate, has lived at Eagle Pond Farm, with its white clapboard farmhouse and weathered barn, in Wilmot, New Hampshire, since 1975. Hall grew up in the Connecticut suburbs but spent his summers at the farm haying, milking, and doing other chores with his grandfather. I got to know Don in 1978 after moving to New Hampshire, when I read *String Too Short to Be Saved*, his memoir of his summers here. The rural life has long been his muse. I started inviting Don to visit the paper I edited, the *Concord* (N.H.) *Monitor*, to talk to staff about poetry and place and journalism. Don has written poetry, essays, criticism, plays, short stories, a novel. You name it, he's done it, including journalism. He's written for *Sports Illustrated*, the *Ford Times*, *Yankee Magazine*, and many, many others. I now come up here about once a month, and Don and I go over to a place we call Blackwater Bill's to eat hot dogs. Don likes his hot dogs with the spicy mustard, and relish, and onions. We sat down at Eagle Pond Farm to talk about Don's work and the writer's craft. Edited excerpts follow. —Mike Pride.

Mike Pride: Do you still read the paper regularly?

Donald Hall: Yeah, I read two newspapers almost all my life. The *New Haven Register* and the *New Haven General Courier*. The *Courier* was the morning paper, the small, poor one. The *Register* was the big one. I moved to Ann Arbor, where I was a teacher at the University of Michigan, [and] read the *Ann Arbor News*, which was not very good. I added the *Detroit Free Press* to it, so I read two papers a day. Then I came up here, and it is the *Concord Monitor*, which is the local paper, and the *Boston Globe*. I should say I read the *Economist* also. The *Economist* is a *Time* magazine that happens to be good. There's a part of me that doesn't seem like the rest of me that wants to know what's happening everywhere. The *Economist* fills me in on the rest of the universe. I get the simple local news from my newspapers.

MP: You don't use the internet at all?

DH: I don't have a computer. I'm probably the last person on Route 4 not to have a computer. I had a fax machine, and everybody I was faxing turned out to be keeping their fax machine only because of me. That was the quickest I had. Everything has to be quick now. I still write a lot of letters and get away with it. I worry about the general speeding up of words in the world. I worry about the intelligent young people, students, for whom reading is too slow. All they want is a bit of information. They can get that very easily from Google. Certainly they can get entertainment through games, television, television on the internet, everything. Everything can be quick and sudden, delayed, or finished quickly.

MP: When I was an editor, I would tell my staff to try to write for the newspaper as though they were writing a letter to an intelligent friend. I'm not even sure that if I said that today to a newspaper staff, they would be able to understand the analogy or the comparison.

DH: A letter? What's that?

MP: For many years, you and I drove together down to Lippmann House and spoke with the Nieman Fellows about what a poet could teach journalists about writing. Why don't we start with one of our favorite subjects, the dead metaphor?

DH: Absolutely. All winter I read in the *Boston Globe* and probably in the *Monitor* about a "blanket of snow." Isn't that wonderful? It always annoys me, of course. There are words that are used in the headlines because they are short. But dead metaphors are something I notice all the time. You can kid yourself so easily. I have written a draft of a poem fifty times, sixty times, and see a gross dead metaphor in it. It's easy enough to do it.

I remember telling a girl over at Cornell one time that I never say "dart" for a person moving quickly because "dart" is English invented in pubs. A dart is an arrow and using that as a verb . . . it's like, "I was anchored to the spot" or "I was glued to the spot" means that a ship in a harbor and Elmer's glue are the same thing. Remember that, and maybe it will help you avoid a dead metaphor.

MP: From a practical standpoint, what you're really talking about is helping writers pick the more precise word, right?

DH: It is precise, because it's not something under the surface, another object. It's looking straight forward. There are people who say that everything in language is originally a metaphor, and I don't understand the thought, but I don't deny it. With prose that is full of dead metaphors, no character can get through. Everything has a veil between the utterance of the speaker and the perception of the reader, the listener. Somehow plainness is more intimate than the word "shrouded," the word "blanketed." A shroud is a shroud, and that's fine. A blanket is a blanket. I can write about it, but don't confuse it with an item that covers.

MP: In your poems often sound is a driving force. To what extent do you think that is applicable to prose in newswriting?

DH: I think sound has been for me the doorway into poetry, and by sound I particularly mean the repetition of long vowels more than anything else. It's always repetition, and repetition sometimes has a slight difference. I always say that I read not with my eyes and I hear not with my ears with poetry. I hear and see through my mouth, the mouth itself. Then a reaction to the sounds, it's kind of dreamy and intimate. It opens up (dead metaphor) the alleyway to the insides. This I particularly apply to poetry, and I think it is the chief difference. In poetry, we have the line break to organize the rhythm and sometimes to give emphasis.

Mix up long and short sentences. Mix up complex and compound and simple sentences. That's easy. It is a matter of rhythm of the dance. There is something bodily about the rhythm of a paragraph, and there is a rhythm within a paragraph. Someone like John McPhee can write four pages without needing a paragraph because he is so terrific on transitions. But he is quite apt to have a four-page paragraph and then a one-line paragraph. That could be wonderful. Newspapers can do that, too, but most newspapermen do not have time to write forty-two drafts of every piece.

The structure of a news story is a kind of form itself: the new news and the background afterwards and so on. An editorial writer is sort of freer to be wild and metaphoric than a news writer. The news writer, you know, the Jack Webb thing, "Nothing but the facts, ma'am." It has to feel like that, but there can still be adjustment in rhythm and the type of sentence to engage the aspects of the reader which do not have to do only with fact but with some bodily joy and pleasure.

MP: You recently stopped writing poetry. How did that happen?

DH: It happened gradually and I didn't know it was happening. Poems used to come in little meteor showers. I would begin three or four poems in two or three days. They'd come to me. I'd be sitting or I'd be driving and I'd pull over to the side of the road and write something down. Then it might not happen for six months, but I had four or five new poems to work on. Rarely, but occasionally, they would turn out to be the same poem. But they felt different. So that stopped, the meteor showers stopped coming.

I knew a lot about poetry and I had been working in it for years. I pushed; I didn't know how to stop. But in 2008, I began the last two poems I wrote and I worked on them a couple of years. But I knew, by that point, pretty certainly that this was the end of it. It had gone slowly. I had done it for sixty years. What am I complaining about?

I began to substitute prose for poetry. When I published a piece in the *New Yorker* called "Out the Window," I talked about getting old and I talked about not writing poetry anymore. Many people wrote me and said, "It is poetry." If you call something poetry to praise it, that's fine, but it's not a poem. It's something else again. It works by the paragraph, within the paragraph by types of sentences. But certainly by rhythm; God, rhythm is utterly important to prose.

I read whole books of prose that are intelligent and full of fact and so on and never does the author ever seem interested in writing anything that's beautiful or that's balanced or rhythmic. It's hard for me to finish those books, intelligent and informing as they may be.

MP: But without beautiful writing.

I love the writing, but I love the rewriting, too. In fact, rewriting is much more fun than writing and that was always true with poems or everything, because the first draft always has so much wrong with it. That's one reason I admire a good newspaper. I cannot imagine being able to do it steadily, completely and finished. If I had been [a newspaper journalist], I probably could have learned how to do it, but it's very distant now from the way I've worked.

MP: What are your writing habits now?

DH: I change individual words, get more precise. One thing that's kind of common is that any verb-adverb combination can be done better with a more exact verb. I take out adjectives. So many times, I qualify. I say, "Some time, I don't remember when," and all you have to say is, "Once something happened" or something. You're always cutting, very seldom adding. But sometimes you realize that you left out something important, and you put it in.

MP: Talk a little bit about "Out the Window," published last year in the *New Yorker*.

DH: One of my dogmas, a lot of people's dogma, is that everything has to have a counter-motion within it. I wrote about looking out the window, sitting passively watching the snow against the barn, loving the barn and watching it. Then I went into the other seasons I could see out the window. It was all sort of one tone, a kind of old man's love of where he lived and what in his diminished way he could enjoy without any sense of loss. I was almost finished with it at one point, and then this wonderful thing happened.

I went to Washington with Linda [his longtime companion], and we went to the various museums. In the National Gallery, there was a Henry Moore carving. I had written a book about Henry Moore. A guide came out and said, "That's Henry Moore, and there's more of them here and there." Thank you.

An hour or two later, we had lunch; this is the National Gallery. When we came out from lunch, the same guy was there. My legs have no balance, and Linda was pushing me in a wheelchair. The same guy asked Linda, "Did you like your lunch?" And Linda said, yes. Then he bent down to me in the wheelchair, stuck his finger out, waggled it, and then he got a hideous grin and said, "Did we have a good din-din?"

And people said, "Did you pop him?" No! We were just sort of amazed and walked away without saying anything more. But then, I thought it was very funny. Because I was in a wheelchair I obviously had Alzheimer's, and it made me think of little pieces of condescension. I thought about this, but especially the story about the guard gave me the counter-motion: "So, you like being old!" or whatever people who condescend to you do.

I got tons of mail about that essay, and people said it's really poetry. But a lot of them talked about the museum guard, and they were sort of indignant, "Why didn't you pop him?" and so on.

MP: You have said that you are revising your essays a great deal more now. What are you looking for in a revision?

DH: I know that when I wrote *String Too Short to Be Saved*, it was soft and luxuriant to remember, and I had room for some images that I remember with pleasure, like "seeing a whole forest of rock maple trees knocked down by one blast of the hurricane, like combed hair." I like that. But many years later, when I wrote *Seasons at Eagle Pond*, a book of essays about life at the farm, my prose had become much more conscious of itself, and sort of showy. I think it takes so much longer, probably, not because of its nature, but because my energy is less, and maybe my imagination needs to go over a set of words many times to get it right. But I don't mind. I like it a lot, and I dream up new things. Some of them are funny. At the beginning, my poems had nothing to do with me, almost all of them. As my life has gone on, one thing I've said is I began writing fully clothed and I took off my clothes bit by bit. Now I'm writing naked.

Poetry, Aging, and Loss:
An Interview with Donald Hall

John Martin-Joy, MD / 2015

Conducted and edited by mail between June and November 2015. From *TriQuarterly* (online). Posted in "The Latest Word" section, September 13, 2016. Reprinted by permission of John Martin-Joy. Available at https://www.triquarterly.org/node/273721.

Donald Hall, former poet laureate of the United States, is the author of *Without, The Painted Bed*, and many other books of poetry. He has won many awards, including the National Medal of Arts and the Robert Frost Medal, and is a member of the American Academy of Arts and Letters. Jane Kenyon was the author of *Otherwise* and *Let Evening Come*; she won the 1994 PEN/Voelcker Award for poetry.

Hall gave up a tenured professorship at the University of Michigan in order to move to Wilmot, New Hampshire, where he and Jane Kenyon lived and wrote for many years—and where he still lives. In this interview, Hall discusses his recent collections *Selected Poems* and *Essays After Eighty*; his experience of aging; his creative and intimate life with Jane Kenyon; his grief over her untimely death of leukemia; and their poetry.

This interview began as an exchange of letters; it has been edited for publication.

Acknowledgments: The interviewer thanks Teresa Gorman for her help in typing portions of the interview. The original Hall letters on which the interview is based are in the archives of the Boston Psychoanalytic Society and Institute (BPSI) in Newton, Massachusetts.

John Martin-Joy: In your most recent essay collection, *Essays After Eighty*, you call old age a "ceremony of losses." If I can start with a shrink-like question, what did you mean by that?

Donald Hall: I chose *ceremony* partly because I want to make the progress of old age a positive thing, for me anyway. Also because its progression is more or less orderly.

JMJ: You lost Jane Kenyon in 1995, and you yourself survived cancer. Yet at eighty-seven, the books keep coming.

DH: Poems stopped, because poems are erotic. The sound and density of poems require more testosterone. But without writing, my life would be empty. When I can write, it is a joy to be alive, and I can look forward to writing more. Now I need a nap after writing much, but that does not stop the necessity. I continue.

JMJ: Your new *Selected Poems* is out now. What does it include?

DH: It contains the poems that I feel best about, and also represents phases of my life. It is short; less is more. I have done three selections before, and the last one (ten years ago) was outrageously long.

■ ■ ■

JMJ: You and Jane Kenyon have written more powerfully than anyone else I know about the experience of grief and intense loss—and of depression. May we talk about her experiences, and yours?

DH: I'm happy to speak of our experiences of grief and loss—and of depression.

JMJ: Poetry was a passion and a calling for each of you, starting early. Did depression find you and Jane early as well, or did it evolve in different ways for each of you?

DH: I think that Jane was depressive from childhood on, but it was a long time before she realized that and sought help in calming it. I'm not sure that I was depressive, really, ever. Certainly, I became depressed, at Jane's death, and could write about nothing else for many years, and screamed and yelled, and had many thoughts of violence—but I believe this was reactive.

Jane had depression with no apparent cause. I believe I was hypomanic. I rose early and took care of things, brought Jane coffee in bed. She went to sleep early and woke up late. As she walked the dog, I was already writing. It took her a while to get upstairs and get to work. Sometimes she was so depressed that she could not work—and neither she nor I thought that it was in response to anything in her world. She felt that her father was also depressive.

I remember the first time she went over the cliff. (Much of the time, she was mildly depressed. I speak of something more extreme.) We had supper at a diner in Bristol, then drove home. In the car she wept. At home she threw herself on the sofa, and depression covered her like a blanket. She told me, "It's not your fault, Perkins!" (My pet name.) She could not bear to have me touch her. I wanted to rub her head or anything.

Twice in her depressions she used doctors—a general practitioner and a psychiatrist—to tell me that it was not my fault! Obviously, she instructed them. They stood and made a short speech to me. I had never thought that it was my fault!

JMJ: How difficult was it for her to get help?

DH: When Jane and I first lived together in Ann Arbor, she wanted psychiatric help. I asked a friend who was a psychiatrist, and it was delicate, because my ex-wife Kirby was a therapist, I believe a very good one. Jane ended up seeing a therapist from the academic specialty at University of Michigan, clinical psychology. They explored, they explored. Jane felt better. I'm not sure the word *depression* had yet been used.

After depression struck so painfully here in New Hampshire, our general practitioner consulted a psychiatrist at Dartmouth-Hitchcock Medical Center, Dr. Charles Solow, and eventually Jane went to him. He was able to provide antidepressants, but he was also a *talker*. He was supportive rather than analytic, but he was empathetic and intelligent. He helped her a lot. Sometimes a new chemical would keep her steady for quite a while, maybe mildly depressed but not acutely. Then she would need to increase the dosage until they could increase it no more. But there were many times when a chemical, or class of chemicals like the Prozac bunch, would not seem to touch her.

JMJ: When I teach medical students about depression, I try to convey something about the experience itself. I've found nothing that connects more powerfully with students than Jane's "Having It Out with Melancholy" and "Back."

DH: Jane wrote many poems about depression or at least out of depression, and gradually worked toward doing the Big One, "Having It Out with Melancholy." It was difficult for Jane to face her illness head on, in that poem, and so extensively. She had that figure of depression raping her. "Having It Out with Melancholy" was the hardest poem for her to write.

Incidentally, "Back" was originally the last poem in the big poem. She sent the big poem to Alice Quinn at the *New Yorker*, and Alice accepted

"Back" for the magazine, appearing not to understand that it was part of a sequence. I suspected that Jane would perhaps have withdrawn it from the *New Yorker*, but as it happened she wrote a different ending, which was perfection, so that "Back" became a separate poem.

JMJ: It might be a cliché to call writing of this intensity therapeutic, yet it has meant so much to so many people who suffer from depression. Did Jane ever speak about what this poem meant to her?

DH: Jane first read her long poem at the Frost Place in Franconia, New Hampshire, one of Frost's summer houses. After she finished it, there was a great line of people who needed to talk to her—depressives, people from the families of depressives. She wept when she read it.

JMJ: There is a point in the poem where she conveys something like absolute bleakness:

A piece of burned meat
wears my clothes, speaks
in my voice, dispatches obligations
haltingly, or not at all.
It is tired of trying
to be stouthearted, tired
beyond measure.

I'm just stunned by that passage whenever I read it. Somehow, a vibrant, creative person has shriveled to a thing, an impersonation—not a person but an "it." Yet there is a part of her that is able to observe it all, almost clinically.

DH: I'm devoured by that section.

JMJ: The passage seems so simple and direct, so heart-rending, that it's easy to overlook how the poetry actually works.

DH: Notice how "A piece of burned meat" could be hamburger left on the stove, but the enjambment into "wears my clothes" works by careful surprise. Note the line breaks in general. Note the assonance of "trying" and "tired."

JMJ: In "Back," she depicts what seems to be an unexpected remission. All at once the poet's self begins to come back:

We try a new drug, a new combination
of drugs, and suddenly
I fall into my life again . . .

I can find my way back. I know
I will recognize the store
where I used to buy milk and gas.

I remember the house and barn,
the rake, the blue cups and plates,
The Russian novels I loved so much,

and the black silk nightgown
that he once thrust
into the toe of my Christmas stocking.

JMJ: That last stanza always catches me off guard. Many of us doctors are uncomfortable talking about sex, so we never learn just how devastating depression can be for our patients' love lives—and how joyful it is when sexual interest returns.

DH: When she was acutely depressed, there was nothing. When she was mildly depressed, orgasm gave her immediate excitement and energy. Afterwards, I would want to cuddle. She would run upstairs to her study in order to work on some poems!

The ending of the poem has something amusing. Every year at Christmas I would put something sexy at the bottom of her stocking. This time it was not a "black silk nightgown." That was not lewd enough! This time it was a teddy—obviously erotic, something in which a girl might strut to arouse her boyfriend. It was sexy and it was comical. When she wrote the poem, she knew the name of the garment—but she was embarrassed to use it. She used something a bit more classy.

JMJ: Had Jane recovered from her depression by 1994?

DH: Jane had not recovered by 1994. She never had, entirely, and she never would. But it was remarkable—she noticed it as much as I did—that in the great pain of her treatment for leukemia, fifteen months of pain and the knowledge that death was more probable than life, she was not deeply depressed. She was hardly happy. There was one time, maybe two weeks, when she was flat-out depressed, as much as she had ever been. The Hutchinson Research Center in Seattle, the bone-marrow place, had a psychiatrist who treated her, and it seemed to help.

On another occasion in Seattle she had a psychotic episode, probably the result of a medication. It began when she was not in the hospital but back in the apartment with me for a bit, and decided one day that I was dying of a heart attack. I merely had vertigo. The phone rang from the clinic, and she told the nurse that I was dying. In minutes, the medics came roaring in. I asked them to give me a quick electrocardiogram, and she simmered down.

The next day she was frantic. We went to the clinic. Suddenly she fell and could not use her legs. The nurses put her into a psychiatric section of the hospital, and she kept muttering depressed but demented thoughts. I offered to stay with her, but she sent me away. When I came back in the morning, it was terrible. She had been awake all night, and had convinced herself that she had no leukemia, that she was a malingerer, that the insurance company would find out and take our house away—and she continually said that she was "wicked." She was, of course, miserable in her conviction. The psychiatrist gave her two pills. Haldol? She slept for two or three hours and woke up sane.

Early in April 1995 after one of her weekly bits of blood work, our oncologist and her head assistant took us into a small room and told us that Jane would die. I had a million questions, panic. Jane only said, "Can I die at home?" We had eleven days, and nothing I could tell you would surprise you.

■ ■ ■

JMJ: Your book *Without* is powerful and is one of my favorites; yet it is almost too painful to read.

DH: *Without* kept me alive after Jane's death. It was as if I could *do* something about her dying.

JMJ: Yes. In fact, helplessness makes an appearance very early in the book:

> He hovered beside Jane's bed,
> Solicitous: "What can I *do*?" . . .
>   . . . when there was
> exactly nothing to do. Inside him,
>   some four-year-old
> understood that if he was good—thoughtful,
>   considerate, beyond
> reproach, *perfect*—she would not leave him.

JMJ: The husband, or poet, in *Without* does so much—buys his dying wife a ring, dons an elaborate sterile suit, imagines throwing himself in front of a bus, and helps her choose poems for her last collection and hymns for her funeral.

DH: I could not leave her. Everywhere, I was with her not for twenty-four hours, but at least twelve hours together when she was being treated in hospital. (Since then, I have heard about husbands who could not stand it and left their dying wives alone.) Out in Seattle the nurses kept telling me that I should take time off, take a little trip . . . and it was not thinkable. Since then, I wonder if my constant attention wore on Jane. I never felt it.

After her knowledge that she would die, our knowledge, we talked about everything. We chose poems for her posthumous collection, and wrote her obituary—but I forgot to talk about the shape and manner of her gravestone—"ours." I regretted it but did the best I could.

JMJ: I just can't bear to quote from the poem that begins "In the last hours." There, near the moment of her death, you seem to be choosing the poem's words so carefully—"hours" is repeated, "Jane" now becomes the more formal and distant "Jane Kenyon." How does one pay attention to poetic technique when the subject is this wrenching?

DH: When I was writing *Without*, I wrote about Jane for maybe two hours in the morning, and the only thing that gave me pleasure was writing about my misery and Jane's suffering. When I finished, I had twenty-two hours to get through. There was no pleasure. If there was "poetic technique," I used it to try to get my feelings through to a reader.

JMJ: And then, minute by minute, life keeps going on:

Tonight the Andover fireworks
Will have to go on without me
As I go to bed early, reading
The Man Without Qualities
With insufficient attention
Because I keep watching you die.

DH: I held up throughout her illness, as I had to do. After she died, after everybody attended the funeral and then went home, I screamed a lot. Living in the country, not near anyone else, I could scream to my heart's content and no one would dial 911.

JMJ: One of the painful things about your next collection, *The Painted Bed*, is the experience the reader has of moving on, with you, to episodes with other women. This is hard after we have lived through your deep connection with Jane—perhaps especially so in "Villanelle," where a new lover's suppleness unmakes the bed.

DH: The title poem in *The Painted Bed* is about Jane and me dying. After half my liver went, in 1992, we both knew I would die. I was sprawled on the painted bed when Jane came in, handing me her poem "Pharaoh" and asking me, "Is it all right? Do you mind?" When I read about my dying, I said something like, "It's weird, but it's a wonderful poem."

The early poems in *The Painted Bed* are about Jane's death, including the metrical poems, which are favorites of mine, "Her Garden" and "The Wish," and also maybe the best poem I've ever written, "Kill the Day." Then there is "Ardor," which speaks of the other women. Many widows and widowers want nothing to do with anybody else, after their spouse dies. Others—not just me, lots of people—become promiscuous. I had nightmares that she had left me for another man. Maybe I was getting even?

When I was seventy, I fell "in love" for the first time, and it was so ridiculous that it ridicules itself. For seven months I had an affair with a twenty-three-year-old fashion model who was interested in somebody famous. I was interested in somebody incredibly young, with skinny legs and enormous breasts. She was the woman in "Villanelle."

JMJ: You seem to be saying that you feel loyalty to Jane, after everything.

DH: I think of her—love and loss—every day.

JMJ: You've continued to write about her. But her presence in your poetry changes.

DH: I can no longer say "you," but "Jane" or "she." In the short-short *Selected Poems*, I reprint the best of my later Jane-poems.

■ ■ ■

JMJ: Before she died, had you ever sought out help from psychiatry or psychology?

DH: For several years before Jane and I even met, I took therapy with the Ann Arbor psychoanalyst M. M. Frohlich. He was the only analyst in Ann Arbor (we had more analysts than in Vienna) who did therapy, and by general consensus he was the best analyst in Ann Arbor. My problem was not depression. It was ignorance of my own feelings. As I have often said, "for 'love,' read 'hate' throughout."

From my early twenties I had read practically everything by Freud and, as you will understand, I started therapy by educating Dr. Frohlich in Freudian doctrine. Often I would confide my understanding to him and he would say that he did not understand anything I said. We took a little sabbatical—and when I hurt enough I came back.

He helped me enormously over the years. I learned that I had never really loved anybody despite a number of "loves." Toward the end I wept one day and wailed, "I cannot love anyone!" Quietly he assured me that of course I could really love someone. So I fell in love with Jane!

JMJ: You've written of how your relationship changed when she became manic.

DH: Jane had brief periods of mania, not many. She loved a ring that she saw in the jeweler's and bought it for four hundred dollars. If we were going out to dinner, she had one place in mind. (Always otherwise she said, "You choose.") Dr. Solow added a small amount of an anti-manic chemical to her diet of antidepressants. You won't be surprised to learn that when she was manic I turned depressed. When I became depressed, on those occasions I understood that I had emotionally profited from being the *steady* one.

JMJ: Did you seek out help after Jane's death?

DH: I was down, up, down, up. I noted manic tendencies when I began a four-hour drive after finishing a reading at midnight, and woke up my friends in the morning. I noticed that after a Jane-celebration in New York, I paid for a dinner of twenty-five people. Then I took the most enormous drop down. It was violent depression. Reading my poems, I fantasized about mowing down my audience with a machine gun. As I drove home from the reading, that image continued in my mind—and it terrified me. I called Dr. Solow, Jane's psychiatrist, and he came to my house and gave me a prescription for a mood stabilizer. At least the violence retreated and did not return.

■　■　■

JMJ: In "Three Beards," in *Essays After Eighty*, you describe how a woman you were seeing suggested that you grow an extravagant beard. I'm not sure your current beard suggests steadiness, exactly. But it certainly is intense looking, and it dominates the cover of the book. How do you feel with the beard?

DH: At first the beard was tidy. Finally I let it grow out and stopped combing my hair. I like the crazy look. When I rubbed testosterone into my chest, my beard exploded.

JMJ: What's your view on what makes for a good essay—and has your view changed since *String Too Short to Be Saved*?

DH: I'm not sure I know what makes a good essay. I ought to, because with my own work (or anybody's), I know which essay is better than another. But like everything else to which you might say "I know," I also know I might change my mind.

I notice total differences in my prose. *String* and *Essays After Eighty* are madly unlike—there's no humor in *String*—in vocabulary, in sentence structure and paragraph structure and most in tone. Even in *Essays After Eighty*'s "Out the Window," much about this farm, the sentences do not resemble the farm sentences of my first prose book. *String* was fifty or so years ago!

JMJ: *Essays After Eighty* artfully describes a number of losses, some potentially quite painful. For example, you report that you're living on one floor of your farmhouse now, but you manage to convey some humor about that—and about the advantages of wheelchairs.

DH: I think I've done remarkably well, adjusting to life on one floor. I'm so glad we didn't put a kitchen or a bed or a bathroom upstairs! Many times I would like to run upstairs and look at a picture or a book or a pile of papers, but I know I can't. I live largely alone and like it. Yesterday my right knee, all bone, was doing something extraordinary, painful and scary. I thought for a moment of having to have somebody stay in this house with me, or having to go into one of those death hostels. There's loss!

Actually I use a rollator to get around in this house, not a wheelchair. I have a portable wheelchair which is handy for certain tasks, when of course I have to get somebody to push me.

JMJ: Your first poem was about death, and at the ripe old age of twenty-five you wrote about your newborn son in "My Son My Executioner," portraying the change of generations as a kind of death. But now you write, "At some point in my seventies, death stopped being interesting." You don't seem to be especially afraid of it.

DH: When I wrote my first poem, and "My Son My Executioner," I didn't exactly feel afraid of death. It's certainly turned up in my thinking. When I was ten or so, a whole bunch of great-uncles and aunts died, and in bed at night I said, believe it or not, "Now death has become a reality!" There was a poet waiting to happen.

I'm not remotely afraid of death. Of course I'm afraid of dying, of pain, et cetera. At eighty-seven only an idiot would be afraid of death.

JMJ: I'm afraid that we're out of time. And we haven't even discussed your grandparents, tenure, alcohol, football games in Ann Arbor, or the Caldecott room. Let alone your visits to the White House.

DH: Each is worth at least a page!

JMJ: Thank you for being so generous and open about all of this, and for sharing your story with others.

DH: You thank me. Has anybody ever noticed that I like to talk about myself?

Additional Resources

Additional Interviews with Donald Hall

Sen, Sudeep (1992). The Making of a Poet. *Span*, August 1992, pp. 25–26. Sen, an Indian poet, discusses Hall's career, American poetry, and the issue of creative writing programs.

Hamilton, Ian (2000). *Donald Hall in Conversation with Ian Hamilton*. London: Between the Lines. A masterful extended interview by a poet who knew Hall well and was not afraid to challenge him.

Tobin, Jean (2004). *Creativity and the Poetic Mind*. New York: Lang. Includes an interview with Hall that focuses on his writing routine and the relation of his creativity to mania.

Hall, Donald (2005). Filmed contributions to www.webofstories.com. Recorded in 2005 at Eagle Pond Farm, these 111 filmed segments cover Hall's entire career. Accessed August 5, 2018, https://www.webofstories.com/play/donald.hall/1.

Cooper, Allan (2018). Three Questions for Donald Hall. *Numero Cinq*. Accessed April 2, 2018, http://numerocinqmagazine.com/2017/01/08/three-questions-donald-hall -interview-allan-cooper/. A brief, perceptive interview.

Selected Works about Donald Hall

"The Yanks at Oxford." *Time*, June 9, 1952, p. 47. Hall, along with critic George Steiner, gained international attention in this brief feature on American writers in England.

"Time's Sweet Praise" [review of *Exiles and Marriages*.] *Time*, December 5, 1955, pp. 120, 122. *Time* championed Hall as a fresh new formalist in an era when older poets were contributing little.

Blanchard, Brian (1977). "Poetic Justice: Prof. Hall Finds the Good Life in N.H." *Michigan Daily*, vol. 88, no. 58, November 13, 1977, pp. 4–5. A warm, insightful portrait of Hall in the post-Michigan years. Accessed April 22, 2018, https://digital.bentley.umich .edu/midaily/mdp.39015071754506/730.

Orr, Gregory (1988). "A Reading of Donald Hall's 'Kicking the Leaves.'" *Iowa Review*, vol. 18, no. 1, Winter 1988, pp. 40–47. An extended analysis of a major poem by a fellow poet whose opinions and presence mattered greatly to Hall and to Kenyon. Accessed April 22, 2018, http://ir.uiowa.edu/cgi/viewcontent.cgi?article=3613& context=iowareview.

Rector, Liam (1989). "The Building of Work and Love" [review of *The One Day*]. *Los Angeles Times*, February 5, 1989. Accessed July 22, 2018, http://articles.latimes.com/1989-02-05 /books/bk-2266_1_donald-hall.

Moyers, Bill (1993). "Donald Hall and Jane Kenyon: A Life Together." *Bill Moyers' Journal*. PBS. Accessed July 22, 2018, https://voxpopulisphere.com/2018/01/01/video-bill -moyers-journal-a-life-together-jane-kenyon-and-donald-hall/.

Simic, Charles (2006). "The Elegist" [review of *White Apples and the Taste of Stone*]. *New York Review of Books*. vol. 53, no. 19, November 30, 2006, pp. 30–32. A comprehensive assessment of Hall by a fellow poet laureate.

Cooper, Allan. "Entering the Golden Room: Review of *The Selected Poems of Donald Hall*." *Numero Cinq*, vol. 8, no. 1, January 2017. Accessed April 15, 2019, http://nu merocinqmagazine.com/2017/01/08/entering-golden-room-review-selected-poems -donald-hall-donald-hall-allan-cooper/.

Pride, Mike (2018). "Donald Hall, a Giant of American Poetry, dies at 89." *Concord Monitor*, June 25, 2018. Accessed July 22, 2018 https://www.concordmonitor.com /Donald-Hall-Poet-Laureate-Wilmot-NH-18399476.

Begley, Louis (2018). "Among the Thirty Thousand Days: An Appreciation of Donald Hall." Posted July 3, 2018. Accessed July 22, 2018, https://www.poets.org/poetsorg /text/among-thirty-thousand-days-appreciation-donald-hall.

Papers of Donald Hall and Jane Kenyon

Donald Hall Papers, Special Collections, University of New Hampshire at Durham. Includes approximately seven hundred cubic feet of material related to Donald Hall, including manuscripts; drafts of poems; essays; and books; letters to and from T. S. Eliot, Adrienne Rich, Robert Bly, and many others; childhood photographs and mementos; recordings; and copies of books by Hall and many others from his personal collection. The collection is still growing. Accessed December 24, 2018, https:// www.library.unh.edu/find/archives/collections/donald-hall-papers-1928–2014.

An item of special interest within the Donald Hall Papers is "Drafts of Donald Hall's Ox Cart Man." This record of an exhibit at the University of New Hampshire Library presents color facsimiles of drafts of the poem, including the handwritten and typed drafts discussed in Hall's 1992 interview with Jay Woodruff. The drafts show Hall's revisions as well as handwritten comments by the poet Louis Simpson (1923–2012). Accessed December 24, 2018, https://www.library.unh.edu/exhibits/eagle-pond /drafts-donald-halls-ox-cart.

Jane Kenyon Papers, Special Collections, University of New Hampshire at Durham. Consists of fifty-five boxes (nineteen cubic feet) of material related to Jane Kenyon, including manuscripts of poems and essays; books; and letters to and from Joyce Peseroff, Hayden Carruth, Robert Bly, and many others. Accessed December 24, 2018, https://www.library.unh.edu/find/archives/collections/jane-kenyon-papers -1961-1995.

Index

Adams, Clover, 133
Adams, Henry, 133
"Adam's Curse" (Yeats), 32
"Affirmation" (Hall), 154–55
"After the Industrial Revolution, All Things Happen at Once" (Bly), 11
"Afternoon at MacDowell" (Kenyon), xii
Akhmatova, Anna, 125
Allen, Harvey, 63, 66
"Alligator Bride, The" (Hall), 30, 36; imagery in, 99
Alligator Bride: Poems New and Selected, The (Hall), ix, 26, 28, 31, 49, 73, 78; process of writing, 36
Ambassadors, The (James), 91
American Academy of Arts and Letters, 162
American Library Association, 105
American Scholar, 105
"Among School Children" (Yeats), 50, 98
Andrew the Lion Farmer (Hall), 65
Ann Abor, Michigan, vii, 46–47, 62, 78, 92, 102, 157–58, 164, 169
Ann Arbor News, 158
"Ardor" (Hall), 169
Ashbery, John, viii, 24, 66, 75, 86, 94–95, 153
Atlantic, 75, 105
Auden, W. H., 4, 8–9, 95
Azarian, Mary, 65

"Back" (Kenyon), 162, 164–66
Back Chamber, The (Hall), 149–50, 153
Baudelaire, Charles, 4
BBC, 86
Beat poets, 22, 23, 65
Begley, Louis, xii
Berry, Wendell, 56, 68
Bidart, Frank, 68, 69
Birkerts, Sven, 76
Black Mountain poets, 22
Blackwater Bill's, 157
Blake, William, 14
Blast, 67
Blue, Marian, xi, 118–29
"Blue Wing, The" (Hall), 30, 33, 34
Bly, Carol, 62
Bly, Robert, 10–11, 23, 43, 49, 64, 67, 68–69, 71, 86, 93, 96–97, 125–26; at Harvard, viii, 24, 75, 78, 85, 94–95, 101, 105, 148, 153; writing workshops/feedback, 38–39, 91–92, 138
Boat of Quiet Hours, The (Kenyon), 127, 145
Boehme, Jacob, 11
Bogan, Louise, 9, 75
Bolcom, William, 48, 58, 59, 88
Bonhoeffer, Dietrich, 102
Bonnie and Clyde, 80
Boston Globe, 135, 158
Booth, Phil, 96
Boston Celtics, 90

Boston Psychoanalytic Society and Institute (BPSI), 163
Boston University, 102
Bowra, Maurice, 94
Boy Scouts, 79
Branch Will Not Break, The (Wright), viii, 10
Bread Loaf Writers' Conference, 16, 81
Bridges, Robert, 5
British Museum, 42, 55
Brooks, Cleanth, 13
Browning, Elizabeth, 145
Browning, Robert, 145
Budweiser, 54
"By the Exeter River" (Hall), 34
Byrom, Bill, xiii, 10–14

Caldecott Medal, 78, 88, 105, 148
Cantos, The (Pound), 20–21, 40
Cameron, Norman, 8
Carnival of Losses, A (Hall), xiv
"Casey at the Bat" (Thayer), 45
Ceremony (Wilbur), 95
Chisholm, Scott, ix, x, 15–36
Ciardi, John, 6, 9, 94
Civil War, 44, 55, 101, 156
Clark, Kenneth, 90
Clark, Tom, 40
"Cloud of Unknowing, The" (anonymous), 102
Colby-Sawyer College, 102
Collected Poems (Kenyon), 162
Collected Poems (Yeats), 40
Columbia University, 6
Concord Monitor, 157–58
Contemporary American Poetry (Hall), 10, 78
Cooney, Barbara, 65, 78
Cornell University, 158
Cowley, Malcolm, 75
Crane, Hart, 4
Crawford, Willie, 90

Creeley, Robert, xv, 22, 24, 65–66, 76, 93, 95
Criterion Book of Modern American Verse (Auden), 9
cummings, e. e., 22–23
Cunningham, J. V., 8
Currier, Kendel, xv

Dark Houses, The (Hall), 28–29, 78
Dartmouth-Hitchcock Medical Center, 164
Davies, J. R. S., xiii, 10–14
Davison, Peter, 24, 75, 95
Dawn, Billy and Marjorie, 54
"Days, The" (Hall), 30
"dead metaphors," 156, 158–59
Deerfield Academy, 94
Detroit Free Press, 158
Dial, 84
Dickey, James, xiii, 86–87, 97
"Digging" (Hall), 29
Doolittle, Hilda "H. D.," 40
Donatello, 42, 88
Drowning with Others (Dickey), 86–87
"Dump, The" (Hall), 48
Duncan, Robert, 66, 93

Eagle Pond Farm, xiii, xiv, 55, 101, 130, 148; future plans for, 143–44; Hall at, ix–xi, 37, 42, 79, 100, 102, 105, 131–32, 135, 157, 162; Hall's childhood at, ix–x, 42, 56, 60–61, 79, 101, 157; Kenyon at, ix–x, xi, xii, 79, 100, 102, 105, 127–29, 135, 144, 162
"Eating the Pig" (Hall), 49
Eberhart, Richard, 69–70, 93, 95
Eckhart, Meister, 52, 102
"Eclogue" (Virgil), 64
Economist, 158
Edna St. Vincent Millay Award, 105, 148
"Eisenhower's Visit to Franco, 1959" (Wright), 10

"Elegy for Wesley Wells" (Hall), 43–44

Eliot, T. S., vii, 4, 6, 19–20, 40–41, 75, 78, 80, 82, 105, 107, 117

Ellis, Dock, 47, 78

Elmslie, Kenward, 95

Emerson, Ralph Waldo, 67

Esquire, 105

Essays After Eighty (Hall), xiii, 162–63, 170–71

"Exile" (Hall), viii

Exiles and Marriages (Hall), viii, 25–26, 28, 78, 105

Faber and Faber, 20

Falk, Colin, 10

"Falling Asleep Over the Aeneid" (Lowell), 96

Fantasy Poets, 85–86

Faulkner, William, 116

Fenton, Dennis, 106

Fenton, Paul, 106, 113, 116

Festival of Britain, 88

Fifties, The, viii, 67, 93

Finklestein, Caroline, 138

Fletcher, Valerie, 82

Ford Times, 157

"Four Classic Texts" (Hall), 64

Franco, Francisco, 13–14

Freud, Sigmund, viii–ix, 71–72, 98–99, 152, 169

Frohlich, M. M., viii, 169

From Room to Room (Kenyon), 127

Frost, Robert, 6, 8, 16, 19, 40–41, 78, 81–82, 85, 95, 117, 165

Frost Place, 143, 165

Fry, Christopher, 75

Fussell, Paul, 51

"Garden, The" (Marvell), 40, 50

"Genesis" (Hill), 86

Gettysburg Review, 142

Ginsberg, Allen, 23, 65–66, 97

Gissing, George, 67

Goatfoot Milktongue Twinbird (Hall), 78

Godine (publisher), ix, 73

"God's Little Mountain" (Hill), 86

Gorey, Edward St. John, 94

Gorman, Teresa, 162

"Grass, The" (Hall), viii

Graves, Robert, 43, 47, 93

Grolier Book Shop, 95

Guggenheim Foundation, 75, 78, 95, 105, 148

Gulf War, 125–26

Gunn, Thom, 86, 97

Hall, Andrew (son), 34–35, 65, 95, 143

Hall, Donald: aging, 161–63; ambition, 153–54; anthologies, xiv, 8–9, 22, 54, 65–66, 78, 85; awards and prizes, viii, xiii, 78, 105, 148–49; birth, viii, 15–16, 78, 148; blurbs, writing, 74–75; cancer, xii, 126, 133–35, 163, 169; childhood, ix–x, 42, 45, 55–56, 60–62, 78–80, 101, 148, 151, 157; critics, poetry, 67–71, 75, 90–91, 154; death, xiv–xv, 156; depression, viii, 141–42, 163, 165–66, 170; early influences, 15–17, 19, 79–81; education, early, 15–16, 32, 47, 80, 88, 92, 97; education at Harvard University, viii, 18, 24, 45, 46, 61–62, 75, 78, 85–94, 95, 101, 105, 148, 153; education at Oxford University, 17, 18, 23, 42, 43, 86, 96; "forgetting" poems, 50–51; freelance writing, 47–48, 71, 79, 90; gender and writing, 125–26; grandparents/older relatives, 15, 28, 34, 42–45, 55–56, 58, 63, 78, 79, 100–101, 131, 148, 153, 156; grief and loss, xii–xiii, 16, 28, 33–34, 43, 131–33, 136–42, 144, 152–53, 162–63, 166, 167, 169–71; imagery in poems, 29–34, 36, 44–45, 51, 98–101, 109, 114, 137, 139–40, 142–43, 160–61; inspiration,

early, 5–7, 16–17, 45, 47; irony, 13–15; legacy, 72–73, 143, 146–47; marriage to Jane Kenyon, ix, xi, 105, 118–29, 145; "Perkins" nickname, 134, 136–37, 164; physical appearance, xii, xiv–xv, 90, 130–32, 170; poetic forms, ix, x, 3–5, 10–14, 17, 23–25, 41, 50–51, 57, 63–64, 66, 69, 93, 96–98, 107–9, 138–39, 142, 151; psychotherapy, viii–ix, 71–72, 99–100, 164, 169, 170; public readings, 7–8, 27, 56, 66–67, 85, 98, 125, 132, 146, 156; publishing industry, 6; religion, 73–74, 101–3, 142; revisions, x–xi, 26–27, 31, 37, 48–49, 50–52, 56–57, 70, 87, 97–98, 106–15, 137–38, 142–43, 160–61; sexuality of poetry, 150, 163, 166; style, 24–25; surrealism, 29–31, 47; teaching, vii, ix, 5–6, 28, 40, 43, 61, 78, 100, 105, 136, 148, 157, 162; technique, 18–19, 157–59, 168; technology, 158; working/writing partnership with Jane Kenyon, xi, 39, 50–51, 68, 113, 118–29, 139, 145, 146, 169; writing process, 25, 27–30, 37–39, 48–49, 51–52, 55, 57, 87–90, 97–100, 106–14, 137–38, 151–53, 159–60; writing workshops/feedback, 38–40, 51, 58, 84–85, 91–92, 113–14, 119–20, 122–23, 127, 138
Hall, Donald Andrew (father), 28, 35, 45, 63, 81, 92, 153, 171
Hall, Lucy Wells (mother), 55, 81, 127, 143, 148, 153, 154
Hall, Philippa (daughter), 81, 143
Hamill, Sam, 51
Hamilton, David, 37–52, 69
Hamilton, Ian, xiii, xiv, 10–14
Happy Man, The (Hall), x, 63, 78; form, 63, 64; imagery in, 100; reviews, 64
"Happy Times" (Hall), 28, 30
Hardwick, Elizabeth, 96
Hardy, Thomas, xii, 39, 40–41, 57–58, 68

Harmonium (Stevens), 85
Harper's, 51
Harvard Advocate, 32, 46, 70, 75, 85, 92, 94–95
Harvard Magazine, 70
Harvard University, viii, 18, 24, 45, 46, 61–62, 75, 78, 85, 94, 95, 101, 105, 148, 153
"Having It Out with Melancholy" (Kenyon), 162, 164
Hay, John, 133
Hebner, Richie, 90
Hemingway, Ernest, 43
"Her Garden" (Kenyon), 169
Heraclitus, 71
Hill, Geoffrey, 86, 97, 123
Hitler, Adolf, 102
Hollander, John, 74
Holmes, John, 96
"Holy Thursday" (Hill), 86
Hope, Bob, 8
Hopkins, Gerard Manley, 5
Horace, 98
Horizon, 41, 88
"Horse Song" (Hall), 58–59
Houghton Library, 40
Hughes, Ted, 145
Hulme, T. E., 11
Huntington, Cynthia, 138
Hutchinson Research Center, 166

Ignatow, David, 139
"In the Kitchen of the Old House" (Hall), 92
"Independence Day Letter" (Hall), 162
Inside Sports, 47
Iowa Review, 37, 52, 68–69, 74
Isis, viii, 85, 86

James, Henry, 43, 76, 83, 91
Jarrell, Randall, 8
Jensen, Jack, 102
Joyce, James, 40

Julian of Norwich, 102
Jung, Carl, viii, 71, 72
Justice, Donald, 50

Kallman, Chester, 9
Keats, John, 39, 40–41, 50, 55, 64, 72, 98, 125, 150
Kenyon, Jane, x, xii, xiii, xv, 38, 103, 148, 150, 162; in Ann Arbor, vii, x, 164; bone marrow transplant, 133, 134, 166; death, vii, xii–xiii, 130–33, 136, 138–39, 142–45, 148, 162–63, 167–69; depression, 134, 141, 163–67, 170; as Donald Hall's student, ix, xi, 121, 122, 136–37, 148; feedback/workshopping poems, 119–20, 122–23, 126; gender and writing, 125–26; grief and loss, 126; marriage to Donald Hall, ix, xi, 118–29; legacy, 144–45; leukemia, xii, 131, 133–35, 148, 162, 166; parents, 127, 128, 140, 164; working/writing part-nership with Hall, xi, 39, 68, 113, 118–29, 139, 145–46, 169; writing process, 124–26, 128–29
Kicking the Leaves (Hall), x, xii, 44, 63, 78, 105, 115; form, 63, 98; process of writing, 97–98; public readings, 125
"Kicking the Leaves" (Hall), ix, x, 49, 73
"Kill the Day" (Hall), 142, 169
Kinnell, Galway, ix, 36, 38, 39, 49, 68, 96, 115, 125, 138
Kizer, Carolyn, 87, 93
Koch, Kenneth, 24, 75, 94, 153
Kray, Betty, 103
Kunhardt, Linda, 161
Kunitz, Stanley, 8

Ladies' Home Journal, 8
Lamont Poetry Selection Award, 78, 105, 148
"Lapis Lazuli" (Yeats), 21
Larkin, Philip, 13

Lawrence, D. H., 14
Let Evening Come (Kenyon), 127, 162
"Letter After a Year" (Hall), 142
"Letter with No Address" (Hall), 142
Levertov, Denise, viii, 65, 66
Lewis, Wyndham, 67
Life magazine, 3, 51, 81
Life Studies (Lowell), 96
Life Work (Hall), xii
Lindbergh, Charles, 32
Lindsay, Vachel, 85
"Lines Written in Dejection" (Yeats), 32
Lippmann House, 158
Lipton, Lawrence, 5, 7
Lockwood, Willard, 86
Loecher, Anne, 148–56
Long River, The (Hall), 25
"Long River, The" (Hall), 30, 150–51
Longman, Green and Co., 10
Lord Weary's Castle (Lowell), 96
Los Angeles Times Book Prize, 149
Lowell, Robert, 95–96, 149
"Lycidas" (Milton), 50
"Lying in a Hammock" (Wright), 13
Lyrical Ballads (Wordsworth), 22

MacLeish, Archibald, 95, 116, 149
"Man in the Dead Machine, The" (Hall), 33–34, 44–45, 73, 98
Mann, Thomas, 87
Marshall (Lenore) Poetry Prize, 149
Martin-Joy, John, viii, xii–xiii, 162–71
Marvell, Andrew, 40, 50, 68, 76, 100
Mattison, Alice, 123
Maximum Poems, The (Olson), 65
Mazzocco, Robert, 64
McDowell, Robert, 70
McHale, Kevin, 90
McPhee, John, 159
Meridian Books, 9
Merwin, W. S., 4, 71, 93, 96–97
Michelangelo, 42, 72, 88, 146

Mid-Century anthology (Ciardi), 9

Middleton, Christopher, 49

"Midwinter Letter" (Hall), 135–36

Miles, Josephine, 93

Milton, John, 50, 146

Montale, Eugenio, 139

Moore, Henry, vii, xiv, xv, 41–42, 72, 78, 105, 107, 116, 146, 161; *New Yorker* profile, 88–90

Moore, Irina, 89

Moore, Marianne, vii, 8, 68, 82, 83–85, 105, 117

Morris, Joan, 58, 59, 88

Morrison, Theodore, 81

Moss, Howard, 6, 112–15

"Mother Marie Therese" (Lowell), 96

"Mount Kearsarge" (Hall), 34

Moyers, Bill, 135

Muir, Edwin, 47, 57–58

Muir, Willa, 47

"My Son My Executioner" (Hall), viii, 31, 34–35, 97, 154, 171

"Names of Horses" (Hall), x, 53–59; feedback regarding, 58; form/line length, x, 56–57; music set to, 58–59; public readings, 56; revisions to, 56–57; writing process, 57–58

Nation, 23, 65, 75

National Book Award, 149

National Book Critics Circle Award, 149

National Book Critics Circle Award for Poetry, 149

National Council of Teachers of English, 93–94

National Gallery of Art, 161

National Medal of Arts, xiii, 162

Near the Ocean (Lowell), 96

necropoetics, xiii

Nemerov, Howard, 8

Neruda, Pablo, 23

New Grub Street (Gissing), 67

"New Hampshire" (Hall), 44–45

New Haven General Courier, 157

New Haven Register, 157

New Poems, 85

New Poets of England and America (Hall), 22, 78

New Republic, 75

New York Review of Books, 75

New York Times, 75, 80, 142–43

New Yorker, 6, 9, 41, 54, 68, 73, 75, 89–90, 94, 105, 113–15, 149, 152–54, 160, 164

Newdigate Prize, viii

Nieman Fellows, 158

92nd Street Y, xiii

Notebook (Lowell), 96

"O Cheese" (Hall), ix

Obama, Barack, xiii, 149

"Ode: Intimations of Immortality" (Wordsworth), 50

"Ode to a Nightingale" (Keats), 98

O'Hara, Frank, 24, 66, 75, 94, 97, 153

Old and New Poems (Hall), 78, 105, 115

"Old Home Day" (Hall), 16, 43

"Old Roses" (Hall), 128

Olds, Sharon, 138

Olson, Charles, 23, 65

One Day, The (Hall), x, 63, 73, 78, 125, 140; form, 63–64; imagery in, 98–99, 140–41; revisions to, x–xi, 63–64; writing process, 98–100

Orr, Gregory, xi, 38, 68, 121

Ortega y Gasset, José, 60

Otherwise (Kenyon), 144, 162

"Out of the Cradle" (Whitman), 40, 50

"Out the Window" (Hall), 155–56, 160, 171; imagery in, 160–61

"Ox Cart Man" (Hall), xi, xiv, 45, 48, 88, 104–17; feedback on, 113–14; form and structure, 107–9, 110; imagery

in, 109, 114; inspiration for, 106; language, 117; music set to, 48, 88; revisions on/drafts, xi, 88, 105–15; title, 109; "Total Dispersal," 106–7; writing process, 106–14
Ox-Cart Man (Hall), 78, 88, 105, 116, 146
Oxford University, viii, xiii, 10, 17–18, 23, 42–43, 61–62, 75, 78, 86, 94–96, 105, 148

Pack, Robert, 9, 65, 78
Painted Bed, The (Hall), xii, 162, 168–69
"Painted Bed, The" (Hall), 169
Paris Review, vii, x–xi, 20, 78, 82–83, 85, 86, 91, 97, 103, 105–6, 116–17
"Pastoral" (Hall), 99
Patmore, Coventry, 5
Peace Corps, 93
Penguin Publishing, 10, 65
PEN/Voelcker Award, 162
Perrine, Laurence, 93
Peseroff, Joyce, 123
"Pharaoh" (Kenyon), 169
Phillips Exeter Academy, 45, 61, 80
Picasso, Pablo, 73
Pinsky, Robert, 68, 115
Pittsburgh Pirates, 90
Plath, Sylvia, 145
Playboy, 47, 156
Plimpton, George, 97
Poe, Edgar Allan, 4, 56, 79
Poet Laureate of New Hampshire, 149
Poet Laureate of the United States, xiii, 149, 162
Poetry, 64, 94
Poetry and Ambition (Hall), 78
"Poetry and Ambition" (Hall), 37, 72, 153
Poetry Society of America, 10, 12, 105, 149
Poet's Theater, 75
"Porcelain Couple, The" (Hall), 162

"Possibility of New Poetry, The" (Bly), 11
Pound, Ezra, 4, 19, 21, 23, 38, 40, 67, 68, 106, 116, 117; *Paris Review* interview, vii, 20, 82–83, 105
Pride, Mike, xiii, 157–61
Proctor Cemetery, xv
"Projective Verse" (Olson), 23
"Prophesy" (Hall), 98
Pulitzer Prize, 76, 149
Putterill, Jack, 101–2

Quinn, Alice, 115, 154, 164–65

Randolph, Willie, 90
Ratiner, Steven, xii, 130–47
"Raven, The" (Poe), 56
Ray, David, xiii, 3–9
Rector, Liam, xiv, 60–77, 138
Reed College, 87
Reid, Alastair, 103
Remembering Poets (Hall), 41, 78, 83–84
"Repeated Shapes, The" (Hall), 34
Rexroth, Kenneth, 66
Rich, Adrienne, viii, 24, 68, 75, 95–97, 153
Rilke, Rainer Maria, 102
Robert Frost Silver Medal, 149, 162
Roberts, Kenneth, 63
"Rocks and Whirlpools" (Hall), 116
Rockwell, Norman, 54
Rodin, Auguste, 89, 116
Roethke, Theodore, 149
Rohfritch, Richard, xiv–xv
Roof of Tiger Lilies, A (Hall), viii, 29, 35–36, 43, 78, 80
Rose, Pete, 90
"Rose, The" (Yeats), 40
Rosenthal, M. L., 115
Rousseau, Jean-Jacques, 93
Rudge, Olga, 82
"Rusticus" (Hall), 60–61
Ruth Lilly Poetry Prize, 149

Salter, Mary Jo, 115
Sandburg, Carl, 85
Sanders, George, 103
Sappho, 125
Sarah Josepha Hale Award, 148
Saturday Review, 6, 75
Seasons at Eagle Pond (Hall), 161
Selected Poems (Hall), 162–63, 169
Servetus, 102
Seventies, The, viii
Seymour-Smith, Martin, 95
Shakespeare, William, 146
Shanks, Michael, 85–86
Shapiro, David, 64
Shapiro, Karl, 8–9
"Shrubs Burnt Away" (Hall), 63–64
Silence in the Snowy Fields (Bly), viii
Simpson, Hallpack, 65–67
Simpson, Louis, viii, 6, 9, 38–39, 58, 68,
    78, 92, 96, 113, 125
Sissman, L. E., 24, 95
"Sister by the Pond, A" (Hall), 51
Sixties, The, viii, 23
"Sleeping" (Hall), 34–35
"Sleeping Giant, The" (Hall), 98, 151–52,
    154
Smith, William J., 149
Snodgrass, W. D., 38, 39, 50–51, 58, 68, 96
Snyder, Gary, 65, 93
Society of Fellows, 62
Solow, Charles, 164, 170
Sound and Sense (Perrine), 93
South Danbury Christian Church, xv,
    102, 156
Sports Illustrated, 157
St. Olaf College, 94
Stafford, William, 93, 138
Stanford University, 5, 43, 61–62, 78, 96–
    97, 105, 148
Stennett, Rennie, 90
Stevens, Leonard and Mary, 80
Stevens, Wallace, 4, 5, 50, 85

Stitt, Peter A., 78–103
"Stone Walls" (Hall), 49
String Too Short to Be Saved (Hall), x, 16,
    35–36, 42–45, 48, 61–62, 89, 146, 157,
    161, 170–71
"Sunday Morning" (Stevens), 50
Swenson, May, 93, 103
Swinburne, Algernon Charles, 4

"Table, The" (Hall), 30
1020 Art Center, 3
Thayer, Ernest Lawrence, 45
"This Bread I Break" (Thomas), 19
Thomas, Dylan, 8, 19, 41, 78, 85, 117
Thompson, Kirby, ix, 164
Thompson, Lawrence Roger, 81
"Three Beards" (Hall), 170
Time magazine, viii, 3, 8, 26, 81, 158
"To His Coy Mistress" (Marvell), 40
To Keep Moving (Hall), 78
Town of Hill, The (Hall), ix, 49, 73, 78
"Town of Hill, The" (Hall), 49, 73
"Traffic" (Hall), 49
"Transcontinent" (Hall), ix
Trilling, Lionel, 76
Turner, Alberta T., x, 53–59

University of Iowa, 5
University of Michigan, vii, ix, 40, 43,
    61–62, 78–79, 100, 105, 121, 136, 148,
    157, 162, 164
University of Michigan Press, Poets on
    Poetry series, 70
University of Minnesota, 93
University of New Hampshire, xiv, 58,
    136, 143
*Unpacking the Boxes: A Memory of Life
    in Poetry* (Hall), xiii
Untermeyer, Louis, 8
"Up from the Grave He Arose" (anony-
    mous), 103
Updike, John, xiv

US Library of Congress Poet Laureate, 149

Variorum (Yeats), 40
"Vatic Voice, The" (Hall), 27
Vendler, Helen, 75
"Villanelle" (Hall), 168–69
Villon, François, 55
Virgil, 64
Vision, A (Yeats), 38
"vocal tradition," 7–8
Voight, Ellen, 138, 142

Wallace, Henry, 94
"Waste Land, The" (Eliot), 73
Weather for Poetry, The (Hall), 78
"Wedding Party" (Hall), 31
"Weeds and Peonies" (Hall), 142–43
Wesleyan University Press, 86
"White Apples" (Hall), ix
White Apples and the Taste of Stone (Hall), ix
Whitman, Walt, x, 8, 40–41, 50, 100
"Whitsun Weddings, The" (Larkin), 13
Whittemore, Reed, 8, 93
Wilbur, Richard, 4, 24, 87, 95, 149
Wilde, Oscar, 94
Williams, Oscar, 8
Williams, William Carlos, 4, 8, 23, 85
Wilson, Edmund, 75, 76

Winters, Yvor, 8, 43, 96–97, 116
"Wish, The" (Hall), 169
Without (Hall), xii, 131, 133, 142, 147, 162, 167; feedback/workshopping, 138; form, 138–40, 142; imagery in, 137, 139–40, 142, 143; revisions, 137–38; writing process, 134–35, 167–68
"Without" (Hall), xii, 141
"Wives, The" (Hall), 29
"Wolf Knife" (Hall), 49
Woodruff, Jay, xi, xiv, 104–17
Woodward, Washington, 45
Woolf, Virginia, 125
Wordsworth, William, 12, 22, 40, 50, 68, 80
World War I, 83
Wright, James, viii, 10, 13, 38, 86–87, 92–93, 96–97
Writing Well (Hall), 71

Xenia (Montale), 139

Yale Series of Younger Poets, 95
Yale University, 80, 102
Yankee Magazine, 105, 157
Yeats, W. B., 4, 21, 32, 38–41, 50, 68, 98, 146
Yellow Room: Love Poems, The (Hall), ix, 49, 78
YM-YWHA, 79, 103

About the Editors

John Martin-Joy is a psychiatrist in private practice in Cambridge, Massachusetts. A candidate member at the Boston Psychoanalytic Society and Institute, he teaches at Beth Israel–Deaconess Medical Center in Boston and Mount Auburn Hospital in Cambridge. He is the author of *Diagnosing from a Distance: Debates over Libel Law, Media, and Psychiatric Ethics from Barry Goldwater to Donald Trump* and of scholarly articles on literature, psychiatry, and ethics.

Allan Cooper has been a full-time poet, translator, publisher, and editor for over forty years. His nineteenth collection of poetry, *Waiting for the Small Ship of Desire*, was published by Pottersfield Press in 2020.

Richard Rohfritch was educated at Wesleyan University, the University of Southern California, and the University of Missouri, St. Louis. He is compiling and editing a new bibliography of Donald Hall, based in part on interviews with Hall at Eagle Pond Farm in Wilmot, New Hampshire.

CPSIA information can be obtained
at www.ICGtesting.com
Printed in the USA
BVHW031355200221
600656BV00003B/14

9 781496 822475